T0989098

YVES LACOSTE is an eminent and internationally respected geographer. He is the editor of the well-known French journal, *Herotte,* and the author of a number of works including *The Geography of Underdevelopment* and *Unity and Diversity of the Third World.*

Yves Lacoste

Verso

Ibn Khaldun:

The Birth of History and
The Past of the Third World

British Library
Cataloguing in Publication Data

Lacoste, Yves
  Ibn Khaldun.
  1. Ibn Khaldun, 'Abd ar-Rahman ibn Muhammad
  I. Title
  907'.2024   D116.7.I3

First published as
Ibn Khaldoun: Naissance de l'Histoire
Passé du tiers-monde
© Librairie François Maspero, 1966

This translation first published, Verso, 1984
© Verso Editions, 1984
15 Greek Street, London W1V 5LF

Filmset in Plantin by
Red Lion Setters
London WC1N 2LA

Printed by
The Thetford Press Ltd,
Thetford, Norfolk

ISBN 0 86091 084 9
      0 86091 789 4 Pbk
ISBN 978-0-86091-789-2

Contents

Translator's Note

Quotations from Franz Rosenthal's translation of Ibn Khaldun, *The Muqaddimah: An Introduction to History*, Bollingen Series XLIII, New York, Pantheon Books, 1958, 3 vols., have occasionally been modified to take account of variations between it and the French translation used by the author: *Les Prolégomènes historiques d'Ibn Khaldoun*, tr. Baron De Slane in *Notices et extraits des manuscrits de la Bibliothèque Impériale*—Académie des Inscriptions et Belles-Lettres—vols. XIX-XXI, Paris 1862-1868. Material not included in Rosenthal is indicated as 'De Slane'. *Histoire des Berbères* indicates quotations from *Histoire des Berbères et des dynasties musulmanes de l'Afrique septentrionale*, tr. Baron De Slane, Algiers 1852-1856, 4 vols.

David Macey.

Preface

Ibn Khaldun?

The encyclopedia gives the following information: 'Ibn Khaldun (Abd al-Rahman), the most famous of Arab historians (born Tunis 1337, died Cairo 1406)'.

In North Africa, the name of Ibn Khaldun[1] still evokes the splendours of the past, even for relatively unsophisticated people. But outside the Arab world, most educated people familiar with the major problems of our own time have never heard of him. He is known only to specialists in the history of the Maghreb and in the development of the science of history. Those historians and philosophers who have had occasion to read his work praise him unstintingly: 'Ibn Khaldun was the greatest historian and philosopher ever produced by Islam and one of the greatest of all time'.[2]

'The work of Ibn Khaldun is one of the most substantial and interesting books ever written'.[3]

'He has conceived and formulated a philosophy of history which is undoubtedly the greatest work of its kind that has ever yet been produced by any mind in any time or place'.[4]

Such comments are more than justified: Ibn Khaldun's work marks the birth of the science of history and is perhaps the most prestigious product of what can only be called the 'Arab miracle'. Ibn Khaldun wrote at a time when what had once been the centre of medieval Arab civilization was in decline. He had no real followers and his work was forgotten for centuries. For my part, I believe that, if Ibn Khaldun's thought is to become more widely known and if it is to be integrated into contemporary thought, we have to do more than simply restore him to his rightful status as one of the founders of History. We are now witnessing major and totally unprecedented events: throughout the world, people are faced with vast and tragic problems which mankind has never previously experienced. The reconstruction of the past is therefore not an end in itself. It is a matter of *contemporary* interest and importance. The content of a work of the past can only be integrated into an active intellectual movement (one which leads to some political understanding of the times in which we live) in so far as it has contemporary resonance and increases our understanding of the problems that face us in the latter part of the twentieth century.

Exploring the thought of Ibn Khaldun does not mean straying into medieval orientalism, plunging into the distant past of an exotic country or complacently entering into a seemingly academic debate. It does not mean turning our backs on the modern world. It is, rather, a means of furthering an analysis of the underlying causes of the most serious of contemporary problems. As we shall see, in his analysis of economic, social and political conditions in medieval North Africa, Ibn Khaldun raises a number of fundamental historical problems. His work sheds light upon a very important stage in the history of what are now underdeveloped countries. He describes very complex social and political structures whose development determined a lengthy historical process and whose effects are still being felt today. In combination with equally determinant external causes, those structures led to colonial domination in the nineteenth century, and colonialism led in its turn to the present situation of underdevelopment.

Provided that they are analysed with care, the most important and original features of Ibn Khaldun's work can now be seen as a major contribution to the study of the underlying causes of underdevelopment. It must, however, be stressed that the relationship between the work of the Maghrebian historian and underdevelopment is far from straightforward. It would be not merely simplistic but quite wrong to think that in the fourteenth century Ibn Khaldun described the characteristics of an objectively underdeveloped country. He was studying medieval structures which slowed down or blocked social, political and economic development. It was only several hundred years later that those structures combined with outside influences to facilitate colonization, and colonization determined the appearance of the phenomenon of underdevelopment.

Fourteenth-century North Africa was no underdeveloped country. Contrary to the opinion of certain writers, underdevelopment has not always existed and does not date back to ancient times: it is a relatively recent phenomenon. We have to be careful not to confuse the situation that 'traditionally' prevailed in North Africa and much of the rest of the world with modern underdevelopment. The underdeveloped countries have of course inherited many features from the past, but those features are now integrated into a radically new combination. Traditionally, what are now underdeveloped countries were characterized by an equilibrium between a very slow rate of demographic growth and an equally slow rate of economic growth. Whereas 'development' can be described in terms of an economic growth rate which since the nineteenth century has out-stripped population growth, 'underdevelopment' in all Third World countries is characterized by a population growth which greatly out-strips the increase in the resources available to the population.[5]

The astonishing demographic growth rate which has characterized almost all Third World countries over the last few decades is a result of modern health programmes. But the inadequate increase in resources is a direct or indirect effect of factors which block the exploitation of exist-ing resources, rather than of any natural lack of potential. Most of these factors relate to colonial domination. And in North Africa colonization was made possible by structures which had existed for centuries.

A discussion of the present situation may seem out of place here and irrelevant to a study of Ibn Khaldun. Nothing could be further from the truth: if we are to analyse the past adequately, we must have a clear pic-ture of the times in which we live. Such considerations enable us to perceive a basic and much older problem which is of direct relevance to the period and the countries studied by the great Maghrebian historian.

Colonialism itself cannot be regarded as the primary reason for under-development: it is neither a necessary nor a sufficient historical cause. Europe has not always had an economic and social lead over the rest of the world by any means. In historical terms, the technological develop-ment of Europe is a relatively recent phenomenon which appeared only in the eighteenth and nineteenth centuries. In other parts of the world, economically advanced societies existed hundreds of years earlier. By the Middle Ages, China, India and the Arab countries had reached a techno-logical level which was equal to or even in advance of that achieved in Europe prior to the Industrial Revolution.[6]

We have, then, to explain why the scientific and technological advan-ces made by the great states of Asia and Africa in the Middle Ages did not lead to a process of economic development comparable to that to be observed in nineteenth-century Europe. This is a very complex question, but also an extremely important one in that it determined the fate of the world for a long time to come.

Very briefly, the answer to the problem would appear to be as follows: if the very complex economic and social phenomenon known as the industrial revolution is to appear, the development of the productive forces must have reached a certain level. What is more important, there must also be a bourgeoisie, a social class capable of co-ordinating the means of production and of bringing about fundamental structural transformations by making innovations and investments. For a variety of historical reasons, the bourgeoisie, which was the essential agent of economic development in Europe, could not emerge or constitute itself as a specific class in most other countries in the world. Historically, the bourgeoisie is a specifically European class. Historically, what are now underdeveloped countries were lands without a bourgeoisie.[7]

It was of course impossible for Ibn Khaldun to raise such problems, which with historical hindsight we are only beginning to formulate today. But—and it is this which gives the true measure of his brilliance— he did to some extent anticipate them. As we shall see, Ibn Khaldun provided an explanation for the sequence of political (and therefore social and economic) disasters which punctuated the history of North Africa over a period of several hundred years. These can now be seen as resulting from the absence of a social group capable of taking over from the forces which, after forging the State, succumbed each time to an ineluctable dismemberment.

Ibn Khaldun came very close to raising the fundamental question of this 'historical absence' and its effects for North Africa, albeit in partial and subjective fashion. This problem—which can now be seen as the historical non-existence of a bourgeoisie—gives his work its universal significance. The history of many underdeveloped countries differs considerably from that of the Maghreb. What they all have in common, however, regardless of the level of civilization they achieved, is that their development was blocked by the absence of those conditions that might have exacerbated their internal contradictions and allowed a bourgeoisie to emerge.

After initial periods of growth, the history of all such countries is characterized by a downturn in economic and social development, or even by a phase of stagnation or outright decline. In spite of past wealth and prestige such countries remained structurally static, and, after a series of often painful major convulsions, they appear to have entered a phase of slumber towards the end of the Middle Ages. On closer examination, their stagnation—which colonialism would subsequently turn to its own advantage—proves to be a period of confused disorder and of unsuccessful attempts to put an end to the turmoil.

Ibn Khaldun lived during this period of simultaneous turmoil and stagnation. He regarded it not as a habitual or 'normal' situation, but as a phase of decline interrupted by vain attempts at renewal.

Ibn Khaldun studied this period of ossification punctuated by intermittent crises, during which the Maghreb acquired many of the essential features that were to mark it until the eve of colonial conquest. The factors analysed by Ibn Khaldun were specific to North Africa, and he was well aware of that fact. No doubt other thinkers also became aware of the relative decadence of their respective countries (above all with the approach of colonialism). But Ibn Khaldun was the only one to produce, several hundred years before the arrival of the Europeans, such a methodical description of the successive crises that arose; he alone looked for the causes of stagnation in the internal structures of the society in which he lived rather than in some divinely ordained plan or in external causes. He found no solution or remedy simply because none was to exist for several hundreds of years to come: those stagnant and restrictive structures could only be destroyed by the action of a force emanating from a foreign and *qualitatively* different society.

Ibn Khaldun's work deals primarily with North Africa, but its significance is universal. In his account of why a series of historical upheavals failed to produce any genuine historical evolution, Ibn Khaldun is describing one form of that structural paralysis which, with the exception of Europe, existed throughout the world for centuries. In Europe, *private appropriation* of the means of production—and this now appears to have been a specifically European factor—exacerbated the internal contradictions and social antagonisms. Europe thus saw a relatively rapid succession of modes of production (over twelve centuries, admittedly): the slave system, the feudal system and the capitalist system.

In most other countries, the economic and social situation was for long periods characterized by forms of social and economic organization deriving from a single mode of production, which Marx baptized the *asiatic mode of production*.[8] The asiatic mode is characterized by the existence of a class capable of appropriating a surplus and exploiting the population without necessarily owning the means of production which, for the most part, remain in the hands of tribal or village communities.

The effect of internal contradictions is lessened because of the non-appropriation of the means of production. Class struggles cannot therefore appear and develop in any clear form, as they did in Europe. This to a large extent explains why historical development elsewhere in the world was slower and more confused than in Europe. A study of these rigid, slumbering societies provides negative confirmation of Marx's thesis that the class struggle is the motor of history.

Ibn Khaldun did not of course see the problem in these terms or on this global scale. Brilliant as he may have been, there were certain questions that he simply could not ask in the fourteenth century. We now have the benefit of hindsight and it no longer takes a genius to compare the evolution of the Maghreb and other underdeveloped countries with that of Europe. Ibn Khaldun could draw no such comparisons simply because the contrasts between these very different patterns of development were as yet embryonic or even non-existent. We have the added advantage that an analysis of an economic and social system as complex as the capitalist system enables us to perceive the specificities of the structures that preceded it both in Europe and in the rest of the world. Finally, the development of the economic and social sciences in the nineteenth and twentieth centuries, together with the work of Marx, has provided us with a conceptual arsenal more sophisticated, accurate and effective than any available in the Middle Ages.

But why should we use concepts that Ibn Khaldun himself could not formulate to analyse his work? It might be argued that we are sinning by anachronism and projecting concepts on to his work simply in order to find them there. If that were in fact the case, might not the work of other early historians look as rich and as modern as that of Ibn Khaldun when examined in the same light? But in fact they do not. Only Ibn Khaldun is so close to our contemporary concerns, and his work is undoubtedly of much greater interest than that of any other early historian. His conception of history is very close to that developed in later nineteenth-century Europe, after the rapid rise of research in the economic and social sciences. The work of other early historians, even that of great historians like Thucydides, St Augustine, Machiavelli and Montesquieu, relies upon a conception of history qualitatively poorer than that of Ibn Khaldun.

The extraordinary thing about Ibn Khaldun is that he raised many of the questions that modern historians are now asking and tried to answer them by analysing economic, social and political structures. He could not establish a precise and complete problematic or forge rigorous concepts, simply because he was working in the fourteenth century and not the nineteenth and therefore had an insufficient basis for making comparisons. He began arguments, but could not finish them or articulate them in any rigorous way. He half grasped essential facts, but could do no more than that in the conditions of his own time. Ibn Khaldun's thought also sometimes seems contradictory. Some of these contradictions are more apparent than real and a careful analysis can resolve them. Others are more serious and should not be ignored for that reason.

It would be anachronistic to see Ibn Khaldun's thought as a coherent or modern whole. The great Muslim historian was no thinker of the Enlightenment. In terms of historical analysis, his approach is rational and scientific and at times he comes close to historical materialism. But in philosophical terms, he was no rationalist: on the contrary, he was by the standards of his time very religious and sometimes clings to a form of mystical obscurantism. This contradiction will have to be analysed in detail.

But using modern concepts to analyse the work of Ibn Khaldun or looking at it in terms of contemporary problems does not mean modernizing his thought or distorting it. It is the only way we can appreciate its richness and discover the true significance of essential notions which he was unable to define with any precision. We have to try and articulate arguments that he could not follow through and recognize his subjective judgements as fragments of an objective analysis which no-one could complete in the fourteenth century. Our task is to reveal a brilliant system of thought which, for historical reasons, was doomed not to fulfil its own premises.

If we compare Ibn Khaldun's views with what we now know with the benefit of hindsight, they are obviously incomplete. But in the domain of serious history none are outdated. The work of Ibn Khaldun has now been studied in Europe for more than one hundred years.[9] As the historical conceptions of those analysing it have developed the richer and the more significant it has come to appear.

The historians of the nineteenth and early twentieth centuries were so obsessed with purely factual history that they understood little of Ibn Khaldun's work, even though they did sense its importance. The emphasis he places on social structures seemed to them to be the mark of a philosopher rather than that of a writer with an eminently scientific and unusually rich conception of history.

Many commentators distorted Ibn Khaldun's analysis of historical developments in a specific place and time and turned it into a general world view that applied to all periods and all countries. In the twentieth century, and especially between the wars, his work was taken up by authors[10] who fraudulently used it to justify their own racist theories and provide a basis for colonial ideologies. Once it had been thus distorted and diminished in scope, his work was praised to the skies by the eulogists of colonialism.

Later critics reacted against this tendency and explained the complexity and richness of his work by relating it to the specific characteristics of North Africa. But at the same time, they tried too hard to recognize the social structures of Western Europe in his writings. The historical development of the Maghreb was forced to fit in with a schema which was for long regarded by Marxists as universal: primitive communism, slavery, feudalism, capitalism. This false generalization, which blocked research into the history of non-European countries, was an expression of the eurocentrism and dogmatism that surrounded Marxian analyses for several decades. Now, however, the increasing interest shown by Marxists in the history of Africa, Asia and Latin America as a result of their increased political importance and because of the gravity of the problems they represent, suggests that research may now develop in a less dogmatic and scholastic way.

Aspects of Marx's thought which have hitherto received insufficient attention have recently been rediscovered, notably in France. Thus, the concept of the 'asiatic mode of production' is now regarded as essential to any understanding of the history of most of the world and has increasingly become the object of detailed research.[11] That research is now beginning to bear fruit and to shed light on the pre-colonial history of America, Asia and Africa. It also allows us to take a much more accurate view of Ibn Khaldun's work.

'History is a dialogue between past and present in which the present takes and keeps the initiative. ... The historian cannot be expected to see a society in the same way that it saw itself. ... Only by relating the past to the present can we make it reveal secrets which it has so far kept from even the most careful investigators.'[12]

If we are to gain any awareness of the immense and dramatic problems that have to be resolved by people who make up three quarters of the world's population, we have to think historically about the reasons for colonization and for the present situation of underdevelopment. We also have to integrate the content of the extraordinary work of Ibn Khaldun into contemporary thought. His work marks the birth of the science of history and provides an account of an essential stage in the history of what we now call the 'third world'.

Part One

The Past of the Third World

1
General Characteristics and Fundamental Structures

Ibn Khaldun (1332-1406) lived at roughly the same time as Froissard, Petrarch, Boccaccio, Duguesclin, Bajazet and Tamerlane. The names alone are enough to evoke a world that was in an intellectual ferment. But they also evoke a confused and violent world characterized by slow transformations and sudden upheavals.

We have to describe the world of the fourteenth century in broad outline, as Ibn Khaldun knew much more about it than might be thought at first sight. It would be quite wrong to imagine the great Maghrebian historian as living in isolation on the western fringes of the Muslim world. Medieval Arab civilization was essentially a trading civilization whose influence extended throughout the known world. It controlled a very extensive trade zone which stretched from the Mediterranean coast to India, China and Japan and which also took in the eastern coasts of Africa and the Western Sudan. North Africa straddled the major trade routes: it was in North Africa that traders from the east and Christian merchants met the Maghrebian traders who brought gold across the Sahara from the Sudan. As can be seen from the contents of his 'Universal History', Ibn Khaldun was well aware of the characteristics and evolution of the various Muslim states, and he also seems to have had a fairly extensive knowledge of the politics of those European states that were embroiled in the Hundred Years War. The most spectacular episode in an already eventful life came about because of the breadth and sophistication of his political and historical knowledge. Late in life, he reluctantly came into direct contact with Tamerlane[1] beneath the walls of Damascus. The Maghrebian historian provided the Mongol prince who had left such an indelible mark on the fourteenth century with such detailed information on so many countries and made such a detailed panegyric of his victories that he became the conqueror's guest rather than his prisoner. Tamerlane was so impressed that he vainly asked Ibn Khaldun to become his historiographer and adviser.

In the fourteenth century, the greatest political entity in the world stretched from the Danube to Annam. It was made up of the various Mongol principalities that had emerged from the empire forged a century earlier by Genghis Khan. Towards 1350, however, the Mongol horsemen were driven out of China by the great Ming dynasty, which was to last until the seventeenth century. India, the north divided up into kingdoms ruled by Turkish Muslims and the south into Hindu principalities, was at the mercy of wave after wave of Mongol raiders. In the Middle East, the great empire of the Caliphs of Baghdad had been no more than a memory for three hundred years, long broken up into rival states. Partly reunited under the domination of the Seljukian Turks, these countries had borne the brunt of the Crusades, which were drawing to an end in the fourteenth century, and of the fearful offensives of Genghis Khan, who destroyed Baghdad in 1258. As a result of these invasions and of their own internal problems, the regions which had once been the very heart of the Muslim world were in the fourteenth century a mere shadow of their former selves.

It was from Egypt, which had been spared from war by the energetic actions of the Mameluke dynasties, that the counter-offensives that drove the crusaders into the sea and halted the Mongol invasions were launched. Egypt enjoyed the most brilliant period of its medieval history in the fourteenth century. Intensive agriculture in the Nile valley produced abundant harvests, and the country's geographical situation meant that all trade between the ports of eastern and southern Asia and the trading cities of Italy had to go through Egypt. Cairo, where the artists, scientists and technicians who had been driven out of Asia by the war took refuge, became a major economic and intellectual centre. Egypt had been spared the wretched fate that had overcome all the countries between the Atlantic and the Indus and was enjoying exceptional prosperity. Cairo was indeed the 'metropolis of the universe', as Ibn Khaldun, who settled there in 1383, put it.

Byzantium was dying a slow death. Following up the Mamelukes' counter-offensive, the Ottoman Turks drove the Byzantines and the crusaders out of Asia Minor and then invaded Thrace, Serbia and Bulgaria. After their victory at Nicopolis (1369), which put the Balkans under Turkish rule for four hundred years, Byzantium's days seemed numbered. But it was given a last-minute reprieve. Despite its rapid expansion, the power of the Ottomans was suddenly shaken. After a series of lightning conquests (Afghanistan, Persia, Iraq, Azerbeidjan, northern India) which took him almost to the gates of Egypt (he did not in fact get beyond Damascus, which he razed after his meeting with Ibn Khaldun), Tamerlane defeated them at Ankara in 1402.

There was no equivalent in either the Muslim or the Christian west to the great states created by the invading horsemen. The west was spared the great devastating raids and the great battles. States there were smaller and more stable, but they were also more fragmented. The centralized monarchies were weakened or fragmented by feudal regionalism and by the actions of the bourgeoisie and the merchant aristocracies of the great trading centres. War became a permanent phenomenon. There were no great invasions or decisive battles, merely a chronic state of war. In many areas, banditry became a major industry. In most of Europe, the Middle Ages ended in a general crisis. In Italy, however, the first flowerings of what was to become the Renaissance were already visible: despite foreign competition, political decline and struggles between rival principalities, economic and political life was flourishing in Genoa, Milan and Florence. But in France, where the Hundred Years War had begun in 1337, the situation was becoming catastrophic. The kingdom was breaking up and both the royal armies and bands of mercenaries were causing widespread devastation in province after province.

In Spain, the Kingdom of Granada was all that remained of Iberian Islam, which had been undermined from within by internal divisions and driven back by the Christian nobility. Granada itself was often reduced to being a fief of the king of Castille. The progress of the *Reconquista* was, however, delayed for a long time as the Aragonese and Castillian nobility repeatedly rebelled against their overlord.

Political instability, the break-up of centralized states, endless wars with no decisive outcome ... all these characteristics of Western Europe were to some extent also found in North Africa, which was also undergoing a prolonged crisis in the fourteenth century. The intellectual and economic role of the great trading centres was also similar. Despite these similarities, the problems arose in a very different manner in the countries of the Maghreb. The specifically feudal structures of European society were very different from those of North African countries. In

Europe, the Hundred Years War was followed by the Renaissance. In North Africa, the convulsions and difficulties continued on a greater or lesser scale until the fifteenth and sixteenth centuries before giving way to a period of relative stabilization both in Morocco and in the rest of the Maghreb, which was by then under Turkish rule.

Before we look at the work of Ibn Khaldun, we have first to examine the basic historical features of North Africa in the Middle Ages and the essential characteristics of its social and political structures.

The content of Ibn Khaldun's work is extremely rich and complex, but not always formulated in precise or coherent terms. It is only once we have grasped the general characteristics and fundamental structures of the medieval Maghreb that we can truly understand the work of Ibn Khaldun.

North Africa was very different from the rest of the medieval Muslim world.

It shook off the authority of the great empires of the east very early, barely a century after the arrival of the Arab conquerors (690-700). A general rebellion inspired by the egalitarian heresy of Kharijism (beginning in 730) marked the end of the rule of the Caliphs of Baghdad and Damascus. From then until the sixteenth century, the Maghreb was a fully independent political unit, although it did remain in close economic and cultural contact with the east. It was neither a remote outpost of the Muslim world nor a sort of backward 'wild west'. On the contrary, North Africa occupied an essential position in Mediterranean and Middle Eastern trade because of a factor which may have been determinant and which was certainly very important for the development of Muslim civilization, and probably also for the somewhat belated development of Western Europe. For six hundred years the Maghreb controlled the gold routes to the Western Sudan. For most of the Middle Ages, Sudanese gold was the main source of precious metal for the merchants of the Middle East and much of Europe. In order to obtain it they imported all kinds of commodities into the Maghreb. Although vital to the history of the Maghreb, this factor is usually overlooked by contemporary historians. They are normally more concerned with explaining North African history in terms of tribal interests, the personal caprices of sovereigns, theological passions or clashes between different 'ways of life'. North African history is all too often presented as 'a jumble of unrelated facts . . . in which we quite naturally concentrate upon the wars'.[2]

The importance of the trade in Sudanese gold during the Middle Ages is, however, fairly well known. A number of Arab historians[3] and geographers (notably Idrisi and el-Bekri) allude to it. And according to Braudel, who also stresses the importance of the gold trade, 'It is an error . . . to consider North Africa as a rural complex. In the fourteenth and fifteenth centuries, towns grew up, sometimes out of all proportion to the surrounding countryside. They looked not only towards the Mediterranean but also to the south . . . '.[4] The gold trade appears to have been the 'main theme'[5] of North African medieval history and the motor of the Maghreb's development.

Why should the Maghreb have played such an important role in a trade which originated in the Sudanese states to the south of the great loop in the Niger and which ended up primarily in the great trading cities of Egypt and the Middle East?

It seems that from the eighth to the mid-ninth century, communications between the Western Sudan and the east went directly across the eastern Sahara. This direct route was presumably particularly important when there was open conflict between North Africa and the rulers of Baghdad during the Kharijite rebellion. But as the Arab historian Ibn Hawqal points out,[6] the direct route was abandoned because of sandstorms (climatic conditions in this part of the Sahara may have worsened) and because of the constant attacks made on the caravans (presumably by the Zaghawa). Sultan Ahmed ben Toulour of Egypt (863-883) banned the use of the direct route between Egypt and the kingdom of Ghana, which meant that all trade had to take the easier route across the western Sahara and through North Africa.

The abandoning of the direct route across the Sahara is one of the most important factors in the development of the Maghreb. It was towards the beginning of the ninth century, when the gold trade linked the Maghreb and the Sudan, that the first North African states began to develop so spectacularly: the Kingdom of Fez, Tahert in the central Maghreb, and the Kingdom of Kairouan in Ifriqiyah (now Tunisia). The vicissitudes of the gold trade explain and provide a connecting link between many of the more important events of the Middle Ages in North Africa. Only the more important changes can be mentioned here, as we are concerned with analysing the work of Ibn Khaldun and not with undertaking a detailed study of the influence of the gold trade on the Maghreb during the Middle Ages, fascinating as that topic might be.[7]

Trade with the Sudan was for the most part a matter of private initiative.

But it also had a direct effect upon the power of the Maghrebian states. Their rulers profited greatly from it, both indirectly by levying various taxes on the transactions, and directly by organizing caravans, either by themselves or in partnership with merchants. For several centuries, the North African states fought for control over the caravan routes and especially over the 'desert ports', the points at which the caravans reached the northern edge of the Sahara. Although some caravan routes from the Niger valley did cross the central Sahara and the Hoggar and then pass through the eastern Maghreb, by far the most heavily used route crossed the western Sahara, which is narrower and less arid. The Atlantic route curved round to Sijilmassa, at the foot of the High Atlas. For several centuries, the gold caravans passed through Sijilmassa and the town was therefore coveted by the rulers of both Spain and the Maghreb. The Caliphs of Cordoba, in particular, held on to their bridgehead in Ceuta and tried to maintain links with Sijilmassa, either through direct action or through a system of alliances. From Sijilmassa, the routes used by the gold caravans either headed northwards towards Spain or eastwards along the edge of the Tell. The towns, staging posts and crossroads which stood along the trade routes often became the capitals of the states that developed in North Africa from the ninth century onwards: Fez, on the road to Spain, Tlemcen, Tahert, La Qalaa, Constantine and Kairouan on the road to the east. The power of each state and its economic importance depended upon its ability to monopolize a major share of the gold trade.

The apparently confused struggles between these states and their tribal allies can for the most part be explained in terms of a desire to exert as much control as possible over the gold routes rather than a desire for territorial gains as such. The way in which the three most powerful states in medieval North Africa developed clearly underlines the direct relationship between political power and control over the main towns along the gold routes. In all three cases, a fairly small group of tribes led by a man whose political and religious vision went far beyond the confines of the tribe were suddenly able to establish a very large state almost immediately after they had taken Sijilmassa. In all three cases, the prime object of their expansion was to conquer other main centres of the caravan trade.

In the tenth century, a group of mountain tribes from Kabylia whose opposition to the ruler of Kairouan took a religious form captured Ifriqiyah and marched on Sijilmassa. This was the beginning of the *Empire of the Fatimids*, who became so powerful that they conquered Egypt and founded Cairo (973). In a series of major offensives against Fez, Tlemcen Tahert and above all Ceuta, the Fatimid rulers and their successors tried to prevent the Caliphs of Cordoba from controlling Sijilmassa and the gold trade.

The origins of the tenth-century *Almoravid Empire* appear to be even more closely connected with control over the gold caravans. Under the leadership of a religious reformer, a group of Saharan tribes who already controlled the routes across the Atlantic Sahara captured the Sudanese towns from which the caravans left for the Maghreb. In 1056, they captured Sijilmassa. After having founded Marakesh, the Almoravids conquered Morocco, part of the central Maghreb and the Muslim kingdoms of Spain (1110).

In the twelfth century, a group of tribes from the High Atlas, again led by a religious reformer, founded the nucleus of the *Almohad State* in the mountains. For thirty years, the Almoravids resisted them successfully, but suddenly collapsed when the Almohads took Sijilmassa in 1145. Immediately after this, the Almohads captured the whole of Morocco, the central Maghreb and then Ifriqiyah and Muslim Spain. Their immense empire, which stretched across the Muslim west from Castille to the Gulf of Gabès, gradually broke up in the thirteenth century. The Almohads fell only when Sijilmassa was captured by their successors, the *Marinids*. The Marinids were unable to control the south of Spain or to reunify the whole of the Maghreb, which remained divided into several kingdoms with shifting frontiers.

Medieval North African states cannot be defined in terms of their frontiers. The state was basically a political centre of gravity exercising a variable degree of control over a group of relatively autonomous tribes. The heart or 'pole' of each state was a major city on the trade routes to which Christian or eastern merchants flocked. In the west, Fez became the capital of Morocco once more under the Marinids. In the central Maghreb, Tlemcen, Bougie and Constantine (all of which traded with the Sudan) became the capitals of three states of unequal size. In the east, Tunis, which was a major centre for international trade, became the capital of Ifriqiyah.

These states were frequently embroiled in confused struggles, the main cause of which was, by the thirteenth or fourteenth century, no longer even masked by religious rivalries. The struggles between them always revolved around control over the gold routes: one of the constant preoccupations of the Marinids, for example, was gaining control over Tlemcen, the goal of some of the caravans arriving from the Sudan.

The events mentioned above are not the major feature of much of North Africa's history during the Middle Ages. They are merely the most outstanding examples that can be chosen from a host of truly significant events. They testify to the close correlation between state policies and the gold trade in the Maghreb between the ninth and the fourteenth centuries.

The existence of such a correlation proves that a major proportion of the revenue of the rulers of these states derived either directly or indirectly from the trans-Saharan trade and from the associated import trade.

The state levied taxes on all trading operations and particularly on dealings in precious metal. But the rulers themselves also took part in trade, either in partnership with merchants or by using agents to carry out transactions on their behalf. The state needed the merchants, but the merchants' need of the state was even greater as it made a major contribution to their safety. The Royal Treasury and private wealth coexisted in a sort of symbiosis which allowed both rulers and merchants to undertake ventures they could not have undertaken on their own. Ibn Khaldun mentions several examples of bankers and money-changers becoming ministers of finance, chamberlains or grand viziers.

This intense economic activity was not primarily based upon the sale of commodities produced in North Africa itself but upon the exchange of gold and commodities from distant countries. The profits which accumulated in the hands of a minority composed of merchants or individuals associated with the ruler did not derive from their appropriation of the means of production, but from their position as intermediaries in the international market. The only conditions required for the realization of profits were those necessary for the circulation of money and commodities.

The importance of merchants' profits to some extent explains the weakness of the tendency to appropriate the means of production. Ibn Khaldun does point out that the great merchants who lived near the towns often owned estates,[8] but their estates were not large as their ability to appropriate land was restricted by the rights of the sovereign and by the collective customary rights of the tribes. A further sign of the relatively slight importance of such estates and of the weakness of any tendency to appropriate the means of production is that slavery played a minor role in North Africa. Outside the Saharan oases, the sugar cane plantations and the plain of Sous in Morocco, most slaves in the Maghreb were not used in production, although large numbers of them were used as servants or soldiers.

Aside from income from trade, the wealth of the ruler and the profits accruing to the privileged minority derived from taxes levied on other sections of the population, either peacefully or by force. The king could raise taxes directly. In order to reward a powerful individual for services rendered (usually services of a military nature) he could delegate to him fiscal powers over a town or tribe, thus allowing him to levy taxes on his own behalf. This system of fiscal concessions was known as *iqta'*.

The fact that the holder of a charter of *iqta'* paid homage to the sovereign suggests a comparison with some aspects of the fief in the European feudal system, but there are in fact considerable differences between the two systems. In western Europe, the holder of a fief was granted a share of political power over each peasant in a given area and the right to own land on a permanent basis. In the Arab world, the holder of a charter of *iqta'* was temporarily granted the power to raise taxes from a given group, but had no right to the land, which remained in the possession of the ruler and which was held in usufruct by the tribes. Nor did he have any right to govern the tribesmen.

The European lord had certain economic, administrative, juridical, political and land rights over a given area and a given number of people; a charter of *iqta'* gave only fiscal rights. The holder was of course often a warrior, like the European feudal lord (if only because that gave him the means to bring in the taxes), and there was a personal basis to his relationship with the ruler. But in the Maghreb, personal vassalage relations affected only a small fraction of the population. Whereas in Europe the feudal system made every peasant directly dependent upon a master, in North Africa every man belonged to a tribe and on the whole it was the tribe that was subject to the chieftain who had been granted the right to raise taxes. The tribe gave every peasant and shepherd belonging to it considerable protection against the warlord-tax farmer.

The survival of tribal cohesion in the Maghreb prevented the *iqta'* system from evolving into a seigneurial system. In certain regions of the Middle East where tribal organization had broken down, chieftains with charters of *iqta'* did, however, find it easier to force the peasants to place themselves under their protection and give up their land. But although widespread in the Middle East, the *himaya* system—under which a powerful individual offered protection to anyone who surrendered himself and his land to him—could not really develop in North Africa because of the strength of the tribes.[9]

As Ibn Khaldun points out, however, personal relations based upon protection did develop in the towns and surrounding areas where the tribal system had almost ceased to exist.[10]

In North Africa, vassalage relations were superimposed upon tribal organizations but did not penetrate them. The ruler's power was to a large extent based upon his own tribal group. He had power over other tribes, but not within them. Whereas in feudal Europe individuals were subject to the personal authority of a suzerain lord, in North Africa the individual's only loyalty was to his tribe and its chieftain. In Europe, relations of dependence were juridical and personal. In North Africa, all that existed was a hierarchy between tribes rather than between individuals. It was a *de facto* and not a *de jure* hierarchy. The leaders of the more powerful tribes who had received charters of *iqta'* and who were directly allied with the ruler often used force to raise taxes from weaker tribes, either on behalf of the ruler or on their own account (and in theory on behalf of the tribe). In extreme cases, this developed into a *razzia* system of raiding parties and booty. The weaker *ra'iya* tribes who paid such taxes were subordinate to the *maghzan*[11] tribes whose chieftains paid homage to the ruler: relationships between the two were often strengthened by marriage ties.

The strength of tribal organizations was one of the distinguishing features of the Maghreb. It can be explained in a variety of ways.

In the Middle East, the dynasties founded by the Umayyad and then the Abassid Caliphs to a large extent adopted the estate system established by the Romans and Byzantines. In North Africa, survivals of ancient structures were much less widespread, partly because Rome and Byzantium never controlled anything but the fringes of the country (primarily Ifriqiyah). Moreover, the Arab conquerors who took over the Maghreb in the seventh century were not following directly in the footsteps of other foreign rulers. The Arab empire extended over areas in which the tribal structures dismantled by the colonizers had been reconstructed over a period of several centuries of effective independence.[12] Finally, the eastern Caliphs' domination over North Africa (710-780) was relatively short-lived, being ended by the Khajirite insurrection.

As Ibn Khaldun points out, the strength of tribal structures in North

Africa can also to a large extent be explained in terms of the dominance of a pastoral economy. This results partly from geographical factors, such as the size of the steppes, which were better suited to stock-raising than to irrigated agriculture, the importance of transhumance between the plains and the mountains and the proximity of the desert. The pastoral economy had survived and had even been strengthened by historical factors, notably the role played by herdsmen in the caravan trade. The tribal system was also eminently suited to ensuring the cohesion of a pastoral group whose movements meant that it could not define itself in terms of a specific or permanently occupied territory.

Ibn Khaldun gives prime importance to a further reason for the survival of tribal structures, namely the warlike customs and abilities which had for centuries characterized most of the (male) population of North Africa. Much more so than in western Europe, most men in the medieval Maghreb were still warriors, especially the men of the *bled*. This was largely an effect of the spread of pastoralism. No matter whether he was truly nomadic or semi-nomadic (raising crops and stock), the herdsman always had a mount, which, given the military techniques of the day, meant that he was either actually or potentially a warrior. Even groups whose herding activities were more restricted were equally warlike. The military skills of the population as a whole strengthened tribal structures by preventing the warlords from extending their authority to any great extent, as they could have done if the population had not been armed. 'Where every free man remained a warrior, liable to be constantly called to service and distinguished from the pick of the fighting-men by nothing essential in his equipment, the peasant had no difficulty in avoiding subjection. . . .'[13]

Finally, the amount of profit that could be made from the caravans also helps explain why few tribal chieftains tried to break up the tribal structures and appropriate the means of production.

In the more densely populated areas of the Middle East (Iraq, Egypt), tribal structures had been weakened. In western Europe, they had disappeared altogether. In North Africa, however, most of the population (with the notable exception of those living in the towns and surrounding areas) still lived within the framework of tribal structures and went on doing so until the nineteenth century. In some mountain areas, the tribal structures took the form of village communities. Although money circulated on a considerable scale and although groups with different 'ways of life' often traded with one another, for the most part each of these tribal groups was still living in an economy that was close to self-sufficiency.

The population as a whole was dominated by a privileged minority which enjoyed considerable wealth but did not own the means of production. As we have seen, the holder of a charter of *iqta'* did not enjoy any particular rights over land or individuals, but merely fiscal power over a group. For the most part the merchant's role was restricted to that of an intermediary between distant markets. The privileged minority is particularly complex and difficult to define: although numerous and powerful, the merchants did not constitute a bourgeoisie. On the one hand, they made relatively little attempt to control the means of production: they did not want to do so (trade being more profitable in the short term) and could not do so as the land belonged to the king and was occupied by the tribes. On the other hand—and unlike the true European bourgeoisie, which although wealthy was as a class subordinate to the aristocracy—merchants in Muslim countries were closely connected with royal power and belonged to an aristocracy. They did not, then, form a bourgeoisie but a merchant aristocracy, often closely connected with the tribal or military aristocracy. Some great tribal chieftains were also caravan traders. In Europe, members of the bourgeoisie who wanted to buy land came up against the power of the landed aristocracy. No such conflict existed in North Africa where the land was not subject to private appropriation.

In Europe, the landed nobility was able to retain power because it was a specialized military force living in the midst of an unarmed population. The right to bear arms became a hereditary privilege, the mark of a caste. In North Africa, almost everyone bore arms and no such caste could develop. There was no nobility in the strict feudal sense.

In Europe, the structures of feudal society were established in a period marked by a decline in monetary exchange. Land distribution was the only possible way in which the sovereign could reward the nobility for their services. The development of private rights over land and individuals was not, however, simply an effect of this historical phase: it also represented a continuation of the slave system, which had been characterized by an even more radical appropriation of the means of production (land and slaves). When trade and monetary exchange recovered in Europe, there was no room for merchants within the landowning military aristocracy, which had developed the stable structures of a hereditary caste. Unable to integrate themselves into this 'watertight' minority, the

merchants formed a distinct class—the bourgeoisie—whose interests
were in conflict with those of the aristocracy

In the Arab countries, the circulation of money never dried up for such
long periods and the merchants were able to retain their position within
the privileged minority. The criterion for membership of this aristocracy
was neither birth, military prowess or ownership of land, but financial
power, no matter whether it derived from trade or from the use of military (tribal) force to raise taxes. This moneyed aristocracy was neither a
caste nor a watertight minority. Anyone who became wealthy could
become a member of it. It was also very unstable. On the one hand, if
merchants went bankrupt, the king could confiscate their fortunes on the
grounds that they had been acquired illegitimately. On the other hand,
the warlord was the *de facto* leader of his tribe but had no *de jure* rights.
Within the tribe, he was theoretically *primus inter pares*. Power could
not therefore be simply or directly handed down from father to son, particularly as polygamy complicated lines of descent considerably. Finally,
unlike the king in the European feudal system, whose real power was
greatly reduced because it was fragmented amongst the nobility, the
North African ruler enjoyed great wealth and had a concentrated state
apparatus at his disposal. He could use other tribes, mercenaries or
slaves to take back charters of *iqta'*, which were granted only on a temporary basis. The North African aristocracy therefore remained relatively unstable and never became a structured hereditary group. Money
was in permanent circulation and it was therefore possible to establish a
permanent centralized state. The existence of the state meant that no
vassal hierarchy could come between the central authorities and their
subjects or displace the loyalties of the peasants.[14]

Conflicts were frequent in North African society, but there was no real
class struggle as such.

There were no basic antagonisms between the merchants and the tribal chieftains. Merchants could increase their profits without antagonizing the chieftains, as they too could take part in trade. Struggles resulting
from the use of military force to collect taxes were common, but such
struggles were between groups of a similar nature. There were no qualitatively different features between dominant and dominated tribes.

The leaders of the stronger groups did of course benefit most from the
iqta' system. But there was no clear distinction between the leaders and
other members of the tribe. Their power was not juridically defined and
they in fact tried to mask their real authority beneath a show of tribal

egalitarianism. Moreover, they shared some of their profits with those who paid them tribute, showing particular generosity to their own clients. One of the most interesting sections of Ibn Khaldun's work provides an analysis of the complex and contradictory aspects of the role of the chieftain within the tribe.

Medieval North African society was not simply a tribal society: the role of the military and merchant aristocracy was essential to it. Nor was it a slave society; slaves were common, but they were rarely used in production. Nor was it a feudal society; despite the existence of complex relations of dependence, the dominant relations of production were not feudal. Only a minority were affected by clearly delineated relations of dependence and, within the tribe, relations between employer and employee remained unstructured and embryonic. Even on the few big estates near the towns there was no seigneurial system and, for the most part, no private ownership of land. In North Africa, there was no real nobility, no professional soldiers (apart from slaves) and no real bourgeoisie.

The dominant mode of production in the medieval Maghreb, as in much of the medieval world, was basically characterized by:

1. the insertion of the vast majority of the population into autarkic or semi-autarkic village or tribal communities;

2. the presence of a privileged minority whose members accumulated large profits but had no right to the private ownership of the means of production.

These, then, are the basic characteristics of what Marx termed the *asiatic mode of production*.

The mode of production found in North Africa does, however, differ considerably from that described by Marx as existing in 'hydraulic societies'.[15] Hydraulic societies (Egypt, Mesopotamia, India, China, Muslim Spain) were characterized by the construction of large-scale irrigation works, or, more generally, by large-scale works built for various purposes. These enormous constructions were built by the entire population working under the orders of a bureaucracy. The population was forced into a generalized *corvée* system by the sovereign, the personification of the higher interests of the community.

Large-scale irrigation works were built in the *huertas* of southern Spain and Egypt, but practically none were constructed in the Maghreb even though North Africa does have a number of great plains (the Ghard plain in Morocco, the Chetif and the Mitidja in Algeria and the Medjerda in Tunisia) which could have been irrigated and used for agriculture.

It is not easy to explain why no irrigation works were built there. It could be argued that the labour force was too small for anyone to contemplate such undertakings. On the other hand, the development of highly intensive agriculture would have led to an increase in the population. The prevalence of a pastoral or semi-pastoral way of life was presumably a further obstacle. But the main reason is that the strength of tribal structures had so weakened the power of the rulers that it was impossible for them to subjugate or mobilize the population. It should be noted that, for the most part, hydraulic societies developed in classical antiquity when ideological and social conditions were such that the population completely accepted the authority of a god-king and his bureaucracy of engineer-priests.

The preconditions for the mobilization of the labour force and for the construction of large-scale works may have existed in North Africa before the region was colonized by the Romans, in the days of the ancient Berber kingdoms. The many megalithic monuments found in the Maghreb, and notably the famous Medracen near Tipasa in Algeria, could only have been built by rulers who commanded a large workforce. Roman domination, which destroyed the power of the Berber kings and introduced the slave mode of production, may have led to the disappearance of developing forms of collective mobilization. That, however, is no more than a hypothesis.

Whatever the reasons, North Africa did not develop along the same lines as the so-called 'hydraulic societies'. If the two are reduced to their bare essentials, the relations of production are of course the same: members of an aristocracy dominating a collectively based society are able to appropriate considerable profits but have no private right to own the means of production, which are still organized within the framework of tribal or village communities. But although North African and Asiatic societies may seem similar in that the relations of production are the same in both, they are in fact similar only in so far as such relations of production differ from those characteristic of the slave, feudal or capitalist modes.

A mode of production is defined not only by its dominant *relations of production* but also by the nature of the means of production. In terms of both agriculture and manufacturing activity, 'hydraulic societies' were typified by much more sophisticated and effective means of production than those found in medieval North Africa.

In hydraulic societies, where the construction of large-scale works led to a considerable increase in production, the wealth of the privileged minority derived from the confiscation of a major surplus. In Maghrebian society, where the level of the productive forces remained relatively low, the undoubted wealth enjoyed by the privileged minority derived from the trading profits made possible by North Africa's exceptional position in relation to the main international trade routes, rather than from the direct confiscation of a surplus from the tribes.

Were the relations of production found in the medieval Maghreb identical to those typifying 'hydraulic societies'? In the latter, peasant communities were subject to a very high rate of exploitation. They were forced to undertake *corvée* labour and kept in a state of generalized collective serfdom by an aristocracy which was in fact a true caste, often of foreign origin, and with virtually no contact with the mass of the population. As well as being inhibited by a religious ideology according to which the powers of the privileged minority were divinely ordained, the peasantry was usually defenceless against armies of slaves. The priest and the warrior-slave were the means by which the aristocracy maintained its exploitation of the peasant masses in 'hydraulic societies'.

Conditions in North Africa were quite different: the privileged minority was not regarded as divine and for the most part it remained firmly integrated into the tribal communities. In most cases, the warlord was also a tribal chieftain and, as Ibn Khaldun stresses, his military strength depended upon the enthusiasm with which his followers supported him. The king himself was merely a tribal chieftain who had taken command of a confederation of tribal groups. In time of conflict, his slaves were faced with a formidable military force made up of mounted herdsmen. Class differentiation was therefore much less developed and the rate of exploitation much lower than in 'hydraulic societies'. In North Africa, the mass requisitions of labour which typified 'hydraulic societies' were not really possible, and this to a large extent explains the absence of major irrigation works in the region.

The characteristics of the tribal communities of North Africa were, then, very different from those of the village communities of 'hydraulic societies'. The two communities were subject to very different forms of exploitation and their ability to resist oppression differed considerably.

They represented two very different forms of communal structure. The tribe was characterized by the existence of blood ties (often imaginary) between its members. It was a much more autonomous social structure than the village community. The tribal group was a form of military organization, and it could defend itself. Its members were armed and knew how to fight under the leadership of their chieftain. As a form of political organization, the tribe was an embryonic state. In North Africa, the 'state' was in a sense a confederation of tribes allied to a sovereign. Being supported by warriors from different tribes, the sovereign did not necessarily have to rely upon an army of slaves. A large proportion of the ruling aristocracy, including the king himself, was still an integral part of the tribal structures.

In contrast, the village communities of hydraulic societies could not defend themselves; as a rule, their members were not armed and had no military leader. The village community was not an autonomous political unit, but simply one of the many elements making up the base of the state. The ruling aristocracy, and especially the king, were quite external to it and had to rely upon armies of mercenaries or slaves to assert their power.

For the most part, the tribe consisted of 'free men' who were proud of the arms they bore and which symbolized their freedom, be it real or illusory. The village community consisted mainly of men who were forced to perform *corvée* labour as well as working on the large-scale constructions ordered by the sovereign. The tribe was characteristic of a society in which the exploiting class had yet to become clearly differentiated and in which forms of exploitation were not accentuated. The village community was one element in a society in which the powers and the characteristics of the privileged minority were very strongly marked.

The differences are considerable. They relate to both the means of production and to the relations of production. We therefore have to conclude that the two societies do not derive from the same mode of production or even from two variants of the so-called 'asiatic mode of production'.

We are dealing with two different modes of production. It would be as erroneous to make no radical distinction between them on the grounds that they both correspond to communally-based societies dominated by an aristocracy, as it would be to argue that slavery and feudalism belong to the same mode of production simply because the means of production are in both cases 'appropriated'.

It would therefore seem advisable to use the expression 'asiatic mode of production' with extreme caution, as referring only to a number of very different modes of production which can be identified neither with slavery nor with feudalism nor with one another. Even within the communally-based modes, a primary distinction has to be made on the basis of the criterion of the productivity or non-productivity of the large-scale works. Such works presuppose the existence of very specific relations of production between a despotic aristocratic caste and subjugated village communities. The aristocracy can force the unarmed population to work on large-scale projects because the ruler is regarded as divine and can rely upon an army of slaves. The work is carried out under the supervision of a technical bureaucracy. 'Hydraulic societies' belong within this major category, as do 'non-hydraulic societies' in which despotic aristocracies force the population to construct non-productive large-scale works.

An analysis of the economic and social structures of North Africa reveals a completely different mode of production. In terms of its basic characteristics, it is not specific to the Maghreb and appears to have existed in other countries too. Its extension adds further interest to the work of Ibn Khaldun, which provides most of the elements of this analysis. In terms of their mode of production, several other societies of considerable historical importance seem to have been similar to the medieval Maghreb. Such societies are particularly interesting in that they played what would now be termed an 'international' role. Just as the Maghrebians were able to establish their control over the trans-Saharan routes, over Spain and even briefly over Egypt, these societies were able to conquer vast areas of territory and thus control a major share of international trade. To take examples outside classical antiquity, we could, for instance, mention the conquests made by the Arab tribes in the seventh and eighth centuries, the conquests made by Seljukian and Ottoman Turks, and the immense empires established by the Mongol tribes. In addition to these spectacular examples, we might cite the equally significant cases of the states established in the Western Sudan: Ghana from the seventh to the ninth century, Mali in the eighteenth and nineteenth centuries, and the Songhai Empire in the fifteenth century. Their power resulted from their control over the gold routes from countries even further to the south.

In all these cases, we find tribally-based societies in which an aristocracy that is still very much integrated into the tribe uses the complex influences it can exert (blood ties, client or vassal relationships) in order to lead a group of armed men to military victory. The subsequent conquests are made, not by slaves, but by free men who think it is in their interests or to their honour to support their tribal chiefs. The aristocracy is not yet a fully differentiated privileged minority, but merely the embryo of an exploiter class. As the tribe conquers more territory, the tribal aristocracy does, however, tend to become more differentiated and to develop into a ruling class which destroys the earlier (theoretical) egalitarianism of the tribe. In historical terms, this development marks the transition from the last classless society to the first class society. The concept of 'military democracy' can be used to characterize these complex relations of production. As we shall see, Ibn Khaldun studied it in detail and saw it as being of primary importance to North African social structures.

The conquests made by the tribal group allow it to levy taxes from its defeated enemies and to establish control over some of the major international trade routes. As an increasingly large share of the profits are more and more openly appropriated by the privileged minority, a state apparatus can be financed to maintain dominance over allied or conquered tribes. The greater part of the profits derive from trading activities. When the means of production do not produce a major surplus, taxation does not produce a particularly great mass of profit, despite the harsh exploitation to which the conquered population is subjected. That surplus alone is not enough to support the structures of a great state. The military power of a group of tribes is not enough, and profits from trade are essential. All the states created on a tribal basis were greatly involved in trade. The strength of the Turkish and Mongol empires derived from their control over the routes to the east and the west. In this respect, the famous alliance between Genghis Khan and the merchants is highly significant.

These societies can, then, be characterized by a combination of the structures of military democracy and those of trade. The privileged minority is directly or indirectly associated with both tribal and merchant aristocracy. But does the phenomenon of military democracy and a tribal aristocracy constitute a true 'mode of production', autonomous in the same sense as the mode characteristic of the communally-based societies which produced 'large-scale works'?

In tribal and trading empires profits derive from trade rather than from the appropriation of a surplus out of what is, after all, a low level of production. The empire owes its wealth to its function as an intermediary

between productive societies. The amount of profit made by the intermediary depends upon the distance between those societies. On the one
hand, geographical distance determines the scarcity of the products
exchanged. On the other hand, the profits are also determined by the
historical distance between societies with very uneven levels of development. Gold is bought cheaply from the producers in Africa or even
extorted from tribal chieftains and then exchanged for high-value
manufactured products in the Maghreb.

Tribal and trading empires whose wealth derives primarily from their
function as intermediaries can, therefore, be characterized as belonging
to an *artificial mode of production*. Many of these states collapsed when
traders ceased to use the routes they controlled. But, as the work of Ibn
Khaldun and others shows, they were also suffering from an internal
crisis.

Certain states founded by warrior tribes and merchants did, it is true,
find a certain stability within structures similar to those of 'hydraulic
societies'. Such was the case of certain parts of the Arab empire (Egypt,
Iraq) and the kingdoms founded in India by the Turkish and Mongol
conquerors. It would, however, be wrong to argue that the structures of
'military democracy' were transformed there into those of 'hydraulic
society'. Within the conquering tribes, tribal structures were certainly
transformed, with a tribal aristocracy that was once firmly integrated
into the tribe being differentiated into a ruling caste. But the Muslim
conquest did not change the life of the majority of the population to any
great extent. In Egypt, for instance, village communities simply preserved the structures of the 'hydraulic societies' established in the Nile
valley in classical times. In order to keep the unarmed peasantry in a
state of serfdom, the privileged minority relied upon armies of mercenaries or slaves whose role was so important that they often took power
themselves.

Basically, then, the structures of 'military democracy' did not really
evolve towards those of 'hydraulic societies'. The latter were much older
and survived only with major transformations.[16]

It would seem that the states founded by warrior tribes and merchants
only survived for any length of time in so far as they conquered truly
productive regions in which hydraulic societies had long been established.

This was not the case in North Africa, where, despite the presence of
considerable natural potential, no hydraulic societies developed. The

Maghreb is of great importance to any debate over the evolution of communally based modes of production. Thanks to the work of Ibn Khaldun, it is possible to study the evolution of the structures of military democracy in almost a pure state.

2

A Politician from a Great Family

Now that we have schematically defined the social and economic characteristics of medieval North Africa, we can begin to analyse the numerous difficulties facing the region in the fourteenth century. Instead of relying upon a theoretical approach we can use a concrete description: Ibn Khaldun's own account[1] of his experiences during the fifty years he spent in the various countries of the Muslim west. The great historian was directly involved in a number of political events and lived in many very different milieux. Ibn Khaldun's account of his life from his childhood to his departure for Egypt, where he spent the last third of his life, is like an exemplary and significant extract from a long film about the vicissitudes of Maghrebian history over a period of several hundred years. It also provides us with a picture of the destiny of an extraordinary individual. Finally, it allows us to grasp some of the reasons that inspired Ibn Khaldun write such an original work before his departure for the east. The implications of his work are universal, but the work itself is inseparable from the man who conceived it and the events he lived through.

The Almohad Empire which unified the Maghreb disappeared sixty years before Ibn Khaldun was born in Tunis in 1332. Its splendours had vanished even earlier, towards the end of the twelfth century. The great era of the Almohads, which marked the apotheosis of medieval Maghrebian civilization, was still remembered as a golden age. That vision of the Almohad Empire was of course somewhat exaggerated, but it has to be said that it was in a sense justified in view of the long period of anarchy, poverty and turmoil that followed it.

Almohad civilization left its mark on many towns, and the three states which dominated political life in the fourteenth century Maghreb were all either directly or indirectly descended from the Empire. In Ifriqiyah, the reigning Hafsid dynasty[2] had been founded by a provincial governor who became independent when the Empire collapsed. In the central Maghreb, the extremely turbulent kingdom of Tlemcen was ruled by the Abd el-Wadid[3] dynasty which was struggling to resist invasions from Morocco. The Abd el-Wadids too were heirs of the Almohads, who had given them the formidable task of maintaining order in the central Maghreb. In Morocco, the rulers of the Marinid dynasty[4] who delivered the final death blow to the disintegrating Empire in 1269 were positively haunted by the memory of the glory of their former adversaries. They tried to emulate them and to continue their work by pursuing a holy war in Spain and attempting to reunify the Maghreb.

By the fourteenth century, however, the unity which had once symbolized the splendours of the Muslim west was a thing of the past. In Spain, the outcome of the Christian *Reconquista* was no longer in doubt. In the Maghreb, the three states were becoming more clearly differentiated, despite the Marinids' efforts to fulfil their great dream of unifying all the lands from Tunis to Fez, and despite the cultural links between them.

The three political entities were far from being coherent units. The death of a king led almost automatically to a struggle over succession to the throne, as the sons of the king's various wives quarrelled and recruited supporters. One of the weaknesses of Muslim kingdoms was that they never succeeded in establishing the principle of transmitting royal power by primogeniture. Such periodical struggles for power obviously did little to encourage that principle.

In theory, royal power was autocratic. In the countryside, however, the kings merely had power *over* the tribes, which remained autonomous and always tried to avoid paying taxes as far as possible. A better measure of the real power of the king was the extent of territory he actually controlled. Usually, he had to content himself with having a purely theoretical authority over the mountain areas and outlying regions. Hence the distinction between the *Bled el-Maghzan*, which was under government control and paid taxes, and the rebellious *Bled essiba*, which refused to pay them. Although rarely aggressive, the *Bled essiba* lived apart from the rest of the kingdom and was organized on the basis of traditional tribal structures.

In the *maghzan* areas, the tribes responsible for collecting taxes carried out *razzias* of their own as well as acting on the king's behalf, and the resultant insecurity was very detrimental to the interests of the peasantry. All these struggles became entangled with government attempts to regain control over the *Bled essiba* and rivalries among the main chieftains. On top of these internal struggles, there were full-scale wars between the rulers of the three capitals. Wars between the states were further complicated by minor tribal wars, vassal rebellions and the plots of pretenders to the throne who readily found tribes to support them. War was therefore a permanent phenomenon, both a real industry and a method of government.

Most of the fighting-men were recruited from amongst the mounted tribesmen, whose mobility was a major reason for their warlike propensities. The Bedouin, who began to move west in the eleventh century, were particularly important in this respect.

Although they were more strictly controlled than the countryside, the cities and even the capitals were frequently turbulent: viziers, chamberlains—effectively the mayors of the palace—and pretenders belonging to the royal family all fought amongst themselves for power and looked for support from Arab and Christian mercenaries. Struggles at court often went far beyond the walls of the *Kasbah* (the fortified part of the city and the centre of political life) and led to popular disturbances. Intrigues, plots, coups d'état and assassinations were commonplace.

Despite the instability and turmoil, the great cities remained major trade centres and continued to play an important role in the life of North Africa. The political, cultural and religious life of the state revolved around them and they attracted large numbers of merchants from both the east and from Christian countries. The cities had relatively large populations for the time: Tlemcen, Constantine and Bougie each had a population of forty to fifty thousand. Fez and Tunis, the capitals of the two largest states, both had more than one hundred thousand inhabitants. The population of the great cities was very mixed and included a floating population which had left the countryside for social or religious reasons or which had been driven away by the reigning instability. The true city-dwellers formed a number of distinct groups: soldiers and officials who lived in the Kasbah, intellectuals, traders, artisans. . . . Various specialist *souks* (narrow streets occupied by artisans and shopkeepers) clustered around the great mosque in the heart of the city. Luxury trades were located close to the mosque; dirty or noisy trades further out.

The Khalduns were a noble family whose distant ancestors came from Hadramaout in Arabia. They settled in Andalusia and the Ibn Khalduns ('sons of Kaldun') were one of the most powerful families in Seville, where they played a considerable role. Many historians speak of the scientific and intellectual fame enjoyed by the Khaldun family, as well as of their importance in political life. They were famed for the bravery they showed during the great battle of Zellaqa (1086), when the Almoravid and Andalusian troops crushed the Christian armies. After having played a major role in the defence of Seville against the Christians, the Khalduns, like many others, left Seville in about 1230, by which time the city was being torn apart by the factional struggles stirred up by the rival great powers. Further resistance became pointless when a rumour that the city was to be surrendered for both local and international political reasons was confirmed.

The Khalduns initially took refuge in Ceuta, where they allied themselves by marriage with one of the most important families, and then left for Tunis. In the midst of the anarchy caused by the death throes of the Almohad Empire, Ifriqiyah seemed to offer the only hope of strength and stability. Abu Zakariya, governor of Tunis and a member of one of the most noble families in the Almohad Empire, had just proclaimed its independence and was laying the foundations of a strong and powerful state. He succeeded in preserving the prestige of the Almohads and his authority was soon recognized by a number of Spanish princes, as well as in large areas of the Maghreb. Right from the beginning of his reign, the ruler of Tunis showed his support for the cause of Spanish Islam by going to the aid of the besieged city of Seville. As well as being the founder of the Hafsid dynasty, Abu Zakariya had for a long time been the Almohad governor of Seville and had connections with many of the great Andalusian families. When they were forced to abandon their homes, many of them therefore made for Tunis. This Andalusian élite was accompanied by a host of clients, including artisans who brought with them their sophisticated techniques and knowledge, and skilled farmers who created small but rich *huertas* on the coastal plains of northern Ifriqiyah.

Being connected with the ruler by a long-standing friendship and being almost related to him, the Khaldun family was given an especially warm welcome in Tunis. As well as being given gifts, favours, land and other marks of friendship, they were soon appointed to important administrative posts. After the death of the first Hafsid ruler, the Ibn Khalduns retained the trust and favours of his successors. The historian's great-grandfather was a skilful minister of finance and paid for his loyalty to the dynasty with his life when a usurper temporarily seized power.

The grandfather of Abd al-Rahman Ibn Khaldun (the historian's full name) held a number of offices and displayed exceptional loyalty to his king in times of difficulty. The king made him his adviser and even entrusted him with the government of the city during his absences.

The Khaldun family were able to play an important role in the administration of the country for a long time, partly because of the ties of friendship between their ancestors and the founder of the dynasty and partly because of the political importance of the Andalusians to the political life of the city. In their attempt to consolidate their power, the Hafsid rulers came into conflict with their vassals, the great tribal chieftains. Although theoretically required to pay tribute to the ruler, the chieftains made a point of regarding him as no more than *primus inter pares*. They demanded considerable and frequent largesse from him, but usually refused to obey him in any real way. Their role was particularly important during the crises that followed the death of a ruler, when they in effect sold their support to the highest bidder and influenced the *ulema* (doctors of the law) who had to legitimize the authority of the new ruler. In order to counterbalance the power of these 'feudal' elements, the Hafsid monarchs tried to use the great Andalusian families against them. They were given key posts in the administration, a domain in which the Andalusian nobility was particularly competent thanks to a cultural sophistication that was vastly superior to that of the tribal chieftains. There was, then, considerable rivalry between the tribal military aristocracy and the intellectuals of the Andalusian aristocracy. The old tribal families often affected an austere puritanism and did not conceal their distaste for the morals and refined culture of their Andalusian rivals.

The Khaldun family also enjoyed considerable intellectual prestige. Thus, the historian's father gave up his political career, partly in order to concentrate upon his research into grammar and philology, but mainly in order to devote his time to mystical meditation. He was one of the most influential members of one of the many religious brotherhoods that developed at this time.

Abd al-Rahman Ibn Khaldun belonged, then, to one of the greatest families in Tunis. His family held an enviable position both in political life and in literary and theological circles. The Khaldun house was a real literary salon, frequented by the greatest names in literature and religion. This meant that the young Abd al-Rahman's education was exceptionally broad. Under the guidance of his father, he was taught by the most competent teachers and his education was enriched by contacts with the most eminent minds of the day. His education was all the more broadly based and varied in that, even as a very young man, Ibn Khaldun displayed the passion for study that was to characterize his whole life. In his autobiography Ibn Khaldun devotes long passages to the various stages in his intellectual training, citing the names of his teachers, stating their origins and qualifications and describing in great detail the knowledge he gradually absorbed. His elementary education was very traditional and included reading the Koran and studying religious traditions and the basic elements of theology. He later acquired a solid grounding in philosophy, logic, mathematics, astronomy and medicine. This extensive education was essential to a young man who, thanks to his family's position, was naturally destined for a position at the very highest level of the administration. He was trained in administrative affairs and taught to draw up official documents in accordance with the standards of the day. It seems that his historical training was especially thorough: history was an essential part of any gentleman's education, but it was also a very necessary discipline for anyone going into political and administrative affairs.

The tranquillity and prosperity enjoyed by Tunis at this time was highly conducive to a thorough and extensive education. After a period of turmoil during which the dismembered kingdom suffered greatly from tribal anarchy, Sultan Abu Bakr had succeeded in restoring order. The city enjoyed an extremely favourable geographical position: it controlled the sea routes between the eastern Mediterranean basin and the western Mediterranean. It was in a sense the point where the Muslim west and the rest of the Arab world met. Of all the towns in the Maghreb, Tunis was most affected by eastern influences, but it also had the closest contacts with Spain and the European merchants. It was one of the rallying points for pilgrims travelling to Mecca. The great number of palaces, mosques and schools under construction testified to the vitality of the city and to its good administration. 'Forgetting the inconsistencies of fortune, the inhabitants of Tunis lived in peace and prosperity, and enjoyed perfect safety beneath the glorious banner raised by the Sultan and under the protection of his justice'.[5] 'The country no longer rang with the cries of sedition.'[6]

The death of the Sultan in 1364 caused consternation. 'Everyone leapt from their beds and ran to the palace to make sure that the news was true. They spent the night outside the royal palace. They seemed drunk, but they were not'.[7] Their fears were not without foundation, as the death of a sultan usually marked the beginning of new upheavals.

Although the late Sultan had let it be known that he had designated one of his sons to be his successor, the interregnum gave ambitious rivals many opportunities. A brother of the heir-designate seized power in a sudden coup and even succeeded in having his brother killed. He came to the throne because he had the support of 'the lowest classes of the population, which he had frequented during a life of debauchery'. According to Ibn Khaldun's account, the 'rabble' was allowed to indulge in all kinds of excesses with impunity once it had ensured the pretender of victory. Although quite typical of the history of North African dynasties, the crisis over the succession was indirectly to provoke an upheaval throughout the Maghreb. The murdered heir was the protegé of Abul Hasan, Sultan of Morocco and one of the greatest Marinid rulers. The events in Tunis gave him a pretext to intervene on a massive scale.

As well as continuing his holy war in Spain (this in fact ended badly with a major defeat at Rio Salado in 1340), Sultan Hasan was trying to fulfil the dynasty's great dream of reunifying the Maghreb. A few years earlier, he had entered into an alliance with the Tunisians and had succeeded in taking Tlemcen in 1337. After that victory he established a sort of unofficial protectorate over Tunis and had sworn that the heir-designate would be crowned. After the murder of his vassal, Abul Hasan used his desire to avenge the victim and punish the usurper as a pretext for direct intervention. Having assembled considerable forces, he conquered the Hafsid state without difficulty and made a triumphal entry into Tunis in September 1347. The unity that North Africa had known in the great days of the Almohads seemed to have been re-established. There seemed every cause for optimism.

Ibn Khaldun appears to have been greatly impressed by the power wielded by the ruler from Fez and by a reunification which seemed to promise a new period of glory for the Maghreb. He describes the Marinids' entry into Tunis in glowing terms: 'The Sultan's troops formed a double line that stretched for three or four miles from their camp at Sidjoum to the gates of the city. The Marinids lined up on horseback under their respective banners and the Sultan rode out of his tent, mounted on a magnificent charger and followed by a magnificent cortège. He advanced to the beat of a drum, with a hundred banners streaming around him. As he passed, the troops fell into line behind him. The earth trembled beneath the feet of this immense army. To my knowledge, a more magnificent day has never been seen'.[8]

Despite the magnitude of the Sultan's achievement, and despite his demonstrations of respect for the holy places of Ifriqiyah, certain groups in Tunis were more or less openly hostile towards the Marinids. The Ibn Khalduns, on the other hand, were thankful that order had been restored and admired the prestige of the scientists and intellectuals with whom the Sultan liked to surround himself. The jurists, writers and scientists who had joined the imperial retinue became guests in the Khaldun household.

The young Abd al-Rahman was to benefit greatly from his contacts with these great minds. Abelli became his favourite teacher and seems to have played a vital role in the intellectual development of the future historian. Abelli was one of the most famous philosophers of the period. He was a follower of Averroes, Avicenna, Farabi and Razes, the great rationalist philosophers, and the author of commentaries on their works. In the fourteenth century, the Maghreb was entering a period of religious reaction when these works were rarely studied, being generally regarded with suspicion. Thanks to Abelli, Ibn Khaldun had the benefit of three years of philosophical training and a rationalist formation that was quite exceptional for what was already an obscurantist period. His master, who lived in the Khaldun household, gave him an extremely good grounding in logic and allowed him to assimilate the teachings of these great philosophers. Ibn Khaldun appears to have been greatly attracted to their doctrines. Abelli's influence on him was so great that when he had to return to Fez, his pupil resolved that he would eventually leave Tunis to rejoin him.

Political life continued during this important period in Ibn Khaldun's intellectual development. Now master of an immense empire, Abul Hasan wanted to re-establish order and to keep a close eye on the 'feudal' leaders, especially those of the great Arab tribes. He forbade the latter to collect taxes from either the townspeople or the peasantry on their own account. In compensation, he promised them regular subsidies to ensure their obedience and retain their services. Such a centralist policy was not in the interests of the great tribal chieftains, who united against the Sultan. When some of them began openly to flaunt his imperial decisions, Abul Hasan decided to subdue them by force. But in 1348 the Marinid army, a heterogeneous coalition of mercenaries, troops conscripted by force and tribal contingents led by their own leaders, abandoned the Sultan. Their defection led to his total defeat at the hands of Arab chieftains whose mediocre forces would never have been victorious on their own. When news of the defeat spread, the whole empire disintegrated. The administration and the leaders who had been left in Fez rose in rebellion. Tunis and Tlemcen recovered their independence. According to Ibn Khaldun, 'Every part of the empire was invaded by hordes of bandits'.[9] In Tunis, the Marinids were attacked and had to take refuge in the Kasbah. Some, including the Sultan's personal secretary, hid in the Khalduns' house. On his return to Tunis, the Sultan tried to ward off the dangers that threatened him from all sides. Despite his valiant efforts he failed, and fled to Morocco. His main enemy had become his own son, who now seized power.

The departure of the Marinids did not restore Tunis to calm. There were constant factional struggles and considerable political instability. The Hafsid prince who had taken the throne fell into the clutches of Ibn Tafrajin, the chamberlain and prime minister who represented the interests of the great tribal chieftains. He had his ruler assassinated and replaced him with a young boy, a puppet he could manipulate as he wished. In the midst of these struggles, a devastating plague broke out in 1348: 'Civilization in both the East and the West was visited by a destructive plague which devastated nations and caused populations to vanish. It swallowed up many of the good things of civilization and wiped them out. ... It lessened the power of the dynasties and curtailed their influence. It weakened their authority. Their situation approached the point of annihilation and dissolution. Civilization decreased with the decrease of mankind. Cities and buildings were laid waste, roads and way signs were obliterated, settlements and mansions became empty, nations and tribes grew weak. The entire inhabited world changed.'[10] The death toll was particularly high in Tunis. Ibn Khaldun lost both his father and his mother, along with most of his friends and teachers.

This terrible epidemic was followed by a disastrous famine in 1350. Ibn Khaldun had spent his youth in a calm and prosperous city and had been brought up in a rich and respected family. All that was destroyed by this series of disasters. There was no longer anything to keep him in Tunis. He plunged himself into his studies with even greater passion than before and decided to rejoin Abelli in Fez. His elder brother could only persuade him to delay his departure for a while.

In 1352, the all-powerful Ibn Tafrajin, perhaps hoping to reconcile himself with a great family, appointed the twenty-year old Ibn Khaldun *Sahib al-alamah* or Master of the Signature. That position made him responsible for inscribing the name, titles and geneaology of the Sultan on official letters and documents. Ibn Khaldun does not seem to have particularly enjoyed being in the service of the king, a young glutton whose greed was encouraged by his chief minister, who wanted to keep him away from affairs of state. Before long, war broke out between the government of Tunis and an independent Hafsid prince in Constantine. Ibn Khaldun left Tunis, where both court and army were on a war footing. He later stated that 'I was so sad at being cut off from my teachers and at being unable to continue my studies that I had long resolved to leave Tunis at the first opportunity'.[11] The rapid defeat of the Tunisian troops allowed him to carry out his project. He remained in hiding until the fighting was over and then went to Biskra to wait for the political situation to become clearer.

At the beginning of 1353, Ibn Khaldun set out for Tlemcen, the temporary seat of the Moroccan court. Abu Inan, the new Marinid Sultan, was, like his father before him, trying to reunify the Maghreb. His troops reoccupied Tlemcen and captured Bougie, but internal difficulties prevented him from marching on Tunis immediately. On the road to Tlemcen, Ibn Khaldun met a military unit that was being sent to Bougie to put down a rebellion against the Marinid governor. The leader of the expedition, a childhood friend of the Sultan, befriended the young man. Ibn Khaldun decided to go with him and took part in the capture of Bougie. In July 1353, a delegation of notables from Bougie set out for Tlemcen to pay homage to the Sultan and Ibn Khaldun went with them, supplied with mounts, fine robes, money and tents by his protector. He was presented to the Sultan during a solemn audience, and despite his youth Abu Inan took an immediate interest in him. The Sultan asked the young Tunisian about political developments in Ifriqiyah. 'I was given gifts of money, robes and fine horses, and I was promised that the fiefs I and my family had held in our home town would be restored to me'.[12] The government of Tunis had confiscated some of their wealth, perhaps in order to punish Ibn Khaldun for his defection.

The very favourable welcome given to Ibn Khaldun can be explained partly in terms of the Chamberlain's affection for him and partly in terms of the political importance of the Khaldun family in Ifriqiyah. Abu Inan presumably also wanted to show his gratitude to those who, like the Khalduns, had remained faithful to his father in his adversities. The scholars and scientists who had accompanied the Marinid army to Tunis and many of whom had been guests in the Khaldun household presumably also drew the Sultan's attention to the merits of a young man who had been one of their most brilliant pupils. It was on their advice that, when he returned to Fez, the Sultan summoned Ibn Khaldun to take part in literary discussions at the imperial court. Presiding over such noble gatherings was one of the most serious duties of any good Muslim ruler and Abu Inan took a great personal interest in such official functions.

Although he had recently married the daughter of an important figure at the Hafsid court, Ibn Khaldun left for Fez, arriving there at the beginning of 1354. The Marinid capital was then at the height of its glory. Traders and artisans were enjoying great prosperity and building was going on everywhere. 'Everyone began to build mansions and palaces of stone and marble decorated with ceramic plaques and arabesques. They passionately sought out silken robes, fine horses, good food and jewels of gold and silver. Well-being, comfort and luxury were everywhere.'[13] The Marinid rulers had just built the new town of Fez Jdid upstream from Fez el-Bali, the old bourgeois and popular town. Fez Jdid was a *maghzan* town with all the political, administrative and military functions of a capital. It also attracted bankers, money-changers and prostitutes, along with others who depended directly on the court for their living. Fez was without doubt the most active town in the Maghreb at this time. It was also a major intellectual centre. The generosity of the sultans attracted scientists and scholars from all parts of the Muslim world, and from Spain in particular. The Marinid rulers built monuments to their glory in the form of *madaris* or colleges. These religious institutions had rich libraries, partly made up of books which had been captured in Spain and which the Christians had agreed to return to the Marinids under the terms of a peace treaty.[14]

These favourable conditions allowed Ibn Khaldun to complete his education by studying with various Maghrebian and Spanish teachers. 'In this way I attained a level of education commensurate with my desires'.[15] As well as taking part in philosophical and literary discussions, Ibn Khaldun had to carry out his responsibilities as private secretary to the Sultan, but showed little enthusiasm for the banal task of transcribing royal decisions. The favours he enjoyed exposed him to jealousy and slander, and his close association with Abu Abdullah, a Hafsid prince from Bougie, began to arouse suspicion. Abu Abdullah had been forced to abdicate in favour of the Marinids and was now a prisoner in a gilded cage. The custom of holding princely hostages, part guest and part prisoner, meant that the various dynasties always had a number of pretenders at their disposal and could use them to ferment trouble in neighbouring kingdoms when the occasion arose. In 1357, Ibn Khaldun was accused (probably with justification) of plotting to help the prince escape. He was arrested, beaten and thrown into prison. Such reversals of fortune were typical of court life. Ibn Khaldun spent two years in prison and was freed only when Abu Inan died on his return from an expedition against Tunis in 1358. Like his father before him, the Sultan saw his power slip away in the very moment of victory. His generals defected and forced him to return to his capital with all speed.

When Ibn Khaldun was released from prison by those who thought it politic to gain the support of the imprisoned opposition, the atmosphere in the palace was sinister. Factional struggles broke out as the Sultan lay dying, with everyone trying to place his own candidate on the throne. The tribal chieftains, all-powerful after the defeat they had inflicted on the Sultan, wanted a pretender who would be loyal to their cause. Led by the grand vizier, they murdered the heir-designate and replaced him with a five-year old boy, who was immediately shut away in the harem. The dying Abu Inan was finally strangled by the Grand Vizier. A struggle for power immediately broke out among the great dignitaries who made and unmade kings by selling their services to the highest bidder. The anarchy at court soon spread throughout the kingdom and the chieftains in the outlying regions also became involved, turning the confusion to their own ends.

Initially, Ibn Khaldun merely watched the struggle for the spoils. Thanks to his intelligence, however, and to his diplomatic skills and the many connections he had established at court, he soon became one of the most active figures in the capital and plunged into a labyrinthine political struggle. The Marinid chieftains rose against the Grand Vizier who wanted to retain power for himself, proclaimed a new sultan and besieged the Vizier's supporters in the 'new town'. Having been named secretary of state to the new sultan, Ibn Khaldun was soon approached by envoys from a third pretender who offered him large financial rewards and an important position if he would get round the most important Marinid leaders. After confused negotiations with the other claimants to the throne the Marinids finally rallied to the latest pretender, who made a triumphal entry into Fez with Ibn Khaldun at his side. Ibn Khaldun had chosen the winning side at just the right moment.

Ibn Khaldun was appointed secretary of state, head of the chancellery and finally *mazalim*, a position which gave him jurisdiction over crimes not covered by religious law. He was twenty-seven. Anxious to remove all possible claimants to the throne, the new Sultan arrested all his brothers and cousins, the princes of the blood and his collateral kinsmen. They were put on a ship under the pretext of being taken to the east and drowned at sea. This act of *Realpolitik* did little good, as the Sultan himself was soon deposed and killed. Although initially confined to the palace, chaos soon spread throughout the town. The Vizier, who was the chief conspirator, put a mentally deficient candidate on the throne. The conspirators soon turned against each other. Some distributed money to the mob, which looted the royal storehouses and set fire to them. Finally, a pitched battle between Christian mercenaries and the Andalusian guard took place in the great audience hall. The townspeople began to attack Christian and Jewish merchants, but were cut down by the Marinid chieftains. Even so, the crisis was not yet over. Although the feudal lords had chosen a new sultan, the Vizier outwitted them and took advantage of his victory to send his original candidate back to the harem and replace him with a more suitable pretender.

When the political confusion finally died down, Ibn Khaldun was still well-placed within the victorious party. In less than four years, five sultans had been placed upon the throne and then deposed. Four of them had been murdered. It is impossible to estimate how many of the relations and allies of these short-lived rulers were killed, either when the pretender they had supported began to eliminate possible rivals after his victory or when he fell from power. Ibn Khaldun played an important political role throughout the period, showing a real genius for intrigue in the midst of this constantly changing spider's web: no sooner had one sultan been placed on the throne than those who had put him there began plotting his downfall.

A general feeling of weariness finally put an end to the crisis. It seemed that the Vizier, who held power by granting more and more expensive concessions with no thought for state interests, would be able to reign for some time at least. (He in fact ruled for six years, and had three sultans murdered in the process. A fourth was about to suffer the same fate when he succeeded in eliminating the Vizier instead.) Realizing that his relations with the present rulers were turning sour, Ibn Khaldun obtained permission to leave the court in Fez. But he was not allowed to go to Tlemcen or Tunis for fear that he might rally support there for one or other of the exiled Marinid pretenders. In December 1362, therefore, he set out for Granada.

An extremely warm and generous welcome awaited him there: 'The

Sultan had had a wing of his palace furnished and carpeted for me. He sent a guard of honour made up of important court officials to meet me. When I was shown into his presence, he greeted me in such a way as to show how much he appreciated my services and gave me magnificent robes.'[17]

Muhammad V of Granada and his Vizier Ibn el-Khatib had been briefly driven out of their capital by a coup and had sought temporary refuge in Fez. It was there, thanks largely to the intervention of Ibn Khaldun, that they obtained the Grand Vizier's help in their attempt to recover their kingdom. Thanks to Ibn Khaldun, they were granted the town of Ronda, the last Marinid stronghold in Andalusia. Using Ronda as their base, they succeeded in driving out the usurper and retaking Granada. Throughout this period, Ibn Khaldun had protected the family of the Andalusian ruler. He thus owed his throne, which he had recovered only a few months earlier, largely to the skills of Ibn Khaldun.

Greatly impressed with the worth and skill of his guest, the king of Granada soon entrusted Ibn Khaldun with an important and delicate mission to Pedro the Cruel, king of Castille. Having set out in 1363, the ambassador was given a sumptuous reception in the magnificent Hall of the Ambassadors in the Alcazar, where the Christian king had taken up residence amongst the traditional trappings of Muslim royal power. Life at the court of Seville was almost Moorish in style and Ibn Khaldun felt quite at home: 'I noticed several monuments to the power of my ancestors'.[18] Being descended from a family that had been forced to flee from Seville and Andalusia, he may have felt a certain bitterness at seeing the Mudejar architecture of the Palace, the Giralda minaret, the Moorish customs and other marks of the recent Muslim past.

Having presented the customary gifts of silks and thoroughbreds with golden harness in accordance with diplomatic tradition, Ibn Khaldun carried out his mission of negotiating a peace settlement between Castille and the Muslim Princes. Such a treaty was all the more vital to Pedro the Cruel in that his forces were tied down by rebellious vassals who had allied themselves with France and Aragon. The Christian king even asked Ibn Khaldun to enter his service, offering him the lands that his ancestors had once owned around Seville. Although both parties were fighting a holy war, it was by no means unusual for Muslims to enter the service of Christian states or for Christians to serve Muslims. A diplomat as skilled and knowledgeable about political life in the Muslim west as Ibn Khaldun could probably have done much to further Castille's

Muslim policy, but Ibn Khaldun refused the offer with suitable expressions of thanks and respect. Perhaps he was aware of the fragility of Pedro's power: he was already fighting his rebellious vassals with his back to the wall. Two years later he was to die in exile, despite the support given to him by the Prince of Wales's Englishmen against Duquesclin and the Castillian rebels. Ibn Khaldun appears to have been very well informed as to the intricacies of European diplomacy during the Hundred Years War.[19] But his political farsightedness is not the only explanation for his refusal of the Castillian offer. In many passages in his writings, he is very harsh on what he calls the 'traitors' who accepted the presence of the Christians rather than going into exile like the Khaldun family. It is quite possible that he refused to serve a Christian government, even on a temporary basis, for ethical reasons.

When, laden with gifts, Ibn Khaldun returned to Granada, he was granted the village of Elvira and the rich irrigated land surrounding it in the Vega de Granada by Muhammad V, who was extremely satisfied by the outcome of the mission. He became the King's confidant and companion. He distinguished himself by reciting brilliant poems in literary gatherings. His eloquence and elegant conceits equalled those of his friend and rival Ibn el-Khatib. Granada was enjoying the most glorious period of its history. Many of the Andalusians who had been driven out by the *Reconquista* had taken refuge there, bringing with them their refined tastes, their knowledge and their technical skills. The city had a population of two hundred thousand and was alive with artisans, goldsmiths, weavers, jewellers and cabinet makers.

During this brief period of calm, Granada was relatively stable and was, despite its weaknesses, a relatively powerful tributary power compared with Morocco. The long period of peace with Castille, which was being torn apart by internal wars, allowed Muhammad V to act as an arbitrator in the struggles in Morocco. He marked the relative stability of his reign and showed his taste for luxury by building the magnificent Court of the Lions and the luxurious apartments that surround it in the Alhambra. In Granada, Ibn Khaldun spent his time in the delightful gardens of the *Generalife*, with its flower beds, water and bubbling fountains. The miracle of water in the middle of the harsh aridity of the Mediterranean summer is a perfect expression of the sensuality and fragility of Andalusian civilization, as are the songs and poems in which mysticism and eroticism mingle together. Maghrebians often cut a sorry figure in the elegant and refined poetic jousts that took place at court.

But Ibn Khaldun, an Andalusian from Tunis, was quite at home in them.

He thought of settling in Granada. Life was very pleasant there. He had a fine house with beautiful gardens in an aristocratic area. The income from the lands he had been granted allowed him to live in great comfort. He brought over his wife and children from Constantine, where they had been waiting for his return.

Ibn Khaldun's life in Granada did not, however, consist solely of pleasure, feasts and poems. He spent long hours discussing problems in philosophy, politics and history with the King. Muhammad V enjoyed playing the part of philosopher-king. At his request, Ibn Khaldun wrote a treatise on logic and a commentary on the work of Averroes. Perhaps he dreamed of turning the King of Granada into a model ruler or an enlightened despot. However, Ibn Khaldun seems gradually to have tired of this life of luxury. Imperceptible at first, his boredom increased as time went by: he was uncomfortable at being removed from political action, the preserve of his friend Ibn el-Khatib, who was extremely jealous both of his own functions and of Ibn Khaldun's friendship with the king. Ibn el-Khatib began to plot and to spread rumours. When all was said and done, Granada was merely the capital of a small tributary state. It was too narrow a setting for the ambitions of someone like Ibn Khaldun. He needed more space and wider horizons.

It was in these circumstances that Ibn Khaldun received a message from an old friend and fellow-intriguer, Abu Abdullah, prince of Bougie. They had become friendly when they were imprisoned together during the reign of Abu Inan. When he later became a minister and an influential figure at court, Ibn Khaldun had persuaded the Sultan of Morocco to free his princely hostage and let him reconquer Bougie. Bougie was at the time controlled by Tunis and not Fez. Causing problems for the Hafsid government was not an unpleasant prospect for the ruler of Fez, at least in the political conjuncture of the 1360s. Thanks to the influence of Ibn Khaldun the exiled Prince was even able to recruit a force of Arab mercenaries. In order to thank him for his services, the Prince offered Ibn Khaldun the position of Prime Minister in his future government. Cautiously, Ibn Khaldun bided his time, waiting to see whether Abu Abdullah's attempts to recover his throne would meet with success. He was finally victorious in 1364, when the city of Bougie rebelled against Tunis.

No sooner had he taken the throne than the new ruler, faithful to his promise, invited Ibn Khaldun to become governor of Bougie. Loyalty aside, it was very much in his interests to have the services of a statesman of such stature. Ibn Khaldun had first to obtain permission to leave Granada from Muhammad V, who let him go reluctantly. In March 1365 Ibn Khaldun left Granada and set sail from Almeria. 'After four days at sea, I reached Bougie, where Sultan Abu Abdullah had prepared a great reception for me. All the state officials rode out to meet me; the townspeople crowded around me to touch me and to kiss my hand. Truly, this was a great day. When I entered the Sultan's quarters, he showered me with blessings and thanks and clad me in a ceremonial robe. The next day a delegation of the dynasty's high officials came to my door to present the Sultan's compliments. ... I then took over the reins of government and zealously devoted myself to organizing the administration and conducting affairs of state.'[20]

Bougie was at this time a rich and active city. Although it no longer had the dominant influence over the whole of the Maghreb that it had enjoyed in the eleventh and twelfth centuries, it was still one of the most important cities in North Africa. Surrounded by a rich and well cultivated plain and with the resources of part of Kabylia at its disposal, it was the capital of a relatively large state. But the city owed its real importance to trade. It was a great entrepôt for Ifriqiyah, Tlemcen, Morocco, the Western Sudan and Europe. The highly lucrative business of piracy had even given birth to joint-stock companies. Ibn Khaldun was once again living in a rich and luxurious environment. Throughout North Africa, the wealthy inhabitants of Bougie enjoyed a reputation for spending their time in revelry, eating well and sparing nothing to make their houses luxurious and their women beautiful. Bougie was also an intellectual and religious capital of such importance that it was often described as a little Mecca, and there were many students in the city. Aside from his political responsibilities, Ibn Khaldun had considerable influence in intellectual and religious circles: the Sultan appointed him to preach in the great mosque where, when he had finished dealing with affairs of state, he would also teach jurisprudence.

Affairs of state did, however, take up a lot of his time, and the political experience Ibn Khaldun gained as governor of Bougie explains many features of his later writings. The population of Bougie was very mixed, being made of Kabyls, Andalusians, Orientals and Christians, and very turbulent. Unlike the citizens of the other great towns, who remained passive in the face of political vicissitudes, the notables of Bougie were active politicians. Various groups would clash with one another (Kabyls versus merchants for instance) and then call for help from one or another ruler, usually a Hafsid or a Marinid. They would then rebel against the foreign governor of the city. On occasion they had even deposed the Sultan and rallied to someone more sympathetic to the dominant group of the moment. According to Ibn Khaldun, the market supervisor (*muhtasib*) played a considerable role in the complex political life of the city, and even what he calls the 'rabble' sometimes intervened.

Abu Abdullah clashed with the *muhtasib* and the leaders of the mob[21] almost immediately after his entry into Bougie. He had them arrested and executed. But that simply led to increased tension between the townspeople and a Sultan whose period of exile and misfortune had not predisposed him to moderation and caution. Ibn Khaldun himself criticized him for the harshness of some of his methods: 'The Sultan was extremely strict and treated the people of Bougie harshly. During the first two years of his reign he had more than fifty of them beheaded.'[22] It is difficult to say precisely what role Prime Minister Ibn Khaldun played in the internal government of the city. But he does state that he carried out his tasks to the satisfaction of all[23] and he seems to have been favourably regarded by at least some of the townspeople.[24]

Quite aside from its serious internal problems, Bougie had equally serious and related external problems. The city was greatly coveted by neighbouring powers because of its geographical position and its wealth. Moreover, Abul Abdullah adopted a very warlike policy. Immediately after his accession, he launched an offensive against territory belonging to Tlemcen, and captured Dellis. His success was short-lived, however, as in order to wage war on the Sultan of Constantine, he had to make peace with the ruler of Tlemcen and give him the hand of his daughter in marriage. The war between Bougie and Constantine was over the territory held by the Dawawidah, an important Arab tribe from which mercenaries were recruited. The Dawawidah were later to play an important role in Ibn Khaldun's life. He took part in this military expedition, which ended badly for Bougie. 'Having suffered a defeat, the Sultan returned to Bougie. He used all the money I had collected for him to pay subsidies to the Arabs.'[25] Like all ministers of his day, Ibn Khaldun tried to find new resources by forcing the rebellious tribes of the *Bled essiba* to pay taxes. 'Lacking the sinews of war, the Sultan sent me to the Berber tribes in their mountain fastness. For several years they had been refusing to pay taxes. I invaded and devastated their lands and took hostages to ensure that they would pay all they owed. The money was very useful.'[26]

In Bougie, however, relations between the Sultan and his subjects were going from bad to worse: 'He was so harsh that he met with general reprobation. His outraged subjects began to hate him and transferred their affections to his cousin Abul Abbas, the ruler of Constantine. He was a wise ruler, an upright man and a father to his people'.[27] 'The people finally lost patience and asked Sultan Abul Abbas to deliver them from the tyranny they were suffering'.[28]

Abul Abbas marched against Bougie in 1366. The city's ruler was aware of the weakness of his position: his subjects no longer concealed their hostility towards him, and the neighbouring tribes had gone over to the enemy. Hoping to ward off the coming storm by making peace proposals, Abu Abdullah set out to meet his cousin. But a sudden attack drove off his escort and he was killed while trying to escape. A delegation from Bougie then asked Ibn Khaldun to act as regent for the late Sultan's young son and to defend the town. The situation was, however, much too serious for Ibn Khaldun to become personally involved in a plan doomed to failure, and he rejected the offer. He took the side of Abul Abbas, who was a true statesman, and surrendered the city to him. 'I gave him possession of Bougie and life immediately returned to normal'.[29]

In the circumstances, Ibn Khaldun seems to have displayed a certain nonchalance, but in his letters to Ibn el Khatib,[30] he was already expressing his increasing fears about the chronic instability of the Maghrebian states. Despite the initially favourable welcome given him by the victorious Sultan, he soon began to feel that he was being watched and even that his life was in danger. Abul Abbas was suspicious as to what the former Prime Minister might do.

The Sultan's suspicions were quite justified. Ibn Khaldun made contact with Abu Hammu of Tlemcen, the son-in-law of the late ruler of Bougie. This Sultan's desire to avenge his father-in-law gave him an excellent excuse to intervene. Ibn Khaldun was an influential figure who was capable of furthering his ends. Having been warned of Ibn Khaldun's dealings with Abu Hammu, the new ruler of Constantine and Bougie was on the point of arresting him when he escaped from the city. Ibn Khaldun took refuge with the Dawawidah, with whom he had first come into contact when he was Prime Minister of Bougie. His younger brother Yahya Ibn Khaldun, less fortunate, was arrested and beaten. All the family's property in Bougie and Constantine was confiscated.

3

From Condottiere to Historian

The Dawawidah, with whom Ibn Khaldun sought refuge, were one of the most powerful Arab tribes and the dominant group within the Ryah confederation, the strongest branch of the famous Beni Hilal. The leaders of the Dawawidah played an important political role and their support was often sought by the various governments of the central Maghreb. They gave the fugitive a warm welcome, no doubt because they wanted the advice of a skilful and well-informed politician who could tell them which side was most likely to win, given the balance of power. If they were to get any booty, it was important to choose the winning side.

The ruler of Tlemcen asked Ibn Khaldun to return to the city and become his Prime Minister, but 'seeing that matters were becoming confused, I did not accept his invitation.'[1] He sent his brother, who had recently escaped from prison, in his place. In the meantime, he spent his own time trying to win the Dawawidah over to the Tlemcen cause and negotiating an alliance between Tlemcen and Tunis so as to be able to attack the Sultan of Constantine on two flanks. Unfortunately, Abu Hammu's expedition against Bougie ended in total failure. His baggage train and even his harem fell into the hands of the victors, who divided the spoils amongst them. After this resounding defeat (August 1366), which in retrospect justified Ibn Khaldun's caution, Sultan Abu Hammu, 'almost dying from shame and grief', had to face up to the pretenders who immediately appeared in his hour of weakness. As for Ibn Khaldun, he decided that safety lay in flight and he went to his friend the Governor of Biskra.

He was not, however, simply running away. Using Biskra as a base and a place to receive emissaries, Ibn Khaldun succeeded in bringing together a sufficiently large group of tribes to restore the Sultan of Tlemcen to power. The Sultan again offered Ibn Khaldun the position of

Prime Minister, and Ibn Khaldun again refused. From now on he was to refuse virtually all government positions, which were often merely ephemeral or illusory, in favour of acting as an intermediary between the tribes he wanted to recruit and the Princes. As a *condottiere* with influence over considerable military forces, his power was in fact greater than when he had been a minister. In addition the eventful life he led amongst the tribesmen was in many ways more peaceful than a life of intrigue at court. Thus, he was even able once more to devote much of his time to study and research.

For four years (1366-1370), Ibn Khaldun acted as an intermediary between the Dawawidah and the government in Tlemcen. He paid out royal subsidies, negotiated alliances, led his tribesmen into battle and experienced all the vicissitudes of military operations, including both victory and defeat. In 1370 he led a delegation of tribal chieftains to Tlemcen, where he finally agreed to take a position in the government once more. Shortly afterwards, war broke out again between Tlemcen and the Marinids. By using intrigues and bribes, the Marinids succeeded in persuading most of the tribes in Tlemcen's army to defect. The situation was so critical that Abu Hammu realized that his only salvation lay in flight and left the capital. The roads had already been cut, and Ibn Khaldun was unable to reach safety in Biskra. He decided to make for Spain, but when he reached Hunayn, the nearest port to Tlemcen, he could not find a ship. Marinid spies soon discovered that he was in the town and informed the Sultan of his presence. A detachment of horsemen was ordered to capture Ibn Khaldun, whose political importance was sufficient to justify such a major expedition. He was also suspected of having been entrusted with certain valuables by the Sultan of Tlemcen.

Ibn Khaldun was taken back as a prisoner to Tlemcen, which had just fallen to the Marinids. He was brought before the Sultan, who violently criticized him for having betrayed the Moroccan cause when he left Fez. Using all his diplomatic skills, Ibn Khaldun explained that he had been forced to leave Morocco because the Grand Vizier was threatening his life. His arguments convinced the Sultan, who had almost been murdered by the same Grand Vizier. Ibn Khaldun also supplied him with detailed information as to the political situation in the central Maghreb and emphasized that he could persuade some of the tribes to rally to the Marinids. He also made suggestions as to how to capture Bougie, the penultimate staging-post on the road to Tunis. The Sultan found this information so invaluable that Ibn Khaldun was immediately released and showered with gifts.

Once he had recovered his equilibrium with a period of retreat in Abu Madyan's sanctuary near Tlemcen (pretending that he intended to renounce the world), the Sultan entrusted him with an important mission. He was given large sums of money, and plenipotentiary powers and told to make for the territory held by the tribes which had remained loyal to Abu Hammu, and bring them over to the Moroccans. Now that he was acting for the Marinid Sultan, Ibn Khaldun displayed the same skills that he had used to support the cause of the Sultan of Tlemcen only a few weeks earlier. This may appear as 'Machiavellianism', an absence of any sense of morality or patriotism. It would, however, be wrong to try to project notions of patriotism (which even in Europe did not appear until much later) on to the Maghreb of the fourteenth century. For Ibn Khaldun, neither the cause of the ruler of Fez nor that of Tlemcen had any particular ideological content. The clashes between the two states were simply a result of the rivalry between their rulers and had absolutely no effect on his deep-rooted conviction that the Maghreb should be unified. Like a true *condottiere*, he always chose to serve the cause which offered him most power at any given moment. And it has to be said that he did the work he was paid for most conscientiously.

Showing great boldness, Ibn Khaldun went to the tribe with whom Abu Hammu had taken refuge and convinced the assembled chieftains that it was dangerous to have the Marinids as enemies. Having won over the majority of the tribes, he even discovered where Abu Hammu was hiding and informed the Marinids of his whereabouts. Led by a Dawawidah contingent raised by Ibn Khaldun, the Marinid forces took the camp by surprise and forced Abu Hammu to flee, abandoning everything, to the distant oasis of Gourara. After this great success, Ibn Khaldun took part in raids against enemy tribes. When that profitable campaign was over he himself led the most important tribal chieftains to the Marinid Sultan, who gave them gifts to reward them for their services—and welcomed the main architect of this tribal alliance with the highest honours.

After taking part in a number of major military operations, Ibn Khaldun returned to Biskra, where he could remain in contact with the main nomadic tribes and observe their movements and their political mood. Biskra was a major centre for the caravan trade and an ideal place for gathering information on the political temperature on the steppes and the fringes of the Sahara. Ibn Khaldun stayed in Biskra as a guest of Ibn Monzi, the regional Governor. The latter, however, soon took offence at the increasingly important role played by his guest. Ever since he had led the Dawawidah to victory, Ibn Khaldun had enjoyed enormous prestige and great authority in the eyes of the tribesmen. But Ibn Monzi was responsible for passing on the subsidies paid to the tribes by the government of Fez. He may have feared that Ibn Khaldun would oust him from his profitable position. Perhaps he was already weaving the threads of the anti-Marinid plots that were later to break out and was afraid of Ibn Khaldun's perspicacity. Whatever his motives, he succeeded in having Ibn Khaldun recalled to the Moroccan court.

Ibn Khaldun left Biskra in September 1372. Reaching Miliana with a small escort, he took the Tlemcen road along the southern edge of the Tell. At this point, the Marinid Sultan unexpectedly died. As usual, a dynastic crisis immediately broke out. Taking advantage of the circumstances, one pretender hastily assembled the Marinid troops camping in and around Tlemcen and led them to Fez to seize power. At the same time, the fugitive Abu Hammu who, fearing a raid by nomads employed by the Marinids, had been preparing to take flight for the Western Sudan, heard the news of his rival's death and instead made for Tlemcen in a series of forced marches. All these events happened very rapidly. The fact that Abu Hammu's return to his miraculously liberated capital coincided exactly with that of Ibn Khaldun, a former minister who had betrayed him and whose zeal had done him so much harm was 'a truly extraordinary event'.[2] As the former Sultan was having all the courtiers he suspected of having betrayed him during his exile executed, Ibn Khaldun attempted to escape to Fez. When he reached Sebdou, his escort was attacked by a detachment sent after him by Abu Hammu, who was determined to capture him and take exemplary vengeance. Ibn Khaldun lost his horse and had to flee on foot. Miraculously he succeeded in hiding and escaping his pursuers. After a two-day march he found a friendly tribe who had remained loyal to the Marinids, finally reaching Fez at the end of November 1372.

The issue of the succession was not yet resolved, and the usual plots and counter-plots were being hatched. Ibn Khaldun found that the all-powerful position of Grand Vizier was now held by an old fellow-intriguer who gave him a very warm welcome, showered him with favours and granted him a generous stipend. Ibn Khaldun took advantage of this temporary breathing-space to return to his historical research and to teaching. He also held an important position as an adviser to the government. Ibn Khaldun found another old friend in Fez: Vizier Ibn el-Khatib, who had been forced to leave Granada after a bitter quarrel with the King. Relations between Fez and Granada being somewhat strained, he had been given a generous welcome. Politically, he was extremely active and appears to have been behind the preparations for a Marinid expedition against Granada. Muhammad V outwitted him by landing a Moroccan pretender he had been holding in reserve on the Rif coast in April 1373. The counter-attack was reinforced by the machinations of a second pretender, who also received support from the King of Granada. The two were soon victorious and divided Morocco between them, one taking Fez and the other Marrakesh. But before long they were at war with each other.

Having initially supported the Prince who had established his court in the southern capital, Ibn Khaldun soon attracted the hostility of the ruler of Fez. Even so, he remained loyal to his friend Ibn el-Khatib and tried to protect him from the danger that threatened. Being the protector of both Moroccan rulers, the King of Granada was now in a position to take vengeance against his former Minister. Despite all the efforts made by Ibn Khaldun and other friends, Ibn el-Khatib was arrested and tried for some blasphemous writings that had been attributed to him. He was tortured and finally murdered in jail by hired assassins. Still not satisfied, his murderers exhumed his body and desecrated it. Ibn Khaldun's position was becoming more and more dangerous. The loyalty and friendship he had shown towards Ibn el-Khatib exposed him to the slanders of his enemies. He was arrested, and freed only when the new Sultan of Marrakesh intervened. This gave him no more than a reprieve, but Ibn Khaldun took advantage of it to place himself under the protection of his friend Wanzammar, an important Arab chieftain with considerable influence at court. It was he who succeeded in obtaining authorization for Ibn Khaldun to leave for Granada, which seemed to offer him a refuge.

Ibn Khaldun arrived in Granada in September 1374. He no doubt hoped that he would be able to explain away his connections with Ibn el-Khatib, obtain a pardon and spend the rest of his days in peaceful retirement. But he found no sign of the generous welcome and the kindnesses of the past. Indeed, he had in a sense walked into the lion's den. Muhammad V had become a cruel autocrat, and the services rendered to him by Ibn Khaldun belonged to a now forgotten past. Ibn Khaldun was greeted very coldly and was unable to dispel the King's suspicions and growing hostility. Messengers from Fez brought increasingly slanderous reports on Ibn Khaldun's activities there. In order to get rid of his 'guest' and bring off a diplomatic coup at the same time, the king of Granada decided to land him on the coast of Tlemcen and leave him to the mercy of Abu Hammu. Early in 1375, Ibn Khaldun was deported to Hunayn, a few leagues away from Tlemcen. It seemed that his fate was sealed.

Fortunately, his friend Wanzammar did not desert him. The vicissitudes of politics had led to a reconciliation between Tlemcen and Wanzammar—who had until then been an ally of the Marinids—and he approached Abu Hammu on Ibn Khaldun's behalf. Once his initial anger had subsided, Abu Hammu realized that it was in his own interests to grant the request of his new and powerful ally and to benefit from the services of an agent of such obvious worth. As a result, Ibn Khaldun was pardoned. Hoping to enjoy a little peace, he retired to the sanctuary of El Eubhad, near Tlemcen. He had only a brief respite, however, as Abu Hammu ordered him to act once more as a *condottiere* and go and recruit troops in the territory occupied by the Ryah tribes.

Having made his preparations, Ibn Khaldun set out for the east. Then he suddenly abandoned his mission and took refuge in the Qalat Ibn Salamah, a mountain fortress belonging to Wanzammar near Taourzout.

Why the sudden change? Ibn Khaldun was probably afraid that Abu Hammu would turn against him again. Although on good terms with Tlemcen at the moment, Wanzammar might break off the alliance at any time. If that happened, Ibn Khaldun would be left without a protector, again exposed to Abu Hammu's anger. Nor would he be able to flee to Fez or Granada, where the kings were hostile to him. And in his home town of Tunis, his enemy Abul Abbas was still in power.

The decision to leave political life cannot, however, be explained solely in terms of Ibn Khaldun's delicate personal position. It seems in fact that he had been contemplating retirement for some time. He had already gone into retreat at El Eubhad on two previous occasions, but had been forced to leave its tranqillity at the express request of the Sultan of Tlemcen. For several years, he had been devoting more and more of his time to study and meditation and becoming increasingly impatient at the way political life interrupted his researches. So he was not forced into retirement by merely circumstantial considerations: it was a deliberate decision.

Ibn Khaldun never gave any real explanation for the radical change in his life, but his withdrawal from political life was to be permanent. After spending almost four years (1375-78) in the Qalat Ibn Salamah, he never again tried to play a diplomatic or military role. He had been seriously ill, and the sordid murder of his brother, the Prime Minister of Tlemcen, had left him disgusted with political life. In 1378 Abul Abbas pardoned Ibn Khaldun for his part in the events of 1365, and he was able to return to his home town where he devoted himself to a life of study and teaching. Fearing that the Sultan might involve him in politics once again, in 1382 he gained permission to go to Cairo to pursue his research. The only posts he would accept were those of teacher and judge, and he continued to work on his 'Universal History'. It was only with great reluctance that he met Tamerlane in 1401. The last third of Ibn Khaldun's life[3] is sufficient proof of the fact that when he gave up political life in 1375 he was acting on the basis of a premeditated decision. The fact that he never gave his reasons may mean that he was not aware of them himself. He certainly did not feel bitter about his decision to give up politics, and appears to have believed that he had struck an excellent bargain with himself.

Ibn Khaldun's decision to give up politics, not to devote himself to mystical meditation but to write a work of history, is an expression of a fundamental new awareness. Ibn Khaldun set out to study not only a sequence of events that had taken place centuries earlier, but also their later consequences. He wanted to study the events in which he had been personally involved, either as an eye witness or as an active participant. And he did so at a time when men's usual perception of the world relied much less upon a historical perspective than it does now. 'The desire to write history is neither the result of a spontaneous intellectual predisposition nor an expression of a general social need. It appears when men are forced by circumstances to admit their own historicity and to ask themselves what it means to belong to a collectivity whose existence is at stake.'[4]

Ibn Khaldun seems to have been meditating upon the underlying causes of historical events for many years, ever since he had given up the governorship of Bougie.

His letters to Ibn el-Khatib reflect his anxiety and perplexity. In them he tries to explain his own personal disappointments and to understand why what should have been a brilliant career was compromised so many times. His own experiences were proof that it was not a question of mere personal misfortune and that his disappointments were simply an expression of some instability that affected the Maghreb as a whole.

Other and better men had failed too: Ibn el-Khatib had been shamefully murdered; Abul Hassan was struck down at the height of his glory; Abu Inan saw his work destroyed as he lay dying ... princes, ministers, courtiers and viziers were defeated just as they seemed to be fulfilling their ambitions. Why were there so many towns in ruins, so much land laid waste, so many monuments abolished, so many roads destroyed? Why did instability and anarchy sweep away the best and the most justified ambitions? 'We were the suns of glory, but the suns have disappeared and the whole horizon mourns for them,' Ibn Khaldun wrote to Ibn el-Khatib.

Ibn Khaldun found no answer to the questions he was asking in traditional political philosophy, which was concerned solely with describing the ideal state. Yet he refused to see his life as being governed by a blind and incomprehensible fate. His introspection did not take the form of bitterness and he did not dwell upon his past failures. By trying to integrate his own experiences into a wider whole he was trying to understand the world in which he lived. 'The decision to write history means that man has become aware of the political dimension of his destiny, that he is aware that he is an active subject'.[5]

In the citadel of Taourzout, overlooking the High Plains, Ibn Khaldun began to ask himself certain questions. He was trying to find an explanation for the darkness that was creeping across the Maghreb like the shadows thrown by the mountains at dusk. As in the letter to Ibn el-Khatib, the theme of the disappearance of light reappears. It is a moving symbol used by a lonely man who was one of the greatest representatives of Arab culture in his attempt to understand the destiny of a country overcome by darkness and chaos.

Ibn Khaldun obviously understood that the Maghreb had long been in a state of crisis. The realization that North Africa was going through a period of serious difficulties was definitely the starting point of the process which led Ibn Khaldun to study history. An important passage in his *Muqaddimah* bears this out: 'The condition of the world and of nations, their customs and their sects, does not persist in the same form or in a constant manner. ...'[6] 'Discussion of the general conditions of regions, races and periods constitutes the historian's foundations. Most of his problems rest upon that foundation, and his historical information derives clarity from it.'[7]

He demonstrates that some major historians, such as Bekri, have failed to observe this principle: '*However, at the present time*—that is at the end of the eighth century[8]—*the situation in the Maghreb, as we can observe, has taken a turn and changed entirely.* ... The Berbers, the original population of the Maghreb, have been replaced by an influx of Arabs, that began in the fifth century[9]. ... A devastating plague ... overtook the dynasties[10] *at the time of their senility, when they had reached the limit of their duration.* It lessened their power and curtailed their influence. It weakened their authority. Their situation approached the point of annihilation and dissolution.'[11] 'When there is a general change in conditions, it is as though the whole world had been altered. ... *Therefore there is need at this time that someone should systematically set down the situation of the world among all regions and races.*'[12]

In this passage, Ibn Khaldun is dealing with changes in North Africa. When he generalizes on the basis of this example, he does so in order to deduce general laws of historical development. He himself states that 'My intention is to restrict myself to the Maghreb'.

Ibn Khaldun certainly had a mass of information at his disposal. During his travels through the Muslim west, he had taken every opportunity of meeting scientists and men of erudition, sometimes even breaking off a political intrigue to pursue a philosophical discussion. He had consulted the great libraries of Tunis, Fez, Spain, Tlemcen and Bougie. But above all he had been involved in major political events for more than twenty years, either as an observer or as a participant. The positions he had held had brought him into contact with kings, viziers and great military leaders. He had lived in palaces and in cities, but he had also experienced the harsh life of the *bled*.

Thanks to his concrete knowledge of the realities of North Africa, Ibn Khaldun realized that the attitudes of kings, the vicissitudes of politics, the destiny of states, living conditions in the countryside, famines, etc. were not isolated problems, but parts of a greater whole: 'These are closely related questions: the strength and weaknesses of a dynasty, the numerical strength of a nation or race, the size of a town or city, and the amount of prosperity and wealth. This is because dynasty and royal authority constitute the *form* of the world and of civilization, which, in turn, together with the subjects, cities, and all other things, constitute the *matter* of dynasty and royal authority.'[13]

A man of letters who had spent his life in his study, far from the realities of politics, might have come to the conclusion that the decisive factors in this greater whole were the decisions made by the great men of this world. But Ibn Khaldun was a man of action and a statesman who had had enough experience to realize that the king proposes but that the 'nature of things' disposes, and that the decisions of a ruler do not have a decisive effect on the destiny of a state.

'It should be known that differences of condition among people are the result of the different ways in which they make their living.'[14] 'I proceeded from general genealogical tables to detailed historical information. ... Thus, this work contains an exhaustive history of the world.'[15] 'I commented on civilization, on the establishment of cities, and on the essential characteristics of human social organization, in a way that explains to the reader how and why things are as they are, and shows him how the men who constituted a dynasty first came upon the historical scene'.[16]

It is impossible to reconstruct Ibn Khaldun's intellectual evolution with any accuracy or to say precisely how his ideas took shape, but it seems probable that he had been questioning the schemas of traditional historical and philosophical thought long before he went into retreat at Taourzout, and that his intuitions suddenly crystallized when he discovered a basis upon which he could provide a coherent answer to his problems. Some indications as to his intellectual evolution can, however, be found in a passage in which Ibn Khaldun describes the work of another historian: 'Judge Abu Bakr al-Turtushi also had the same idea in the *Ibar Siraj al-Muluk*. He divided the work into chapters that come close to the chapters and problems of our work. However, he did not achieve his aim or realize his intention. He did not exhaust the problems and did not bring clear proofs. ... He does not verify his statements or clarify them with the help of natural arguments. In a way, al-Turtushi aimed at the right idea, but did not hit it.'[17]

This and other similar passages give some idea of what must have been a long, slow search for the truth: 'When I had read the works of others and probed into the recesses of yesterday and today, I shook myself out of my complacency and sleepiness. ... I followed an unusual method of arrangement and division into chapters. From the various possibilities, I chose a remarkable and original method.'[18] 'We ... were inspired by God. He led us to a science whose truth we ruthlessly set forth. If I have succeeded in presenting the problems of this science exhaustively ... this is due to divine inspiration. ... If, on the other hand, I have omitted some point ... the task of correcting remains for the discerning critic, but the merit is mine since I cleared and marked the way.'[19]

Full of joy at having arrived at a certain understanding of the times in which he lived, Ibn Khaldun resolved to devote himself to his historical research.

Ibn Khaldun's thought probably evolved considerably during the period leading up to the composition of *The Muqaddimah*. Initially, he probably concentrated upon his own disappointments, the tumultuous events he had lived through and the chaos that affected the Maghreb. He wanted to understand the underlying causes of the turmoil. Why were the Maghrebian states so chronically unstable? Why had all attempts to establish a centralized monarchy ended in failure?

In his attempt to understand the anarchy into which the kingdoms of the Maghreb had been plunged, he had to go beyond the incoherence of purely factual history, make generalizations and establish correlations between various categories of events. This approach led him to a global conception of history, to an analysis of social and political structures and to a study of their evolution: 'It should be known that history, in matter of fact, is information about human social organization, which is itself identical with world civilization. It deals with conditions affecting the nature of civilization as, for instance, savagery and sociability, group feelings, and the different ways by which one group of human beings achieves superiority over another. It deals with royal authority and the dynasties that result in this manner and with the various ranks that exist within them. It further deals with the different kinds of gainful occupations and ways of making a living, with the sciences and crafts that human beings pursue as part of their activities, and with all the other institutions that originate in civilization through its very nature.'[20]

Ibn Khaldun transformed a random collection of apparently unrelated and meaningless events into a coherent whole governed by a complex but logical evolution. This system provided a rational explanation for the confused events of history. The search for a rational explanation for the turmoil in North Africa led to a conception of history as science.

Ibn Khaldun wrote the great part of his *Muqaddimah* at Taourzout between July and November 1377, but went on adding to it until he died.[21] *The Muqaddimah*, or 'Introduction to History', consists of three volumes. The first two were written between 1375 and 1378. The third[22] was written much later, perhaps in Egypt, but in terms of North African history and historical method it is less important than the first two.

The first two volumes contain an exposition of Ibn Khaldun's concept of history as an analysis of the social and political structures of the Maghreb. The extremely varied elements that make up the subject-matter of history are genetically integrated into an exposition of this rational system. Volumes I and II provide the frame of reference for the so-called *Histoire des Berbères*, a factual account of seven hundred years of North African history.[23] In terms of Ibn Khaldun's initial conception of his work, *The Muqaddimah* and the *Histoire des Berbères* are meant to complement one another.

The starting point for Ibn Khaldun's meditations on history was, then, his awareness of the crisis affecting the Maghreb in the fourteenth century. In his search for its underlying causes he evolved a general concept of society and of its overall development. This much more general problem became his major concern and he structured[24] his work in terms of it, but in doing so he strayed somewhat from the initial object of his research.

4
The Myth of the 'Arab Invasion'

Many contemporary historians and specialists in North African history give the impression that the major interest of Ibn Khaldun's work is that it provides us with a complete explanation of the crisis that put an end to the social and economic development of the Maghreb. They argue that the crisis was the result of the gradual invasion of North Africa by nomadic Arab tribes from the east, first the Beni Hilal and then the Beni Solaym. According to C.A. Julien, the most famous specialist in North African history, the 'Hilalian invasion' was 'the most important event of the entire medieval period in the Maghreb'.[1] It was, he writes, 'an invading torrent of nomadic peoples who destroyed the beginnings of Berber organization—which might very well have developed in its own way— and put nothing whatever in its place.'[2] It must be stressed at the outset that *The Muqaddimah* does not provide a systematic account of this crisis, the effects of which were still visible in the fourteenth century. Ibn Khaldun gives no methodical account of the underlying causes of this destructive phenomenon. The *Histoire des Berbères* describes a series of upheavals and crises, and several unsuccessful attempts to establish a centralized monarchy. But the problem of a Crisis with a capital 'C' is never raised. The Hilalian invasion is not the main theme of the *The Muqaddimah*. Ibn Khaldun refers to it simply as one of the causes of the turmoil.

The encyclopedic *Muqaddimah* contains a section on methodology, an analysis of political and social structures and a general synthesis, but basically it does not describe the spectacular collapse which modern historians claim to have discovered. Ibn Khaldun was not studying a major localized event such as an invasion and its aftermath; he makes no systematic distinction between the character of the Maghreb before and after the crisis. But he does make a methodical analysis of the permanent political and social structures that characterized North Africa. And, according to Ibn Khaldun, the arrival of the Hilalian tribes did not alter those structures to any great extent. No space is given to a detailed study of the Hilalian invasion in the systematic and analytic framework of *The Muqaddimah* or in the *Histoire des Berbères*, each chapter of which deals with a different dynasty.

The lengthy modern accounts of the Hilalian invasion do not, therefore, derive directly from Ibn Khaldun. It is, of course, quite legitimate to formulate a thesis by collating scattered data. But the theory that the 'Arab invasion' was the determining factor in the crisis of medieval North Africa is less than legitimate, as it takes into account only part of the data provided by Ibn Khaldun. The modern historians who established this theory left aside all the facts that did not support it. Yet both the facts and the information provided by Ibn Khaldun are often in complete contradiction with the 'Arab invasion' thesis.

Ibn Khaldun does of course mention the arrival of the nomadic Arabs and the destruction they wreaked on several occasions: 'However, at the present time—that is, at the end of the eighth century[3]—the situation in the Maghreb, as we can observe, has taken a turn and changed entirely. The Berbers, the original population of the Maghreb, have been replaced by the influx of Arabs that began in the fifth century.[4] The Arabs outnumbered and overpowered the Berbers, stripped them of most of their lands, and also obtained a share of those that remained in their possession.'[5]

Taken out of context, this much-quoted passage does appear to provide a sound basis for the 'Arab invasion' thesis. But what are we to make of the following statement from the same author? 'The Berbers on the African shore constitute the native inhabitants of the region. Their language is the language of the country, except in the cities. The Arab language there is entirely submerged in the non-Arab native idiom of the Berbers.'[6]

If the Arabs from the east were really conquerors who drove out the Berbers, how could the Arab language be 'submerged'?

The Muqaddimah does contain certain famous and much-quoted passages condemning the behaviour of the Arabs. Thus, Ibn Khaldun writes that 'Places that succumb to the Arabs are quickly ruined',[7] and that 'It is noteworthy how civilization always collapsed in places the Arabs took over and conquered, and how such settlements were depopulated and the very earth there turned into something that was no longer earth.'[8] But in other related passages Ibn Khaldun praises the moral qualities and political virtues of the Arabs, claiming that they are 'closer to being good than a sedentary people'. There is no way we can evade this apparent contradiction.

Ibn Khaldun is too good a historian to forget that the Arabs founded great and stable empires in both the east and the west. In a number of important passages he demonstrates that all the kingdoms and viable political organizations founded in North Africa were established by 'nomadic' or 'Arab' peoples or by tribes with very similar socio-political characteristics. The Almoravids, for instance, were true Saharan nomads; the Fatimids were originally peasants from Kabylia; the Almohads were a mountain tribe from the Moroccan High Atlas. As we shall see, Ibn Khaldun is quite right to classify them together. We are not, then, dealing with 'nomads', 'Bedouins' or 'Arabs' but rather with groups having similar political and social structures though very different 'ways of life'.

Ibn Khaldun does make a methodological distinction between two major groups which are usually referred to as 'Arabs' or 'Bedouins' and 'sedentary groups' respectively. But the truly radical distinction is between the rural population, the people of the *bled*—a category which includes both nomads and sedentary farmers—and the townspeople and farmers who live near the towns. Ibn Khaldun does criticize the destructive Arabs who were robbers and incapable of founding a state, but he does so in order to contrast them with the 'good' Arabs who did found empires.

For reasons that remain unclear, the terminology used by Ibn Khaldun is not very precise. The confusion is not simply a matter of translation problems. His work is often used as a source of quotations rather than being studied in detail. It is extremely complex and often seems to be contradictory. We have to grasp the true meaning of passages which form part of the same argument but which are obviously contradictory if taken out of context. In his classification of human groups, Ibn Khaldun stresses the differences between them and ignores similarities or dissimilarities between their 'ways of life' and we have therefore to try to grasp the real criteria he uses. Despite the obvious complexity of the issues involved, the vast majority of historians of North Africa still subscribe to the thesis that the 'Arab invasions of the eleventh century' destroyed the achievements of the sedentary population. They make a systematic distinction between the foreign nomadic invaders (usually and wrongly described as 'Arabs') and the sedentary Berber population, the native victims of the invasion.

The thesis of the Nomadic-Sedentary, Arab-Berber antagonism appears with the colonization of Algeria. According to J. Berque 'The Arab-Berber antithesis became a cliché by 1845.'[9] Carette's *'Recherches sur les origines des migrations des principales tribus de l'Afrique septentrionale'* launched the theme of the 'Arab invasions of the eleventh century' in 1853. The French translation of *The Muqaddimah* published in 1863 was invoked to provide definitive corroboration of what was by then almost an official thesis. One of the greatest Arab thinkers confirmed (or seemed to confirm) the views of the historians of the colonial period. The Arab invasions may not, as has so often been claimed, be the 'decisive event' in the history of the Barbary states, but they certainly became the main theme of North African historiography from the nineteenth century onwards. According to G. Marçais, 'The entire life of North Africa was deeply and permanently marked by this catastrophe.'[10] For Julien, the arrival of a destructive nomadic people was the most important event of the entire medieval period in the Maghreb.[11]

In the writings of E.F. Gautier, the nomadic-sedentary opposition becomes even more important, takes on still greater resonances. The invasion assumes 'the proportions of an apocalypse', an 'immense catastrophe', 'the end of a world'.[12] The struggle between the two groups becomes an eternal, cosmic battle. According to Gautier, the entire history of North Africa from classical antiquity onwards is a duel between 'two biological species which always behave in totally opposite ways'. 'Throughout the two millenia separating classical antiquity from our own day, the Maghreb has always been divided into two irreconcilable halves: nomads and sedentary groups. The nomad's instincts are quite different (from those of the sedentary farmer). His way of life means that he is a communist. The harshness of his life means that, when led by his prince, he is a disciplined soldier, at least for the duration of the battle. But it also means that he is permanently dissatisfied and always eager for new conquests. Politically, he is an anarchist, a nihilist. He has a great predilection for disorder and for the opportunities it affords him. He is destructive and negative. Even his victories accomplish nothing as he destroys their fruits in an unaccustomed orgy of extravagance.'[13]

Despite their official nature, the thesis of the nomad's historical guilt and the theory of the eternal opposition between nomadic and sedentary groups are in contradiction with a number of elementary points of geography.

There is no basis in reality for any such *total*, metaphysical opposition between nomadic and sedentary groups, even though novelists have found it a fertile source of inspiration. From ancient times until the beginning of the nineteenth century, one of the major features of the areas was the importance of semi-nomadic groups who practised both stockbreeding and farming, their activities at any given moment depending upon the seasons and upon where they were. There were, of course, completely sedentary arboriculturalists and pure nomads, but such groups were extreme cases and rarely came into direct contact with one another (except in Tunisia, for example). The vast majority of the population came in between these extremes. The interests of farmers and herdsmen were interconnected. Although some passages in Ibn Khaldun do suggest that nomadic and sedentary groups were irreconcilable, others could easily be used to support the more convincing argument that farmers and herdsmen coexisted in harmony.

The simplistic opposition between nomadic Arabs and sedentary Berbers is equally fallacious, as any geographer or anthropologist would recognize. But the fact remains that this worn-out argument is still used. It is therefore worth pointing out that not all nomads were 'Arabs' and that not all Berbers were sedentary by any means. The number of authentically 'Arab' groups who came from Arabia and settled in the Maghreb was very small. The people known as 'Arabs' in the Maghreb were in fact Arabic-speaking Berbers who retained many of their original characteristics. Although some of the Berber-speaking population were truly sedentary (in Kabylia, the western Rif and the western High Atlas), others were nomadic or semi-nomadic (as for instance in the mountains of the Central Atlas and the western High Atlas). In an attempt to get around this fact, which completely invalidates the equations between Arab and nomadic and Berber and sedentary, E.F. Gautier tries to divide the Berbers along linguistic lines.[14]

Even if we do accept the existence of some sedentary-nomadic opposition, it does not correspond to any major ethnic or linguistic divisions. Moreover, herdsmen and villagers were capable of coexisting within small but highly unified political and social formations. Brunschwig has shown that during the Middle Ages there were tribes in Ifriqiyah made up of complementary but equal sedentary and nomadic fractions.[15]

The political distinction between nomadic and sedentary groups is equally artificial. There are no known examples of conflict between purely sedentary and purely nomadic groups. On the contrary, all recorded conflicts appear to have been between singularly disparate groups.

'Nomadic factions and sedentary groups entered into alliances against other nomads who were allied with other sedentary groups. Bedouin sheikhs and rulers of cities formed alliances against other Bedouins and their urban allies. The mutually hostile blocs formed in this way had nothing to do with notions of origins or ways of life. Contradictory as their respective mentalities and aims may have been, the nomads no more tried to undermine sedentary institutions in any systematic way than the sedentary groups tried to wipe out nomadism'. Such is Brunschwig's view of Ifriqiyah, the country which suffered most at the hands of certain nomadic groups.

Even if we restrict the argument to the extreme examples of arboriculturalists and long-distance camel nomads, the conflict between their interests is much less serious than has sometimes been suggested. On the contrary, there are many cases in which their interests coincided: the nomads guarded and guided the caravans and were responsible for most transport in North Africa. They supplied the towns with food and contributed to the existence of some trade-based rural economies. They provided a skilled labour force that was much appreciated and greatly sought after at harvest time. Marçais cites specific examples of nomads and villagers entering mutual contractual agreements to farm land in the Constantine area. All too often compared to plagues of locusts, the Beni Hilal 'were taking an active part in the life of the country barely a century after their arrival and were contributing to the wealth of those they had once reduced to poverty.'[16] Brunschwig cites other similar cases. Stock breeding was far from being simply a cause of conflict or from being detrimental to the interests of the sedentary population.

These brief remarks are enough to show that the nomadic-sedentary distinction has to be regarded with a certain scepticism. North Africa did, undoubtedly, go through a prolonged period of turmoil. But was that turmoil basically the result of the 'nomadic invasion'? And was there in fact an 'invasion'?

Modern historians usually describe the arrival of the nomads in terms of an invasion or a flood: 'Waves of nomads broke over the country without ceasing, trailing women and children after them and thrusting back those who had gone before them.'[17]

The 'Hilalian invasion', which is often presented as being as irresistible as the invasions led by Tamerlane or Genghis Khan and on the same scale, was in fact very different. The Arab nomads were not the destructive conquerors of legend. There are no grounds for describing their arrival as a 'flood'. There were relatively few of them: about fifty thousand, according to the most reliable estimates. Although they did cause considerable destruction in the southern part of Ifriqiyah, the only area they actually conquered, in other areas their movements bore no resemblance to a conquest. Except in southern Ifriqiyah, they created no states and did not overthrow any established governments. In other regions, the only battles that took place along the routes taken by the 'invaders' were those in which they suffered heavy defeats.

Besides, it is by no means proven that the tribes' main aim was to march westwards. On the contrary, they were mainly concerned with moving from north to south, from the Tell to the edge of the desert in search of new pastures for their herds, and had no desire to stray outside their traditional territory. 'They moved from north to south in the same way that water follows the movement of the tides, and very rarely moved parallel to the coast.' (Marçais)

The Arab tribes moved west against their will and were pressurized into doing so by various rulers of the Maghreb. Far from trying to drive the tribes back, the rulers wanted them to come. Arab tribes were often forced to leave their own territory and settle in other areas. When the Almohad sultan inflicted a major defeat on the Arab tribes at Sétif in 1152 he was not trying to halt their advance. On the contrary, he was trying to force them to settle in Morocco and enter his service.

As a general description of the movements of the Arab tribes across North Africa from the eleventh to the fourteenth century, the term 'invasion' is, then, totally inaccurate. Although something of an exaggeration, 'deportation' might still be a more accurate term. In most cases, the tribes were invited to come to the Maghreb, or even recruited.

'It would be wrong to imagine the Berber sultans as having been in constant conflict with the Arabs. ... Their presence was frequently considered desirable. ... The large-scale movements of the tribes were usually organized in order to bring in forces that could serve the state rather than to repress neighbouring tribes that were considered a threat. ... The nomads were brought from every corner of the empire and stationed at the weakest point. ... Their departure was considered an irreparable loss and they were granted concessions to make them stay' (Marçais). The history of North Africa shows that, far from behaving like Gautier's 'anarchists and destructive nihilists', the nomadic tribes almost always worked in association with the governments. 'Emergent dynasties were virtually forced to gain the support of a powerful nomadic

group' (Marçais). The rulers of Morocco and Tunis often allied themselves with nomadic tribes, and for the sultans of Tlemcen, such alliances
were a regular policy. Marriage ties, the role played by the nomads in
gathering taxes and maintaining order, and their participation in military expeditions all point to the closeness of the association.

It is clear, then, that the theories of the Hilalian 'invasion' and of the
basic nomadic-sedentary clash are both incorrect. One of the most curious
features of North African historiography is the survival of these erroneous theories, despite all the efforts of the most eminent historians.

It would, of course, be absurd to go to the other extreme and to argue
that the nomads caused *no* destruction and were invariably devoted supporters of law and order. They did play an important role in insurrections and dynastic struggles. But, just as it would be wrong to see the
nomad-government alliance as a specific feature of the nomadic way of
life, it would be wrong to see participation in insurrections as being
restricted to the herdsmen.

It is certainly the case that nomads played an important political role
during the Middle Ages. They were mobile and owned riding camels,
which meant that their military potential was much greater than that of
the sedentary population. Most fighting-men were recruited from
amongst the ranks of the herdsmen, with no distinction being made
between true Arabs and Arabized Berbers. If some of the herdsmen in a
given area supported the authorities, pretenders would look to other
pastoral groups for support. Nomadic mercenaries provided most of the
forces used in struggles between rival rulers, rulers and pretenders and
between local chieftains, and there was considerable competition to
recruit them. Nor was the role of the nomads purely passive: their leaders were cunning and often took advantage of the weakness of their
employers to demand more money for their services or even to act on
their own behalf.

As the political instability developed into a permanent state of war, it
would seem that the political importance of the tribes increased along
with their numbers. Their herds represented a mobile form of capital
ideally suited to an unsettled situation, in that they could easily be moved
away from marauding bands. Harvests and plantations, by contrast,
were frequently plundered. The destruction was no doubt in part the
result of anarchic and spontaneous actions on the part of the troops. But
usually it was organized by governments which wanted to punish the
local population for their political actions or force them to pay taxes.

The destruction caused by the herdsmen seems to have been the result of actions carried out on the orders of the rulers they served rather than of their personal initiative. The nomads' domination over a frequently exploited and oppressed sedentary population did not result from a conflict between two ways of life. The subordination of the sedentary population was usually the result of government policy: nomadic groups were rewarded for their services by being given the right to raise taxes. As Marçais has shown, spontaneous looting was relatively rare and was usually the work of the poorer tribes. Nor is it irrelevant that many North African chroniclers see the contrast between the poverty and insecurity of the government-controlled *Bled el Maghzan*, in which nomadic mercenaries were active, and the relative wealth of the *Bled essiba*, which refused to pay taxes and where nomadic and sedentary tribes coexisted more or less peacefully, as a perfectly natural phenomenon. In many respects, the actions of some nomadic tribes in North Africa correspond to those of the mercenary forces employed in fourteenth-century Europe.

The developing role of the nomads and their movement into North Africa during the Middle Ages was an effect of the political and social organization of the Maghreb, rather than a prime or determinant cause. In the Middle East, where natural and technical conditions were similar to those in the Maghreb, the role of nomads was much less important.

Arabs from the east were not the only group to play this military and political role in North Africa. The sultans often used Berber tribes in the same way. Being more closely connected with the towns and the royal courts, which were the main centres for the spread of Arabic, the mercenary Berber tribes of the *Bled Maghzan* obviously tended to become Arabized more rapidly than tribes which lived in outlying areas where they were safe from royal troops and tax-gathering raids. It is also possible that the sultans who were looking for mercenaries preferred tribes from the east to older tribes who had been settled in one area for a long time simply because the former were more mobile.

It is now possible to demonstrate that the simplistic and erroneous theory of the Hilalian invasion does not appear in Ibn Khaldun's work. On the contrary, the fourteenth-century writer shows, with a perspicacity and accuracy that modern historians would do well to imitate, the real process whereby the so-called 'invasion' took place.

Ibn Khaldun describes the beginnings of the 'invasion' in the opening pages of his *Histoire des Berbères*: 'It was only towards the middle of the fifth century of the Hejira that Africa was invaded by groups from the

Hilal and Solaym tribes. As soon as they arrived, *they made contact with the established governments . . . their history is bound up with that of the ruling powers.*'[18] It was in 433 (1051-52 AD) that the Arabs came to Ifri-qiyah: 'Mounes-Ibn-Yahya-es Sinberi, Emir of the Ryah,[19] was the first to come. El-Moez[20] *immediately tried to win his support.* He called him to him, declared that he was his friend and married his daughter. *He then proposed that he brought in the Arabs* from their outlying camps so as to overwhelm the princes of the Hammad family,[21] his collateral relatives and *those who had rebelled against him* in the eastern part of the empire. After some hesitation, Mounes agreed and sent for the Arabs. The nomads then began to devastate the countryside.'[22]

This passage alone makes it clear that it was the ruling monarchs who invited the nomads into their realms so that they could use them as mer-cenaries. Ibn Khaldun stresses that before long the same methods were being used against rebellious vassals: 'When el-Moez retreated to Mahdya after having abandoned Kairouan, he lit a fire that was soon to rage throughout Ifriqiyah. The victors divided the cities amongst them-selves and appointed their own governors. *They distributed the surround-ing lands amongst the nomads.*'[23]

Similar conclusions could be drawn from the following passage, which is only one of the many that could be cited. Ibn Khaldun was well aware of the links between the rulers and the so-called invaders: 'Sultan Abu Hammu[24] began to make preparations for a new expedition to thwart the plans of the rebels. He sent emissaries to the Arabs, poured money into the tribes and granted them sufficient territory to satisfy all their needs.'[25]

Ibn Khaldun gives an accurate description of the results of these poli-cies: 'The central Maghreb is still in the state I have described so often. The Arabs are the masters of the plains. The authority of the Abd el Wadids does not extend to the outlying areas of the empire or beyond the coastal regions they ruled in the past. The power of the Arabs has weak-ened the dynasty. The Abd el-Wadids helped to make them strong by giving them money, granting them vast areas of land and surrendering a large number of towns to them. The only way they can control them now is to involve them in tribal quarrels and set them against one another'.

He uses other examples to show that the power of the nomadic tribes derived from their alliance with the government and that they never made any real offensives on their own initiative: 'That branch of the Zanatah known as the Beni Badin . . . became devoted supporters of the

Almohads as soon as they achieved power. The Beni Badin were much closer to the dynasty than their rivals. . . . In the central Maghreb they controlled more of the plateaux and more of the coastal area than any other branch of the Zanatah. During their summer migrations, they were allowed to go much further than any other nomadic tribe. They made up part of the Almohad army and were responsible for defending the Empire's frontiers.'

It is quite clear, then, that according to Ibn Khaldun the importance of the 'nomadic' tribes (Arabs and Berbers alike) was to a large extent an effect of the political organization of the Barbary States during the Middle Ages. There would, however, still appear to be a contradiction between those passages in *The Muqaddimah* in which he anathemizes robber 'Arabs' and those in which he praises the political virtues of those 'Arabs' who founded states.

As noted previously, there is no historical basis for the theory that there was a basic antagonism between nomads and sedentary groups or between Arabs and Berbers. It is a myth. Some serious historians have gone on believing in it, however, even though the results of their own research contradicted the theory in a number of ways. Thus Marçais, one of the greatest experts on the problems of the Arabs in North Africa, subscribed to this view, even though he himself had collected a host of facts which prove that there was no real 'invasion'. He never demolished the fables about the 'Arab invaders' by collating his objections and reservations. Gautier, meanwhile, made the 'invasion' an obligatory *leitmotiv* of all historical accounts of North Africa and an official theory.

This refusal to accept the mass of evidence, the stubborn repetition of the error, and the insistence on making it a central theme in any account of Maghrebian history cannot be accidental. The myth did not arise by chance. It was deliberately forged and inculcated into the framework of colonial ideology. From the very beginning of the conquest of Algeria, French generals tried to drive a wedge between 'Arabs' and 'Kabyls', and they succeeded in doing so. Abd el-Kader would never have been defeated in 1847 if the Kabyls had not remained neutral. But they were not attacked until 1851. It was in Morocco that this 'pro-Berber' [26] and anti-Arab policy was organized most methodically. Its most spectacular and most serious manifestation came in 1953 during the so-called revolt of the Berber mountain tribes against Muhammad V, who was thought to be too sympathetic to the nationalist movement.

Turning the Arabs into destructive invaders was one way of legitimizing the 'French presence'. In the work of Louis Bertrand[27] (Academician and official bard of the *Gouvernement Général de l'Algérie*) the Christian Barbary states are symbolized by St Augustine and are represented as having fallen to invaders from the east and then being restored to the bosom of the Christian west by France. Officials who had to make speeches about France's 'civilizing mission' were only too glad to exploit this fanciful argument.

Attempts were made to set the seal of history and geography on these literary fantasies. E.F. Gautier was the theoretician of the Nomadic-Sedentary antagonism. Gautier had been at Galliéni's side during the savage repression of the Fahavalo revolt in Madagascar in 1897. He was a professor at the University of Algiers and one of the most brilliant ideologues of colonialism. Gautier did his best to prove that nationalist feelings had no legitimate place in North Africa: Nomads, Arabs and Orientals had 'a biological and not a historical conception of the past and of history. The Arab is proud of his family, his clan and his tribe; the difference between this and our sense of patriotism is obvious. . . . A fatherland is a geographical country; only a settled population can love the land.'[28]

The Arab, therefore, has no right to a country of his own: QED. The fate of the Berber is no better, at least not according to Gautier: 'The most obvious feature of the Maghreb is the absence of any emotional basis on which to build a feeling of nationhood. We have to accept that this individualistic flaw is incurable.'[29] There is of course no basis for such gratuitous and partisan statements.

Because of the eternal struggle between nomad and sedentary groups, 'the modern Maghreb is a complex of incompatible and irreconcilable elements' and only foreign domination can weld it into a cohesive whole. 'Not only has the Maghreb never been a nation; it has never been an autonomous state. It has always been part of an empire.'[30] 'The people of the Maghreb have always been a conquered people . . . they have never succeeded in driving out their masters.'[31]

It is amazing to hear an academic come out with such a tissue of historical untruths. It is not true that North Africa has always been part of a foreign empire: between the eighth and the sixteenth centuries the countries now known as Algeria and Tunisia were ruled by native dynasties. Morocco was independent from ancient times until the twentieth century. Roman domination was no more than a brief localized episode, and the sovereignty of the Caliph of Damascus never existed except in theory. This eternally conquered people once ruled both Spain and

Egypt. Just think what could be written about France if *only* the period of the Hundred Years War was taken into consideration!

The falsification of history not being enough, purely racist arguments were also used. According to Gautier, 'Of all the white races in the Mediterranean area, the Maghrebian race must be the most backward by far. ...This race has no positive individuality.'[32]

But surely Ibn Khaldun, whose greatness was evoked to lend more weight to the anti-Arab theories attributed to him, was a Maghrebian? And surely there can be no doubt as to *his* worth? Gautier thinks otherwise: 'The oriental mind is quite different from ours. The oriental has no sense of critical rationalism, no sense of reality'. Ibn Khaldun wanted to understand—a very western ambition for a Muslim. 'This oriental had a sharp, critical mind. In other words, he had a western sense of history.'[33]

Gautier goes on quite imperturbably with his falsehoods: 'Muslim civilization suffers from a curious paralysis of the historical sense'.[34] 'During the Middle Ages, the humblest of our historians wrote history in the same way that Monsieur Jourdain wrote prose; without realizing that he was doing so. It never occurred to even the most enlightened Saracen to do so.'[35]

It might, however, be pointed out that if Ibn Khaldun and Froissard are compared, the representative of the Western Mind does not come out too well. Just as Louis Bertrand saw the Maghreb as a Christian country under Oriental domination, Gautier turns Ibn Khaldun into a western-style thinker. 'He has a western conception of history. ...Ibn Khaldun's stay in Andalusia brought a breath of our Renaissance into his oriental mind.'[36]

Why the stubborn refusal, which flies in the face of all the evidence, to admit that Arab civilization could produce historians? Why try to disassociate Ibn Khaldun from this caricature of the Arab world? Because, as Paul Valéry put it, history is a dangerous science. Gautier inadvertently admits his true motives when he writes that 'In order to have a sense of history, one must belong to a nation.'[37] He uses the most laughable arguments to prove that 'Arabs' have no sense of history, thereby 'proving' that Maghrebians have no legitimate claim to a country of their own. Finally, according to Gautier, 'The Maghreb never changes'. It would be euphemistic to describe this as wishful thinking.

Gautier was not the only contributor to this colonial ideology. Bouthoul also sees the struggle between nomadic and sedentary groups as being at the origin of the so-called dilemma facing North Africa: 'Freedom and Barbarism or Servitude and Civilization.'. The only governments stable enough to 'impose peace upon these irreconcilable groups ... were governments which could rely upon aid from a powerful foreign state. Whenever North Africa was left to itself, it always experienced the same vicissitudes'.[38]

Even C.A. Julien, that eminent socialist, subscribes to the same views: after a preamble dealing with geography and prehistory, he offers the following comment on North African history: 'No matter how far back in time we go, the entire region always seems to have been afflicted with a congenital inability to be independent'.[39] The supposed unfitness of Maghrebians for independence and the nature of Gautier's 'eternally conquered people' became keystones of colonial ideology. Given that there could be no doubt as to the fact that, after the Kharijite insurrection of the eighth century, the Maghreb became independent of the eastern dynasties, the migrations of a few Arab tribes who reached North Africa in the ninth century and entered the service of native rulers had to be transformed into an Arab 'invasion' to give credence to the theory of the Maghreb's congenital unfitness for independence.

In terms of colonial ideology, the theory that the Barbary States were conquered by the Arabs was important for two reasons. Firstly, it meant that the French were merely the latest to conquer a land which had always been conquered and which, it was hoped, would always remain so. Secondly, it provided a historical basis for a policy of turning Arabs and Berbers against each other.[40]

It is not surprising that the supporters of colonialism, hardly renowned for singing the praises of the great names of Arab civilization, should have given such importance to Ibn Khaldun. They could have hoped for no better confirmation of their fraudulent theories.

5
The Crisis of the
Fourteenth Century

Although the Arabs did not really conquer or even invade North Africa, and although there was a slow Arabization of the Berber population rather than any real antagonism between nomadic and sedentary groups, it remains true that North Africa went through a long period of turmoil and serious difficulties. In order to understand why, we have to situate the period carefully. According to those who argue that there was an Arab invasion and that the nomads were responsible for it, the eleventh century represents the fateful transition from prosperity to decadence.[1] As Ibn Khaldun shows, Ifriqiyah certainly did go through a difficult period in the eleventh century. But in the twelfth century it experienced several long periods of prosperity under the Hafsid dynasty, despite the presence of the Arabs. The decadence of the rest of the Maghreb did not begin in the eleventh century; on the contrary, it was during the eleventh century that the Almoravids (who were after all nomads) established their powerful empire. In the twelfth century, the empire of the Almohads, who forced the Arab tribes to come to Morocco in 1152, was at the height of its glory. This was the heyday of the Maghrebian civilization. Despite these incontrovertible facts, which completely invalidate the 'invasion' thesis, many historians persist in saying that there was a crisis in the eleventh century simply because the Beni Hilal arrived in Ifriqiyah in 1052. Given that they see the Arab nomads only as destructive conquerors, the crisis *must* have begun when they arrived in the Maghreb, despite all the evidence to the contrary.

The real difficulties facing Ifriqiyah in the eleventh century began long before the arrival of the Beni Hilal. They can to a large extent be explained in terms of the war between the Almoravids and the Sudanese kingdom of Ghana, and the subsequent disruption of the gold trade. When the Almoravids conquered Ghana and gained control of Sijilmassa, they diverted the gold trade to Morocco and away from Ifriqiyah and the central Maghreb. The contrast between the power of the Almoravid empire and the signs of a coming depression in Ifriqiyah and the Hammadid kingdom[2] is very striking.

In the fourteenth century, the decline of the Maghreb became more general. The power of the kings looked increasingly fragile and attempts at establishing a centralized monarchy failed repeatedly. More and more pretenders appeared and palace revolutions became more frequent. Governors became ever more insubordinate and were increasingly tempted to secede. The *Bled el-Maghzan* shrank at the expense of the *Bled essiba*, where the tribes were able to keep the troops responsible for tax gathering at bay. The military tribes were constantly being courted by sultans and pretenders and their power increased accordingly. Their chieftains were granted charters of *iqta'* on a more permanent basis and were allowed to tax wider areas. Such fiscal concessions weakened the central authorities, which became less and less capable of resisting the claims of the great chieftains. The kingdoms seem to have lost much of their former power during the fourteenth century. Speaking of this period, Ibn Khaldun notes that the plague of 1348 'overtook the dynasties at the time of their senility, when they had reached the end of their tether.'[3]

In these North African states which, as we have seen, were characterized by the structures of 'military democracy', the power of the sultans was to a great extent based upon profits from trade between the Western Sudan, the East and Europe. But in the fourteenth century, the Maghreb gradually lost control of the gold routes. The gold trade between Egypt and the Sudan no longer had to go through North Africa.

In the mid-thirteenth century, the reigning Mameluke dynasty in Cairo began to try to extend its authority over the Upper Nile Valley, which had until then been controlled by Christian states. In 1316, the Christian kingdom of Nubia fell to the Egyptian armies and the road to the south was opened up. The Arab tribes of Upper Egypt, who were closely related to those who had reached the Maghreb in the eleventh century, thus had access to the savannah zone which stretches from the banks of the Nile to the Atlantic coast. The great trading centres of the east had direct access to the gold-producing kingdoms of the Western Sudan and no longer had to rely upon the Maghrebians. South of the Sahara, this development led to the decline of previously important states (the Empire of Mali experienced serious difficulties in the fourteenth century) and to the rise of previously minor states in the central Sudan, such as the Songhai and Bornou Empires. Significantly, several Sudanese kings who made the pilgrimage to Mecca were officially recognized by the Caliph of Cairo. Increasingly, the gold caravans by-passed the Maghreb and the decline in trans-Saharan trade was symbolized by the decline of Sijilmassa, which had once been the main desert port.[4] Control over Sijilmassa had been the source of the power of a series of dynasties in Morocco, but from the fourteenth century onwards the town was increasingly outside the zone of influence of the rulers of Fez. This had something to do with their relative weakness, but it was mainly an expression of their lack of interest in the town now that it had been by-passed by the caravans that had once given it its extraordinary importance. Some of the tribes of the Western Sahara now turned to looting, whereas they had previously been involved in the caravan trade and had let the merchants travel in safety provided that tolls were paid. The downturn in trade forced them to look for other sources of income and as Marçais notes, 'Brigandry appears to have been the work of weak tribes rather than strong ones'. The threat of looting became an additional reason for avoiding what had until the fourteenth century been the busiest routes. The increasing scarcity of gold had serious consequences for the countries of Western Europe. Christian merchants had once travelled to the great trading centres of North Africa in order to exchange manufactured products for gold. Now that the gold trade bypassed the Maghreb, the Europeans tried to reach the gold-producing areas themselves. In 1323 the Genoans reached Madeira and the Azores, and by the end of the century the Portuguese were pushing further down the coast of Africa. From 1450 onwards they succeeded in diverting part of the gold trade to the Gulf of Guinea.

The decline in the trade in gold between North Africa and the Western Sudan was the cause of most of the difficulties experienced by the Maghrebian states in the fourteenth century. In an attempt to compensate for their loss of income from trade their rulers resorted to various expedients that were profitable in the short term but disastrous in the long term. Ibn Khaldun describes the methods they used in a number of passages, and notably in a chapter entitled 'Commercial activity on the part of the ruler is harmful to his subjects and ruinous to the tax revenue.'[5] These disastrous methods which, as Ibn Khaldun shows, were used when the kingdoms fell into decline, are in sharp contrast with the collaboration between merchants and rulers in periods of prosperity.

Now that they had lost much of the income once derived from customs duties and taxes on trade, the sultans found it more and more difficult to pay their auxiliaries. In exchange for the latter's services, they granted them the right to levy taxes in a given area or, more frequently, from a given tribe. The *iqta'* system seems to have been rare in periods of prosperity. G. Marçais[6] points out that the first charters of *iqta'* were not granted until the second half of the twelfth century and that they became more common in the fourteenth. As a result, the sultans had less room to manoeuvre and the power of the tribal chieftains increased accordingly. The chieftains became much more independent. They could also make much more money by extorting taxes from weaker tribes than by accepting the subsidies paid to them by the government. On several occasions great chieftains rebelled because the sultans wanted to return to a system of monetary payment and withdraw the charters of *iqta'* they had been granted. Ibn Khaldun gives an eye-witness account of two such full-scale insurrections led by chieftains who wanted to keep their charters of *iqta'*. Overestimating his strength, the Marinid Sultan Abul Hasan decided to consolidate his power by forcing the chieftains to stop taxing the peasantry directly and accept payment by the government. A few years later, his son Abu Inan tried to do the same thing. Such measures would have placed the chieftains under the control of the Sultan and they therefore defected or even rebelled. 'After his conquest of Ifriqiyah in 1347 Abu Hasan treated his subjects haughtily. Under the Hafsid government they had not been treated in that way. In his dealings with the nomads he adopted a very different system to that used by the former dynasty. Realizing that the Arabs had used their power to gain concessions over several extensive areas of territory and a large number of towns, he took them away from them and indemnified them by giving them state subsidies and increasing their *jibaya*.[7] Shortly afterwards, he reduced the amounts he was giving them. Touched by the complaints of those farmers who still suffered as a result of the tyranny of the Arabs and still paid tribute to the nomads, he forbade them to pay it and forbade the Arabs to demand money. The Arabs began to distrust the Sultan. Groaning under the harshness of his administration, they waited for a favourable opportunity to take their revenge.'

During the dynastic crises when pretenders to the throne began to fight, the tribal chieftains became masters of the situation and extorted all they could from the rival pretenders. It is not, then, surprising that such crises should have become more frequent, even when the reigning sultan was still alive. Rival pretenders would appear, each supported by a group of tribes or by a neighbouring state. Provincial governors would declare themselves independent, even when there was no power vacuum at court.

As such conflicts became more frequent, the pretenders turned to the military tribes more and more often, and their power increased accordingly. Deprived of much of their normal income from taxation, the sultans had to resort to illegal measures. Chieftains who had been granted charters of *iqta'* often followed their example and began to abuse their powers. Agriculture gave way to pastoralism, as it was easier for the tribes to flee with their herds than to hide their harvests during *razzias*. As the plains came increasingly under the control of the tax-gatherers, the tribes left them and sought refuge in the mountains where mounted troops could not reach them. Increasingly, the *Bled el-Maghzan* was restricted to the plains where the ruler's agents and the great tribal chieftains could gather taxes more easily. Royal authority was forced to rely upon auxiliaries. The *Bled essiba*, the dissident zone which usually escaped taxation, was usually more peaceful and wealthier, even though it covered the most remote and barren areas of the kingdom.

Ibn Khaldun makes a detailed analysis of the extortion that characterized the North African states during the period of their decadence: 'Injustice brings about the ruin of civilization . . . attacks on people's property remove the incentive to acquire and gain property. People, then, become of the opinion that the purpose and ultimate destiny of acquiring property is to have it taken away from them. When the incentive to acquire and gain property is gone, people no longer make any efforts to acquire any. The extent and degree to which property rights are infringed upon determines the extent and degree to which the effort of the subjects to acquire property slackens. . . . The disintegration of civilization causes the disintegration of the status of dynasty and ruler, because their peculiar status constitutes the *form* of civilization and the form necessarily decays when its *matter* (in this case, civilization) decays.'[8] 'The proven fact is that civilization inevitably suffers losses through injustice and hostile acts . . . and it is the dynasty that suffers therefrom. Injustice should not be understood to imply only the confiscation of money or other property from the owners without compensation and without cause . . . it is something more general than that. Whoever takes someone's property, or uses him for forced labour, or presses an unjustified claim against him, or imposes upon him a duty not required by the religious

law, does an injustice to that particular person. People who collect unjustified taxes commit an injustice. Those who infringe upon property rights
commit an injustice. Those who, in general, take property by force commit an injustice. It is the dynasty that suffers from all these acts, in as
much as civilization, which is the substance of the dynasty, is ruined
when people have lost all incentive.'[9] 'One of the greatest injustices and
one which contributes most to the destruction of civilization is the unjustified imposition of tasks and the use of subjects for forced labour. ... An
injustice even greater and more destructive of civilization and the dynasty
is the appropriation of people's property by buying their possessions as
cheaply as possible and then reselling them at the highest possible prices by
means of forced sales and/or purchases. ... If no trading is being done in
the markets, the subjects have no livelihood, and the tax revenue of the
ruler decreases or deteriorates, since ... most of the tax revenue comes
from customs duties on commerce. ... It should be known that all these
practices are caused by the need for money on the part of dynasty and
ruler. ... The ordinary income does not meet the expenditures. Therefore, the ruler invents new sorts and kinds of taxes, in order to increase
the revenues and to be able to balance the budget. ... The need for
appropriating people's property becomes stronger and stronger. In this
way, the authority of the dynasty shrinks until its influence is wiped out
and its identity is lost and it is defeated by an attacker.'[10] 'At this stage,
the soldiers have already grown bold against the dynasty, because it has
become weak and senile. ... The dynasty ... attempts to remedy and
smooth over the situation through generous alliances and much spending for the soldiers ... '.[11] 'In the later years of dynasties, famines and
pestilences become numerous. As far as famines are concerned, the
reason is that most people at that time refrain from cultivating the soil.
For, in the later years of dynasties, there occur attacks on property and
tax revenue and, through customs duties, on trading. Or, trouble occurs
as the result of the unrest of the subjects and the great number of rebels
who are provoked by the senility of the dynasty to rebel. Therefore, as a
whole, little grain is stored.'[12]

According to Ibn Khaldun, the extortion he describes in such detail,
and which leads to unrest and disorder, was not the result of a normal or
permanent situation. Again and again, he stresses that these practices
and difficulties appeared when the kingdoms entered a period of decline,
as they did in the fourteenth century.

Ibn Khaldun is not describing states which were constantly struggling with financial difficulties, but states which were established during a period in which poverty was unknown. As Ibn Khaldun shows, the state apparatuses were established on the basis of relatively abundant resources, which could be obtained without the state having to oppress or pressurize traders and farmers. The only logical explanation for the relative prosperity enjoyed by these states when they did not exert any great fiscal pressure, is the size of the income they could derive from international trade. In Western Europe, the extreme fragmentation of political structures was largely a result of a fall in the circulation of money. In North Africa, however, the permanent existence of a centralized state meant that governments needed a much greater income.

The decline in the volume of trade forced the North African states, which required a relatively high budget if they were to function, to tax the population increasingly heavily. This proves that, prior to the period of 'decadence', a major proportion of the state budget must have derived from taxes on trading profits. The taxes permitted by Islamic tradition were not enough to supply the states with the resources they needed if they were to last and if their apparatus was to function properly. These states never established a regular, efficient fiscal system. So they had to resort to illegal methods and to what Ibn Khaldun calls 'injustice'. Violence and war were the only ways they could extort the resources they needed. In the long term, this draconian, excessive taxation was catastrophic, and it did not even provide the states with the revenue they required for survival.

Popular resistance to tax-gathering raids can to some extent be explained in terms of the structures of 'military democracy'. The cohesion of the tribes prevented the spread of the share-cropping system[13] which would have allowed the landowner to appropriate a greater part of the harvest. But the relatively non-intensive nature of the mode of production in North Africa meant that there was in any case little surplus to appropriate. As their income from trade decreased, the states therefore began to decline. During the period of their prosperity, the Maghrebian states appear to have derived most of their revenue from trade. Its loss seems to have been the primary cause of the decline and decadence of the North African states in the fourteenth century.

Ibn Khaldun, however, does not mention the role of trade as one of the factors contributing to the prosperity of the North African states. He makes no allusion to the changes in the trans-Saharan trade. He never makes the point that the decadence of these states in the fourteenth century may have resulted from the decline of the gold trade. This is a curious omission, as he obviously knew about the trade in gold between the Sudan and the Maghreb. He was acquainted with the writings of geographers like el-Bekri and Ibn Batuka and his own writings contain valuable information about the Sudanese kingdoms from which the caravans left for North Africa. He describes the magnificence of the Kings of Mali and Ghana who made the pilgrimage to Mecca and distributed the cargo of gold they had brought to finance their journey. He stresses the huge profits that could be made from trade with the Sudan: 'The merchants who dare to enter the Sudan country are the most prosperous and wealthy of all people . . . the goods of the Sudan country are found in only small quantities among us, and they are particularly expensive. . . . The same applies to merchants who travel from our country to the East.'[14] He also mentions the social and political role of the rich merchants: 'they have the protection of rank . . . they have obtained the wealth that helps them to associate with the people of the dynasty and to gain prominence and renown amongst their contemporaries. . . . They are . . . too proud to have anything personally to do with . . . business manipulations, and they leave them to the care of their agents and servants. . . . These merchants will thus be remote from . . . bad character qualities since they have nothing to do with the actions that bring them about.'[15]

Ibn Khaldun certainly stresses that the state suffers when there is a decline in trade, but does not argue that the state goes into decline when the great merchants are less active.

Ibn Khaldun regards the financial difficulties of the state as resulting from increased expenditures rather than from a decrease in revenue. The increase is, he believes, due to the increasingly luxurious tastes of the king, his court and its dignitaries. In addition, increasingly large sums have to be paid to mercenaries, military tribes and their chieftains to suppress the frequent rebellions. Yet Ibn Khaldun himself states that expenditure was higher when the kingdoms were in their heyday than when they were in decline. Expenditure could then be covered without the state having to oppress and ransom the population: 'The ruler and his entourage are wealthy only in the middle period of the dynasty.'[16] Life at court was more luxurious when the kingdom was at the height of its power. The sultan could build much more imposing palaces, fortresses and mosques. His military expeditions were on a larger scale, even though the level of taxation was much lower.

Ibn Khaldun's description of the evolution of the dynasties leads one to the logical conclusion that the transition from greatness to decadence did not result simply from the internal factors he examines, but also from external factors which led to a reduction in state revenue.

If we collate the different elements analysed by Ibn Khaldun we come to the conclusion that the general period of decadence experienced by the Maghrebian countries in the fourteenth century must have been in part the result of the decline of the trade which formerly made them great. Why, then, does Ibn Khaldun never deal explicitly with the external causes of the crisis?

The explanation may be that he was not studying the fourteenth century as such. Ibn Khaldun probably came to history as a result of thinking about contemporary problems. Gradually, he began to take a much broader and more general view and to analyse North African political and social structures. As he extended his ambitions to understanding 'human social organization, which itself is identical with world civilization', he became less interested in his own period. By the fourteenth century, the three main states in the Maghreb were obviously in crisis. But empires had been created in earlier centuries also, and they too had declined and collapsed after a period of glory. The splendours of the Almohad epoch of the twelfth century gave way to the turmoil that affected not only Morocco but also the central Maghreb and Ifriqiyah in the first half of the thirteenth century.

What Ibn Khaldun could not of course know was that the crisis of the fourteenth century was very different from its predecessors. Earlier crises had led to the rise of new empires. Most of the symptoms were the same. But we now know that the crisis that began in the fourteenth century was to be much longer and much more general: it lasted for more than two hundred years. We also know that it did not lead to the rise of states comparable with those of the Middle Ages in terms of power or level of civilization. The Hafsid kingdom did enjoy peace and relative prosperity throughout much of the fifteenth century; but even its prosperity pales in comparison with the great Muslim civilizations of the past.[17]

The long crisis that began in the fourteenth century opened up a weak and decadent Maghreb to foreign influences. The Portuguese based themselves in Moroccan ports and established what was effectively a protectorate over the Atlantic plains. They were followed by the Spanish who, after destroying the Kingdom of Granada in 1492, captured every port on the Mediterranean coast from Melilla (1492) to Tunis (1532) and established their authority over the kingdom of Tlemcen.

The central Maghreb and Ifriqiyah escaped Christian domination only because they were conquered by the Turks in 1520-50. Turkish rule then lasted for three hundred years until the arrival of the French. Despite the anarchy raging in the country, and despite the fact that the Spanish and Portuguese controlled vast areas, Morocco finally shook off both Christians and Turks by turning them against one another. It was only during the reign of Sultan Saadien al-Mansur (1578-1603) that Morocco regained any stability and power. Significantly, this renaissance coincided with Morocco's seizure of Timbuctu and Gao in 1591 and with the defeat of the Askia dynasty in the Sudan, which had previously been allied with Cairo. After this expedition, gold poured into Morocco. Al Mansur, who was immediately nicknamed 'The Golden' struck a famous gold coin to mark his victory. But no regular trade was established with the Sudan, and Morocco relapsed into anarchy, although strong rulers did on occasion establish a certain temporary stability.

We can now see the true nature of the crisis that began in the fourteenth century. At the time it looked like a repetition of the temporary difficulties that had arisen in earlier periods, but it in fact marked the beginning of a long period of decadence. There was no way that Ibn Khaldun could realize this, as the symptoms of the crisis were not noticeably different from those that had announced its predecessors.

Yet he may have sensed, however vaguely, that a major change was taking place: 'However, at the present time—that is at the end of the eighth (fourteenth) century—the situation in the Maghreb, as we can observe, has taken a turn and changed entirely.'[18] 'When there is a general change of conditions, it is as if the entire creation had changed and the whole world had been altered. ... Therefore, there is a need at this time that someone should systematically set down the situation of the world among all regions and races, as well as the customs and sectarian beliefs that have changed for their adherents. ... This should be a model for future historians. ... In this book of mine, I shall discuss as much of that as will be possible for me here in the Maghreb.'[19]

The lasting and devastating effects of the great plague of 1348 may have given Ibn Khaldun some idea of the dimensions of the crisis in the Maghreb: 'A destructive plague ... overtook the dynasties at the time of their senility. ... It lessened their power. ... Their situation approached the point of annihilation and dissolution. ... Civilization decreased with the decrease of mankind. Cities were laid waste. . . . The entire inhabited world changed.'[20]

Unable to go any further because of his lack of hindsight, Ibn Khaldun inevitably came to the conclusion that the historical significance of this crisis was not radically different to those that had occurred earlier. Although the earlier crises had not affected all the states in the Maghreb at once, they had displayed analogous symptoms and had been preceded by periods of financial difficulties. Those periods of difficulty were caused by the disruption of the gold trade. In the fourteenth century, however, the disruption occurred at a continental and not merely a regional level. Trade between North Africa and the Sudan declined considerably, then almost ceased completely.

Perhaps Ibn Khaldun was not aware of the decline of the gold trade. He was not, in any case, in a position to appreciate its importance. Even if he was aware of it, he may have chosen to ignore it in order to concentrate upon the features common to all the crises that had punctuated the history of North Africa in the Middle Ages.

It can be demonstrated that Ibn Khaldun was trying to draw general conclusions from his investigation into the causes of the constant crises in the Maghreb. In his desire to ignore the particular in favour of the general, he omitted to mention one other important transformation. Most of the dynasties that succeeded one another between the ninth and the fourteenth centuries were established by victorious tribes or groups of tribes, as were the Kingdom of Tlemcen, and the Iddrissid, Fatimid, Almoravid and Almohad empires. But these had all been cemented together by a specific religious tendency which marked them out from both orthodoxy and the main heterodox tendencies. In a period when the influence of religion was all-important, this ideological particularism enabled the states to impose a common superstructure upon a heterogeneous group of tribes. The king had an advantage that often proved decisive when it came to retaining the loyalty of chieftains and groups who might otherwise have been tempted to transfer their allegiance to other monarchs, but did not do so because that would have meant renouncing their beliefs. Ibn Khaldun stresses that 'Religious propaganda gives a dynasty at its beginning another power in addition to that of the group feeling it possessed as a result of the number of its supporters'[21] and that 'Dynasties of wide power and large royal authority have their origin in religion based either on prophecy or on truthful propaganda.'[22]

This was obviously of prime importance in the history of the Arabs and of Islam.

But this important factor was absent in the Maghrebian states of the fourteenth century. After the collapse of the Almohad Empire in the thirteenth century, orthodoxy spread throughout North Africa and none of the later dynasties displayed any religious particularism. The disappearance of the particularism that had cemented together the earlier kingdoms further contributed to the weakness of the states from the fourteenth century onwards. Tribes, chieftains and ministers could switch their loyalties much more easily than before.

Ibn Khaldun makes no allusion to this additional factor which made the Marinid, Abd el-Wadid and Hafsid kingdoms so much more fragile than the politico-religious dynasties that went before them. This suggests that he was not trying to explain the crisis of the fourteenth century as such. He could neither grasp its long-term significance nor shed any light on why it was so different from earlier ones.

Similar reasons can be invoked to explain why Ibn Khaldun showed no particular interest in another important event which made the fourteenth century a turning point in the history of the Maghreb: the change in the routes taken by the gold caravans. Ibn Khaldun had insufficient distance from events to realize that in his lifetime, the Maghreb was moving from a period of greatness into one of decline. He merely sensed the gravity of the oncoming crisis.

It was all the more difficult to appreciate the importance of the change in that in the Maghreb the fourteenth century was characterized, not by the appearance of new creative elements, but by the disappearance of a basic factor: the gold trade. The role this played in political life was all the more difficult to appreciate in that it was so indirect. The fourteenth century was marked by the survival of many old factors and pre-existing structures. Their influence was considerable even when they were combined with other major causes; but when those causes disappeared, it became overwhelming.

It is quite understandable, then, that a fourteenth-century historian should have identified this lasting crisis with earlier temporary episodes. But it would be quite wrong for a modern historian to do the same.

In his attempt to distinguish the necessary from the contingent and the general from the particular, and in his examination of the links between long-term historical developments and events which, although apparently random, were in fact part of a general conjuncture, Ibn Khaldun thus gave priority to *permanent* and *internal* factors. Conversely, he minimized *external* factors whose effect was *temporary*. Although it recounts the events of factual history in great detail, *The Muqaddimah* is not really a study of long-term historical developments. Such developments would not have been visible at the time. *The Muqaddimah* contains an analysis of the permanent political and social structures of the Maghreb and an analysis of the interplay between those structural elements. They determine the foundation of empires, and their rise and fall. They also determine the evolutionary cycles that punctuate North African history.

Despite the importance of the gold trade as an external factor, internal factors and structures are all-important. The Maghrebian kingdoms experienced difficulties that cannot be explained in terms of external influences alone. Even though the Almoravid Empire controlled the trans-Saharan routes, it eventually broke up. Even though the victorious Almohads controlled the gold routes, ultimately they too failed to prevent the spread of the gangrene that destroyed their Empire. Its destruction resulted from internal processes, as did the failure of the various attempts that were made to establish a centralized monarchy from the thirteenth century onwards. The vicissitudes of the gold trade did have major repercussions for the history of medieval North Africa; but only because of the specificities of the internal structures of its states and their relative fragility.

6

The Development of the State

The value of Ibn Khaldun's work derives primarily from the sophistication of his analysis of the political and social structures of medieval North Africa. It is, then, particularly galling to see that most commentators give a picture of that analysis schematic to the point of being caricatural, if not downright erroneous.

According to most authors who have studied *The Muqaddimah*, Ibn Khaldun makes a basic distinction between nomadic and sedentary groups and bases his whole conception of historical development upon that distinction. Thus, they claim that Ibn Khaldun argues that only nomadic tribes were sufficiently tightly bound together to found states, that the solidarity born of the rigours of nomadic life enabled their chieftains to conquer and found empires. The stability of the state was based upon the solidarity that united its founders. They were not slow to take advantage of the benefits of political power and in their search for comfort became rich and sedentary. They became weak and cowardly and were concerned only with their own comfort. As they developed a sedentary mentality and a taste for wealth, they gradually lost their former military prowess and sense of solidarity. Becoming weaker and less united, they became incapable of preserving the cohesion of the tribe, which broke up into fragments. Another nomadic tribe made up of men closer to the rigours and isolation of desert life would then defeat them, found a new state, and so on. Most modern commentators have thus reduced Ibn Khaldun's thought to a cyclical theory, with psychology as the main factor in historical developments.

It might seem surprising that they should see any mark of genius in such 'theories' (which are in fact theirs rather than Ibn Khaldun's), as they are, after all, of somewhat limited value. If it is reduced to this, Ibn Khaldun's work does seem to confirm the official theory of an opposition between nomadic and sedentary groups. However, the 'official' view that the nomads were destructive anarchists and the source of all evil is in direct contradiction with the 'theory' that the same nomads were the only group capable of founding states ... and that is merely the most obvious contradiction.

The meaning of certain crucial elements in Ibn Khaldun's thought has to be examined very carefully.

What in fact are the two groups he contrasts with one another? They are not two fractions of the rural population, each characterized by a different 'way of life.' Ibn Khaldun does not, as is so often claimed, make any basic distinction between nomadic and sedentary groups. His views are much more complex and far-reaching. He did not study the rural population alone, but the entire population of the area, and its various social, intellectual and material activities (material in the sense of production and consumption). He uses the term *'umran* to refer to this totality. Both De Slane and Rosenthal translate this as 'civilization', which limits Ibn Khaldun's concept considerably by suggesting an explicit comparison with 'barbarism' or 'savagery'. The word *'umran* derives from the Arabic root *amr*, meaning to live somewhere, to live with someone, to cultivate land, to make prosperous, to have a house, to have a fixed abode. The meaning of *'umran* is, therefore, very complex: it covers everything from the geographical and demographic notion of *oikoumene* (the inhabited world) to sociability. Ibn Khaldun defines what he means by *'umran* on several occasions: 'Savagery and sociability ... the different ways by which one group of human beings achieves superiority over another ... royal authority and the dynasties that result ... the different kinds of gainful occupations and ways of making a living ... all the other institutions that originate in civilization through its very nature.'[1] Ibn Khaldun thus uses the term *'umran* to refer to economic and demographic problems as well as to cultural, political and social activities. It refers to the totality of human phenomena.

Within this totality, he makes a basic distinction between *'umran badawi* and *'umran hadari*. Strictly speaking, the former expression can be translated as 'life in the desert', 'Bedouin life' (*badawi* = Bedouin) or 'nomadic life'. Both De Slane and Rosenthal translate it as 'nomadic life'. *'Umran hadari* has often been translated as 'life in the towns' or, more loosely, as 'sedentary life'.

Ibn Khaldun, however, uses *'umran badawi* to refer to complex realities that go far beyond the framework of nomadic life. In his description of those who live in conditions of *'umran badawi*, he writes that 'Some people adopt agriculture, the cultivation of vegetables as their way of making a living. Others adopt animal husbandry, the use of sheep, cattle, goats, bees and silkworms.'[2] He is referring to the life of the rural population as a whole, and definitely not to nomadism alone. Some authors believe that Ibn Khaldun extends the concept of *badiya* ('Bedouin' in the strict sense) to include all geographical areas accessible to nomads: the countryside, the plains, the desert, in short everything outside the major towns.[3] The opposition between *'umran badawi* and *'umran hadari* thus expresses the contrast between rural and urban life.

According to Mushin Mahdi[4] this is not a static distinction and should be understood in the sense of a general evolution. He translates *'umran badawi* as 'primitive culture' and *'umran hadari* as 'civilization', a suggestion which has caused a certain amount of controversy. According to Mahdi, *badawi* derives from the Arabic root *b-d*, meaning 'start' or 'beginning'. (To support his argument Mahdi cites the Koran 9: 11, 24: 31 and 85: 13, along with Dozy's *Supplément aux dictionnaires arabes* I 59, and Lane's *Arabic-English Dictionary*). He argues that the primary meaning of *badawi* is 'primitive' and, by derivation, 'rural'.

Many passages in Ibn Khaldun appear to confirm this view: 'Civilization may be either desert civilization (*'umran badawi*) as found in outlying regions and mountains, in hamlets near suitable pastures in waste regions, and on the fringes of sandy deserts. Or it may be sedentary civilization (*'umran hadari*) as found in cities, villages, towns ... I have discussed desert civilization first, because it is prior to everything else.'[5] 'Both Bedouin (*'umran badawi*) and sedentary (*'umran hadari*) people are natural groups. ... Differences of condition among people are the result of the different ways in which they make their living. Social organization enables them to co-operate to that end and to start with the simple necessities of life, before they get to conveniences and luxuries. Some people adopt agriculture, the cultivation of vegetables and grains. ... Others adopt animal husbandry. Those who live by agriculture or animal husbandry cannot avoid the call of the desert. ... Their social organization and co-operation for the needs of life and civilization, such as food, shelter and warmth, do not take them beyond the bare subsistence level, because of their inability to provide for anything beyond these things. Subsequent improvements of their conditions and acquisition of more wealth and comfort than they need cause them to rest and take it easy. Then, they co-operate for things beyond the bare necessities. They use more food and clothes, and take pride in them. They build large houses, and lay out towns and cities for protection. This is followed by an increase in comfort and ease, which leads to the formation of the most developed luxury customs. ... Here, now, we have sedentary people.'[6] 'The existence of Bedouins (*'umran badawi*) is prior to, and the basis of, the existence of towns and cities (*'umran hadari*).'[7]

The translation of *'umran badawi* as 'nomadic life' (which is too restrictive) and of *'umran hadari* as 'sedentary life' (which is too loose) is in direct contradiction with the explicit distinction made by Ibn Khaldun between the rural and the urban population. It also fails to take into account one of the basic themes of *The Muqaddimah*. The opposition between *'umran badawi* and *'umran hadari* is not static and does not represent a distinction between two impermeable and antagonistic types of society. It is presented in terms of a general evolution: *'umran badawi* is the first stage, *'umran hadari* the later or higher stage. Nomads belong to *'umran badawi* and represent its most rudimentary form. 'For those who make their living through the cultivation of grain and through agriculture, it is better to be stationary than to travel around. Such, therefore, are the inhabitants of small communities, villages and mountain regions.'[8]

Ibn Khaldun makes a clear distinction between sedentary farmers, semi-nomadic groups and the camel nomads of the desert.[9] Within the more highly evolved *'umran hadari*, Ibn Khaldun makes a distinction between those who live in the countryside near the towns and the true townspeople, pointing out that they have reached different levels of development. He also establishes a hierarchy between the level of civilization in small towns and great cities: 'The more numerous and abundant the civilization (population) in a city, the more luxurious is the life of its inhabitants in comparison with that of the inhabitants of a lesser city.'[10] 'Luxury increases in a city with a large population'.[11] 'The inhabitants of small cities are found to be in a weak position.'[12] 'Cities in remote parts of the realm, even if they have an abundant civilization, are found to be predominantly Bedouin (*'umran badawi*) and remote from sedentary culture (*'umran hadari*) in all their ways. This is in contrast with the situation in towns that lie in the middle ... of the realm.'[13]

According to Ibn Khaldun, the degree of *'umran* depends not only upon the size of the towns but also on the length of time over which they have evolved.

But—and this is an important feature of Ibn Khaldun's thought—there is a limit to their development. Refinement and culture are the highest goals of *'umran hadari*, but they also mark its culmination and the beginning of its decline: 'Sedentary culture (*'umran hadari*) is the goal of civilization. It means the end of its life span and brings about its corruption. ... Royal authority and the foundation of dynasties are the goal of group feeling ... sedentary culture is the goal of Bedouin life (*'umran badawi*). ...Any civilization has a physical life, just as any individual created being has a physical life. Reason and tradition make it clear that the age of forty means the end of the increase of an individual's powers and growth. When a man has reached the age of forty, nature stops growing for a while, then starts to decline. ... The same is the case with sedentary culture in civilization, because there is a limit that cannot be overstepped. ... When elegance in domestic economy has reached the limit, it is followed by subservience to desires. From all these customs, the human soul receives a multiple colouring that undermines its religion and worldly well-being.'[14] 'The goal of civilization is sedentary culture and luxury. When civilization reaches that goal, it turns towards corruption and starts being senile, as happens in the natural life of living beings.'[15]

Ibn Khaldun believes that civilizations begin to decline after a period of some sixty years. How are we to explain the fact that he cannot imagine any possibility of a long-term development? As a man of the fourteenth century, Ibn Khaldun lived in a society that was beginning to stagnate, and it was impossible for him to arrive at the modern conception of progress as being made up of successive and cumulative developments. Such a conception could only develop when historical dynamism became visible, and it results primarily from recent social and economic developments. But that in itself is not an adequate explanation.

The developments described by Ibn Khaldun relate primarily to forms of consumption: luxury goods, clothing, sophisticated cuisine, refined pleasures, relatively sumptuous houses, social accomplishments. ... He makes little or no mention of developments in productive activities. He does, of course, believe that the transition to *'umran hadari* is made possible by developments in production. On several occasions he mentions the rise in productivity that results from a more extensive division of labour. But he rarely goes beyond that. Some of his economic ideas are extremely important (notably his theory that value is based upon the price of labour),[16] but he is primarily concerned with studying social structures rather than production. Thus, the section he devotes to agriculture[17] is one of the shortest in the entire *Muqaddimah* and he does not deal with the very different levels of productivity attained by the different farming methods (wet, dry cultures) used in the various Mediterranean countries. Although economic development and the extension of the division of labour are factors contributing to the transition from *'umran badawi* to *'umran hadari*, once the latter stage has been reached there is very little change at the level of production. The only changes relate to the growth in luxury and comfort, and that is in the long term extremely prejudicial.

It should be pointed out that, in his explanation of the decline of *'umran hadari*, Ibn Khaldun invokes political, social and moral factors rather than economic causes. Once they have reached this stage of refined civilization, the townspeople become depraved. They are concerned only about their comfort and their pleasures: 'The sedentary person cannot take care of his needs personally. He may be too weak, because of the tranquillity he enjoys. Or he may be too proud, because he was brought up in prosperity and luxury. ... He also is not able to repel harmful things, ... because he has no courage as a result of his life of luxury and his upbringing. ... He thus becomes dependent upon a protective force to defend him.'[18]

Although Ibn Khaldun often compares the evolution of *'umran* with the biological cycle of a living being, a people that has reached the highest level of *'umran* does not die of natural causes. It falls because it is defeated by a conquering people with the 'primitive' characteristics of *'umran badawi*. The conquerors lay the foundations for a new state, which in its turn evolves towards the refinements of *'umran hadari*. It is, then, social and political rather than economic causes that put an end to the evolution of *'umran hadari*. But Ibn Khaldun provides no explanation as to why the new state does not take over from where its predecessor left off and continue to evolve rather than reverting to the elementary stage of *'umran badawi*.

To sum up:

1. Ibn Khaldun envisages only a brief cyclical evolution that takes place over a period of about one hundred years.

2. He pays relatively little attention to the development of the productive forces.

3. He stresses the social and political reasons for the decline of the state.

These three points would seem to indicate a major absence in Ibn

Khaldun's analysis of historical developments, and it would be difficult to justify them. But if we recall that he was not primarily concerned with the long-term development of Maghrebian society or with civilization as a whole, we can accept that they are in the main correct. At the same time, other and more debatable aspects of his analysis become somewhat clearer.

Ibn Khaldun is not primarily concerned with studying society in general. He is mainly concerned with explaining the destinies of the various *states* which appeared and then disappeared in North Africa during the Middle Ages: 'I chose a remarkable and original method. ... I commented on civilization, on the establishment of towns, and on the essential characteristics of human social organization, in a way that explains to the reader how and why things are as they are, and shows him how the men who constituted a dynasty first came upon the historical scene.'[19]

Maghrebian civilization as a whole would have to be studied over a period of several hundred years, but the dynasties lasted for much shorter periods—on average, about one hundred years.

Ibn Khaldun sees the development of civilization as being closely connected with that of the state. 'The sedentary stage of royal authority follows the desert stage. It does so of necessity.'[20] 'The duration of the life of a dynasty does not as a rule extend beyond three generations.'[21] 'A dynasty grows up and passes into an age of stagnation and thence into retrogression.'[22]

In his study of the evolution of *'umran*, which he subordinates to the various phases of political life, Ibn Khaldun is not concerned with the characteristics of the population of the empire as a whole. To a large extent, he is concerned solely with transformations within the group which founded it, ruled it and dominated the other tribes. He often uses 'people' or 'population' to mean 'tribe' or 'ruling tribe', and the importance of tribal structures in North Africa should not be forgotten. The content of *The Muqaddimah* is strictly determined by the realities of the Maghreb: 'My intention is to restrict myself in this work to the Maghreb, the circumstances of its races and nations, and its subjects and dynasties, to the exclusion of any other region. This restriction is necessitated by my lack of knowledge of conditions in the East and among its nations'.[23]

'If ... one group feeling (tribe) overpowers another and makes it subservient to itself, the two group feelings (tribes) enter into close contact, and the defeated group feeling (tribe) gives added power to the victorious group feeling (tribe), which, as a result, sets its goal of superiority and domination higher than before. In this way, it goes on until the power of that particular group feeling (tribe) equals the power of the ruling dynasty. Thus, when the ruling dynasty grows senile and no defender arises from among its friends who share in its group feeling, the new group feeling takes over and deprives the dynasty of its power, and, thus, obtains complete royal authority.'[24] 'The group to which a dynasty belongs and the people who support and establish it must of necessity be distributed over the provinces and border regions which they reach and take into possession. Only thus is it possible to protect them against enemies and to enforce the laws of the dynasty relative to the collection of taxes, restrictions and other things'.[25] 'One of the various tribal group feelings (tribes) must be superior to all others, in order to be able to unite them against enemies, and to weld them together into one group feeling comprising all the various groups.'[26]

Given that the state apparatus is based upon the ruling tribe, we can see why Ibn Khaldun gives such importance to the political reasons for the decline of empires. He stresses the essential role played by political factors in the transition from *'umran badawi* to *'umran hadari* for similar reasons: 'Luxury is the consequence of wealth and prosperity; and wealth and prosperity are the consequences of royal authority and related to the extent of the territorial possessions which the people of a particular dynasty have gained.'[27]

The conquest of a kingdom allows a few ruling tribes to raise taxes from the mass of the population and to enjoy considerable wealth, which they spend on luxuries and comforts. Ibn Khaldun's description of *'umran*'s evolution towards a civilization orientated solely towards pleasure and well-being does not refer to the population as a whole, but merely to a *privileged minority*, namely the small group of tribes which rule the kingdom and form the ruler's entourage (clients, etc.). When he comments that 'when royal authority is obtained by tribes and groups, the tribes and groups are forced to take possession of the cities'[28] he is obviously referring to the ruling tribe or tribes and to the ruler's entourage. General terms such as 'people' or 'nation', as used by De Slane and, to a lesser extent, by Rosenthal merely add to the ambiguity. Most of Ibn Khaldun's work deals only with groups that founded empires. When he states that 'The sedentary stage of royal authority follows the stage of desert life'[29] he is referring only to the ruling group: the vast majority of the population does not enjoy the advantages of power, and continues to live in accordance with the ways of *'umran badawi*.

The transition from *'umran badawi* to *'umran hadari* affects only the privileged minority which holds political power. For Ibn Khaldun, the difference between the two stages relates more to social and political structures than to a way of life or a geographical context. All the states that were established in medieval North Africa were founded by tribes with characteristics deriving from *'umran badawi*. Once *'umran hadari* replaced *'umran badawi* within a tribe that ruled an empire, it rapidly fell into social and political decline. Its decline meant that it could be conquered by a new *'umran badawi* tribe from the *bled*. In its turn, that tribe would evolve towards *'umran hadari* and then decline.

A tribe can only conquer and hold an empire if it has the social and political characteristics Ibn Khaldun refers to as *'asabiya*. In practical terms *'asabiya*, which gives a tribe the strength to found a state, can only exist within the context of *'umran badawi*. The conquest of power, which leads to the emergence of a sovereign who can raise taxes and to the appearance of *'umran hadari*, also leads to the disappearance of *'asabiya* and thus to the inevitable decline of the state.

The essentially political concept of *'asabiya* is central to Ibn Khaldun's analysis, but it is also a complex notion which requires careful study.

Most authors who have written on Ibn Khaldun have not, however, examined the concept in any great detail. Some simply define *'asabiya* in terms of one or another of its political effects. Others arbitrarily give it a meaning which makes it synonymous with other very general sociological concepts. Yet others translate it by terms that evoke some of the circumstances that allow it to develop. Virtually everyone who has written on Ibn Khaldun has his own interpretation of *'asabiya*. Some authors simply use a variety of approximations. If we examine these interpretations critically and relate them to the content of *The Muqaddimah*, we will gradually be able to clarify the complex meaning of *'asabiya*.

In their attempts to define *'asabiya* in terms of its effects, various authors have translated it as 'the vitality of the State',[30] 'the life force of the people' or '*Lebenskraft*.'[31] There is indeed a link between the vitality of the state and *'asabiya*: when the latter disappears, state structures begin to break up. But Ibn Khaldun stresses that *'asabiya* exists prior to the formation of the state and begins to decline as soon as the tribe has taken power. In that sense, Erwin Rosenthal is quite right to say that *'asabiya* is the motor of the development of the state ('*Die 'Asabija als motorische Kraft im staatlichen Geschehen'*).[32] His formulation is interesting and accurate, but much too general and abstract.

'Patriotism',[33] 'national awareness' and 'national feeling'[34] are both erroneous and anachronistic. Aside from being too general, such concepts are much too modern to be applied to medieval North Africa, where there were no real nations and tribal structures were dominant.

'Asabiya has also been interpreted as a particular expression of universal sociological notions such as 'public spirit',[35] 'social solidarity',[36] 'group cohesion', 'common will' and 'solidarity, in the strong sense'.[37] De Slane translates *'asabiya* in a number of ways, but usually gives 'esprit de corps', and Rosenthal renders it as 'group feeling'. These interpretations rightly stress one of the constituent elements of *'asabiya*, namely a certain form of solidarity. But it is not nearly so broad or so general as these translations might suggest. *'Asabiya* is in fact inseparable from the phenomenon of tribalism.

According to Toynbee, *'asabiya* is 'the basic protoplasm out of which all bodies politic and bodies social are built up.'[38] This formulation has the advantage of stressing, or even over-emphasizing, the importance of *'asabiya*, but it is still insufficiently explicit and too general.

Although all these interpretations bring out the importance of *'asabiya*, they tend to overstate it by making it synonymous with a general notion of social solidarity. If that is the case, how are we to explain the fact that, according to Ibn Khaldun, townspeople, who are not necessarily lacking in cohesion have no *'asabiya?*

By making *'asabiya* synonymous with social solidarity in the most general sense, such interpretations completely miss the essentially tribal nature of the phenomenon. They also miss one of its most important constituent elements: the vital role of the chieftain who rules the tribe.

Some authors bring out the role of the chieftain by translating *'asabiya* as 'nobility'[39] or 'aristocratic structure of society'. But not all aristocratic societies are based upon *'asabiya*. Expressions such as 'solidarity in battle' or 'warlike attitude'[40] bring out the military element which is certainly essential to the notion of *'asabiya*. But not all military organizations or formations are characterized by *'asabiya*.

In an attempt to specify the nature of *'asabiya* by specifying its base, 'blood ties',[41] 'agnatic solidarity' and 'agnation'[42] have all been suggested as translations, although the last two terms are in fact over-restrictive. Such interpretations stress only one element in this complex notion at the expense of its other elements. And, as Ibn Khaldun demonstrates, social organizations can be based upon blood ties without necessarily being characterized by *'asabiya*.

According to Helmut Ritter,[43] Ibn Khaldun uses *'asabiya* in the sense of Machiavelli's *virtù*, as meaning, that is, an innate disposition towards political power and aggression, the combination of a will to power and cunning that characterizes leaders. It is because they combine these aptitudes that leaders can impose their views upon a group of men and sway their opinions. It is quite accurate to say that the leaders of groups with *'asabiya* display *virtù*. Being a psychological trait, *virtù* is, however, a universal characteristic of leaders of men, whereas not all human groups which follow leaders are characterized by *'asabiya*. *'Asabiya* refers to the influence of leaders of men in a very specific historical context.

According to some authors[44] *'asabiya* means 'tribal fanaticism'. It does in a sense cover that notion, but it is not reducible to fanaticism. Ibn Khaldun could have used the well-known term *hadija* to describe that form of tribal behaviour. Others[45] argue that *'asabiya* is a form of tribal solidarity found amongst non-Arabic indigenous groups who were fighting against Arab domination. It would thus mean tribal solidarity, as opposed to *'umran*, the cognate solidarity between all Muslims. Although all these notions contain an element of truth, they are either too specific or too broad. Moreover, they do not coincide with the realities of North Africa, where the only power struggles were those between Berber dynasties, all of which were Arabized to some extent. Besides, if Ibn Khaldun had wanted to stress political opposition towards Arab domination, he would have used *shu'ubiya* rather than *'asabiya*.

Finally, some authors use 'nomadic way of life' on the grounds that *'asabiya* is characteristic of *'umran badawi* tribes. *'Asabiya* is certainly a characteristic of some nomadic groups, but Ibn Khaldun stresses that it can also characterize sedentary groups. The mountain tribes from the High Atlas which founded the Almohad Empire, for instance, had a high level of *'asabiya*. It is also possible to challenge these interpretations on the grounds that if Ibn Khaldun had wanted to describe the qualities or nature of nomads, he could have used the term *muruwa*, which refers precisely to such notions. And, as we shall see, according to Ibn Khaldun not all nomadic tribes have *'asabiya*.

Our brief examination of the many interpretations of the notion of *'asabiya* underlines its importance and complexity. It also shows that most of the translations are accurate up to a point. But they are not entirely satisfactory as they are at once too specific and too general. They are too specific in stressing only one of the constituent elements of *'asabiya,* which is a complex combination of very different factors.

Certain authors have grasped the complexity of *'asabiya,* and used a variety of terms to translate it. Thus, in his translation of the *Muqaddimah,* De Slane usually translates the expression (used almost five hundred times by Ibn Khaldun) as *esprit de corps.* But as Khamiri[46] has shown in a detailed study, De Slane uses other expressions in some passages: family (I, 234-5), kinsmen (I, 265), group of friends (I, 243), devoted group (I, 199), community (I, 274), a people animated by a sense of its own dignity (I, 299), sympathy (I, 239), fellow feeling (I, 234), zeal and ardour (I, 277), feeling and interest (I, 297), patriotism (I, 262, 340, 352, I, 141, 107), tribal spirit (I, 255, 259, 282, 286, 307, 333, II, *79), national spirit (142, 282, 336, 349, 353, 375), national feeling (142, 282, 336, 349, 353, 375), party (this is used very frequently), strength (I, 265), power (I, 281), support (I, 403), army (II, 121).

Ibn Khaldun could have used much more specific words or expressions for most of these notions. The fact that he did not do so indicates that he is describing a combination of elements and not a relatively simple phenomenon.

The root of the term *'asabiya,* which is used so frequently in *The Muqaddimah,* is *-s-b,* meaning 'to bind'. The word appears relatively early in Arabic literature and is even found in a *hadith* (tale of the Prophet): 'Does *'asabiya* mean loving one's people?' 'No', replied the Prophet '*'asabiya* means helping one's people in unjust actions.' Ibn Khaldun thus takes a word with a basically pejorative meaning and uses it as a technical expression: it does not refer to feelings or a psychological attitude, but to a very complex socio-political reality with important psychological implications.

Virtually all the above-mentioned interpretations of *'asabiya* are both too specific and too general. They tend to turn into a phenomenon that exists in all places and all times, and virtually ignore the extremely specific historical context within which Ibn Khaldun inscribes it: he places considerable limitations on its spatial extension. According to Ibn Khaldun, *'asabiya* is specific to North Africa and explains both the survival of tribal phenomena and the political instability of the region.

'At any time ... there is much opposition to a dynasty and rebellion against it, even if the dynasty possesses group feeling (*'asabiya*) because each group feeling under the control of the ruling dynasty thinks that it has in itself enough strength and power. One may compare what has happened in this connection in Ifriqiyah and the Maghreb from the beginning of Islam to the present time. The inhabitants of those lands are Berber tribes and groups with a high degree of *'asabiya*.'[47] Ibn Khaldun sees this as explaining why the Muslim armies had such difficulty in conquering North Africa, where the population was in a constant state of rebellion.

'Iraq at that time was different, and so was Syria. . . . All the inhabitants were a mixed lot of town and city-dwellers. When the Muslims deprived them of their power, there remained no one capable of making a defence or offering opposition.'[48] 'The Berber tribes in the West are innumerable. All of them are Bedouins (*'umran badawi*) and members of groups and families. Whenever one tribe is destroyed, another takes its place and is refractory and rebellious as the former one had been.'[49]

'On the other hand, it is easy to establish a dynasty in lands that are free from group feelings (*'asabiya*). Government there will be a tranquil affair, because seditions and rebellions are few, and the dynasty does not need much group feeling. This is the case in contemporary Egypt and Spain. They are now free of tribes and group feelings. . . . Royal authority in Egypt is most peaceful and firmly rooted, because Egypt has few dissidents or people who represent tribal groups.'[50] 'The same is the case in contemporary Spain.'[51] Ibn Khaldun explains that the ruler of Spain can hold power with only a small group of supporters because there are few tribes in the country and, consequently, very little *'asabiya*.

Ibn Khaldun thus makes it quite clear that he does not see *'asabiya* as a general notion or as the basis of all governments in all societies, as he notes that it does not exist in much of the Muslim world. More importantly, it does not exist in the areas with the most powerful and stable states.

We therefore have to reject all interpretations which turn *'asabiya* into a general, permanent sociological notion. Basically, Ibn Khaldun restricts it to North Africa. When he invokes *'asabiya* to explain events in other countries, he makes it quite clear that he is referring to past events (usually the great Arab conquests of the seventh century) or to a political conjuncture of the past.

He does often use *'asabiya* as a general theoretical formulation, which might give an impression of universality, were it not for the passages cited above. It is unlikely that *'asabiya* was found only in North Africa. The fact that other conquering tribes established empires (the Mongol Empires, for instance) can be explained in terms of similar phenomena.

This may explain why Tamerlane took such an interest in Ibn Khaldun: the origins and characteristics of his tribal empire were quite similar to those of the Maghrebian states. The fact that when Ibn Khaldun wrote *The Muqaddimah* he simply intended to write the history of the Maghreb itself may also explain why he sometimes uses general formulations.

In Egypt, Ibn Khaldun added chapters dealing with the oriental dynasties, whose problems were very different to those of the Maghreb, to the first two volumes of *The Muqaddimah* and to his *Histoire des Berbères*. The precise application of his concepts is restricted to the Maghreb; they are only tangentially applicable to the history of some other lands. We must therefore examine the meaning of *'asabiya* in the specific context of the history of the medieval Maghreb.

What, then, are the component elements of the complex notion of *'asabiya*? *'Asabiya* is characteristic of *'umran badawi* in the Maghreb and it disappears with the development of *'umran hadari* and luxury. Tribal structures are a precondition for its existence.

Ibn Khaldun clearly relates the existence of *'asabiya* in North Africa to the survival of tribal organizations, and its absence in Iraq and Syria to the fact that there are no longer any real tribes in those countries.

'Only tribes held together by group feeling (*'asabiya*) can live in the desert.'[52] 'Desert habits (*'umran badawi*) preserve the power of group feeling and the habits of luxury wear it out'.[53]

'Group feeling results only from blood relationship or something corresponding to it'[54] 'Pedigrees are useful only in so far as they imply the close contact that is a consequence of blood ties and that eventually leads to mutual help and affection. ... When common descent is no longer clear ... it has become useless.'[55]

The *'asabiya* of the cohesive tribal group is usually expressed in war-like activities: 'The hamlets of the Bedouins are defended against outside enemies by a tribal militia composed of the noble youths of the tribe who are known for their courage. Their defence and protection are only successful if they are a closely-knit group of common descent. This strengthens their stamina and makes them feared, since everybody's affection for his family and his group is more important than anything else. Compassion and affection for one's blood relations and relatives exist in human nature as something God puts into the hearts of men. It makes for mutual support and aid (*'asabiya*).'[56] 'Group feeling produces the ability to defend oneself, to protect oneself and to press one's claims. Whoever loses his group feeling is too weak to do any one of these things.'[57]

When the tribe becomes less warlike, it loses its *'asabiya*. 'Weakness and docility break the vigour and strength of group feeling. The very fact that people are meek and docile shows that their group feeling is lost. ... Those who are too weak to defend themselves are all the more weak when it comes to withstanding their enemies and pressing their claims.'[58] 'A tribe paying imposts did not do that until it became resigned to meek submission. ...Imposts and taxes are a sign of oppression and weakness which proud souls do not tolerate, unless they consider the payment of imposts and taxes easier than being killed and destroyed. In such a case, the group feeling of a tribe is too weak for its own defence and protection. ... When one sees a tribe humiliated by the payment of imposts, one cannot hope that it will ever achieve royal authority.'[59] 'Group feeling gives protection and makes possible mutual defence, the pressing of claims, and every other kind of social activity.'[60]

If *'asabiya* is to exist and develop, the tribe must have or develop what Ibn Khaldun calls *riasa*, the de facto power of an aristocracy, the tacit but real authority of a great family: 'Leadership is vested in one particular family among the tribe, and not in the whole. Since leadership is the result of superiority, it follows necessarily that the group of the particular family in which leadership is vested must be stronger than that of all the other groups,'[61] 'Even if an individual tribe has different "houses" and many diverse group feelings, still there must exist a group feeling that is stronger than all the other group feelings combined, that is superior to them all and makes them subservient, and in which all the diverse group feelings coalesce, as it were, to become one greater group feeling.'[62]

Referring to the role played by the chieftain in a tribe with *'asabiya*, Ibn Khaldun states that he 'must, by necessity, have superiority over the others in the matter of group feeling. ...Such superiority is royal authority. It is more than leadership. Leadership means being a chieftain, and the leader is obeyed, but he has no power to force others to accept his rulings.'[63]

This passage, which is very important if we are to understand the meaning of *'asabiya*, suggests a clear distinction between egalitarian tribes, in which the chieftain has only moral authority, and the tribe with *'asabiya*, in which the chieftain has succeeded in asserting his dominance. Only tribes which are no longer egalitarian and which have developed *'asabiya* constitute a political force capable of making their chieftains heads of states. Solidarity based upon blood ties is not, then, *'asabiya*, but merely a precondition for its development.

The fact that Ibn Khaldun points out that a kind of *'asabiya* can some-times exist in towns proves that it means primarily the political power wielded by a chieftain. In general, the urban way of life and luxury des-troy tribal cohesion, but a form of *asabiya* can still develop in cities: 'When senility befalls a dynasty...the inhabitants of the city have to take care of their own affairs. ...They revert to the council (govern-ment). ...Everyone vies with everyone else. They try to have followers, such as clients, partisans and allies, join them. ...One of them achieves superiority. He then turns against his equals. ...He obtains sole control of the entire city. ...As a rule, such leadership goes to members of great and noble houses.'[64]

How does the chieftain establish his authority over the tribe? Partly by means of the profits he makes from trade. But wars also allow him to appropriate a major share of the booty and to acquire an unchallenged authority over those who pay him tribute. The chieftain therefore involves the tribe in conflicts so as to enrich himself and retain control over the tribesmen. As less and less of the wealth is shared, the old egali-tarianism disappears and the warriors, in theory equal, are transformed into vassals. The power of the tribal aristocracy increases at the expense of military democracy.

One very important factor can precipitate this evolution. The ruler asks the tribal chieftain to come into the *Bled el-Maghzan* to carry out military operations or to bring in taxes on behalf of the state. As well as receiving support from the ruler, the chieftain now also makes considerable profits from *jibaya* (forced tax collection) and plunder. In exchange for these servi-ces, the government grants a charter of *iqta'*, usually to the chieftain him-self. The super-imposition of an organization which in some ways recalls a 'feudal' political structure upon the old tribal structure completely des-troys the latter and confirms the authority of the chieftain.

The chieftain's new found wealth attracts both kinsmen and a host of clients or vassals who help him to 'subdue' the tribe. The tribesmen are persuaded to take part in new military expeditions, sometimes at great cost to themselves, and most of the profits go to the chieftain and those around him. Blood ties give way to vassal relations. Vassal relations[65] initially develop between chieftains and their clients and between the chieftain and members of the tribe he serves. 'Clients and allies belong in the same category as relatives. ...The reason for this is that a client-master relationship leads to close contact exactly, or approximately in the same way, as does common descent.'[66]

Within the dominant tribe, blood ties begin to lose their former egalitarian connotations. Paradoxically, greater emphasis is placed upon blood ties as they become purely formal and begin to mask the vassal relationship that is gradually replacing them. The principle of blood ties between chieftain and dependents had to be maintained. The dependents are warriors: the chieftain needs their help and cannot afford to antagonize such a dangerous military force. The existence of blood ties works to his advantage and he demagogically stresses their importance.

The solidarity which is being undermined by the growing power of the chieftain has to exist if he is to be able to rely upon it in his military ventures. In order to maintain at least an appearance of solidarity, the tribe is constantly drawn into conflicts with other groups. The excitement of battle fosters a feeling of unity in the face of an illusory common danger. *'Asabiya* does not therefore mean social solidarity in general, but rather a very specific form of social organization which allows a tribal aristocracy to control the forces of a military democracy. *'Asabiya* gives the tribal chieftains great power, but it is an ambiguous power. It has its roots in the tribe, but undermines the egalitarianism that gives the tribe its cohesion. The chieftain in fact rules vassals who do not as yet realize that they are vassals or that equality within the tribe is disappearing. They still receive the crumbs of victory, and this, together with the imperative of the old tribal solidarity, makes them go on supporting the ruler who is becoming their master.

In North Africa, *'asabiya* played an important political role, amongst both Berber and Arabized groups. It was most important during the Middle Ages, but in some cases continued to play the same role until relatively recent times. Thus, even at the beginning of the twentieth century in the Berber mountains of Morocco, the chieftain or *Amghar* would surround himself with an armed band of *imedoukal* who were not dissimilar to the *gasindi* of the Middle Ages. Similar phenomena could also be observed amongst the Arab tribes. The armed group guarantees the chieftain's authority over the rest of the tribe. *'Asabiya* combines vassal relations and the tribal solidarity of a military democracy subordinated to a tribal chieftain who is gradually becoming a feudal lord.

This interpenetration of blood ties and vassalage is not specific to North Africa. During what Marc Bloch calls the first feudal age, a similar imbrication of kinship and vassalage was found in Western Europe. Bloch stresses the importance of lineage, kinship and 'friends by blood' in the early stages of European feudalism and shows that blood ties and the associated vassal relations represented a considerable political and military force. Thus, Joinville attributes the feats of valour performed at Mansurah by Guy de Mauvoisin's force to the fact that it was comprised only of knights belonging to his lineage.

According to Bloch, the first feudal age was characterized by an unstructured imbrication of vassalage and kinship. 'The period which saw the expansion of the relations of personal protection and subordination characteristic of the social conditions we call feudalism was also marked by a real tightening of the ties of kinship. ... The centuries which later witnessed the progessive breakdown or metamorphosis of authentic feudalism also experienced—with the crumbling of the large kinship groups—the early symptoms of the slow decay of family solidarities. ... The tie of kinship was one of the essential elements of feudal society; its relative weakness explains why there was feudalism at all.'[67]

North Africa differs from Western Europe in that no co-ordinated hierarchical network of vassalage developed there because kinship ties and tribal structures, which no longer existed in Europe, remained much stronger. In the Maghreb, the vassal system never became structured. It usually remained embryonic, except in those tribes which founded empires. Even so, it was a temporary and relatively incomplete phenomenon.

According to Bloch, two factors were essential to the establishment of a true feudal regime. Knightly vassals had to be virtually the only professional warriors and vassal relationships had to replace other means of exerting authority. In the Maghreb, the presence of warrior herdsmen and *montagnards* made it impossible for a professional warrior class to emerge. The vassal system could not emerge because of the strength of tribal structures and the permanent nature of the state structures imposed upon the tribes.

The existence of military democracy meant that the tribe was the only armed force and that all political undertakings had to be based upon the tribe. Without tribal support it was equally impossible to escape from the power of a sultan, to overthrow a dynasty or to support a state whose ruler was the chieftain of the dominant tribe. The tribal aristocracy was strong only in so far as it remained integrated into the tribe that supported it. In both North Africa and those countries conquered by tribal empires, *'asabiya* was 'the motor of the development of the state'.

'When a person sharing in the group feeling has reached the rank of chieftain and commands obedience, and when he finds his way open toward superiority and the use of force . . . he cannot achieve his goal except with the help of the group feeling which causes the others to obey him. . . . Royal authority is the goal of group feeling. When group feeling attains that goal, the tribe achieves royal authority, either by seizing actual power or by giving assistance to the ruling dynasty.'[68]

Military democracy and the role of the tribal aristocracy are therefore the essential elements of *'asabiya*. It is the solidity of their tribal structures rather than their rural existence which explains why 'savage nations are better able to achieve superiority than others.'[69]

Although *'umran badawi* is a precondition for the existence of *'asabiya*, it is not found in all rural communities, and Ibn Khaldun stresses that there are tribes without *'asabiya*. These are mainly tribes which have been defeated, which cannot defend their own territory and which have agreed to pay taxes.

It is also important to note that tribes in which the chieftains cannot assert their power have no *'asabiya* either. Such egalitarian tribes include the camel nomads, whom Ibn Khaldun describes as Bedouins or Arabs in the strict sense of the term. He uses the term to refer, not to Arabic-speaking groups, but to the Bedouin tribes which retained the nomadic way of life they had followed in Arabia when they reached North Africa. 'In the West, the nomadic Berbers and the Zanatah are their counterparts. . . . The Arabs, however, make deeper incursions into the desert and are more rooted in desert life . . . because they live exclusively on camels.'[70]

The Bedouins represent the most primitive form of *'umran badawi*, characterized by egalitarianism and the fragility of the chieftain's power.

'Because of their savagery, the Arabs are the least willing of nations to subordinate themselves to each other, as they are rude, proud, ambitious and eager to be the leader. Their individual aspirations rarely coincide.'[71] 'It is difficult for them to subordinate themselves to each other, because they are used to no control and because they are in a state of savagery. Their leader needs them mostly for the group spirit that is necessary for purposes of defence. He is, therefore, forced to rule them kindly and to avoid antagonizing them. Otherwise, he would have trouble with the group spirit, and such trouble would be his undoing and theirs.'[72] 'This race has never produced a leader capable of ruling it.'[73]

These Bedouin tribes are characterized by the survival of the very egalitarian structures which prevent the power of the chieftain (an essential part of *'asabiya*) from developing. It will be noted that in the chapters of *The Muqaddimah* that deal with the Bedouins, Ibn Khaldun rarely uses the term *'asabiya*, and that when he does so he is referring to 'purposes of defence', as when in time of danger the warriors of the tribe are forced to accept a leader.

The weakness of the tribal aristocracy determines the absence of any long-term or large-scale policies. As Ibn Khaldun explains, the only time when this anarchy ceases is when a religious ideology arises within the tribe, religion being the indispensable ideal form of any major political movement. But after the twelfth century, there were no religious innovations in the Maghreb. 'The Arabs are by nature remote from royal leadership.'[74] 'The Arabs are of all nations the one most remote from royal leadership.'[75] After the expansion of Islam, 'they remained as Bedouin in the desert, ignorant of royal authority and political leadership. ... At times they achieve superiority over weak dynasties. ... But their domination leads only to the ruin of the civilization that they conquer.'[76] 'Savagery has become their character and nature. They enjoy it, because it means freedom from authority and no subservience to leadership. Such a natural disposition is the negation and antithesis of civilization.'[77]

The weakness or even the absence of *'asabiya* amongst the Bedouin tribes explains Ibn Khaldun's poor view of them. Tribes without *'asabiya* cannot create states, and their actions are therefore destructive. In tribes controlled by an aristocracy, a chieftain who wants to use his conquests as a basis for further progress and who wants to found a lasting kingdom has to restrict looting and preserve wealth. Having no political ambitions, the Bedouins 'plunder whatever other people possess' and 'recognize no limit in taking the possessions of other people'. Failing to see the importance of links unknown to their rudimentary way of life, they destroy everything to satisfy their immediate elementary needs; 'The Arabs need stones to set them up as supports for their cooking pots. So, they take them from buildings which they tear down to get the stones. ... Wood, too, is needed by them for props for their tents and for use as tent poles for their dwellings. So, they tear down roofs to get the wood.'[78] 'They use force to make craftsmen and professional workers do their work ... and do not pay them for it ... labour is the real source of profit ... the sedentary population disperses and civilization decays. ... Furthermore, the Arabs are not concerned with laws. They are not concerned to deter people from misdeeds or to protect some against the others. They care only for the property that they might take away from people through looting or imposts. ... Under the rule of the Arabs, the subjects live as in a state of anarchy, without law. Anarchy destroys mankind and ruins civilization since . . . the existence of royal authority is a natural quality of man. It alone guarantees their existence and social organization.'[79]

Why are these destructive tribes, which have no political aims, characterized by anarchic egalitarianism and a low level of *'asabiya*? According to Ibn Khaldun they are camel nomads who live in precarious circumstances on the edge of the desert. 'They are in a state of savagery.'[80] 'They are used to a tough and hard life.'[81] Their poverty determines the survival of very egalitarian structures. If a privileged minority is to emerge and exercise something more than a moral influence over the tribe, there must be a surplus available for appropriation. No such surplus exists in these poverty-striken groups.

Although they too had been camel nomads, the Almoravids did develop *'asabiya* and a ruling aristocracy because they could derive profits from the caravan trade. With the more advanced level of *'umran badawi* found amongst groups which owned cattle and sheep and amongst semi-nomadic tribes who practised both farming and stock breeding there was a surplus. Privileged leaders could appear because they could appropriate much of the surplus product. The absence of *'asabiya* and of any constructive policies amongst the Bedouin thus results from the extremely rudimentary nature of their productive activity.

In his study of contemporary Bedouin civilization in the Middle East, R. Montagne shows clearly how the authority of the chieftain begins to increase when the tribe settles in less arid areas. In the desert, the chief is simply *primus inter pares* and his influence is purely moral. In regions where more productive agriculture and stock breeding leads to a major increase in production, the chieftain appropriates the land and the herds, and becomes surrounded by clients and servants. He becomes the master of the tribe.[82] The true nature of *'asabiya* can thus be specified in negative terms. It cannot be identified merely with a nomadic way of life, or with *'umran badawi* in any absolute sense. It does not simply mean tribal solidarity or the survival of blood ties. It corresponds to a certain level of social and political structures within the tribe and to a certain level of economic development. *'Asabiya* is a form of military democracy which appears when a *de facto* aristocracy emerges within a tribal community.

In the nineteenth and twentieth centuries, Ibn Khaldun's comments about 'wolfish Arabs'[83] and 'wild untameable animals and beasts of prey'[84] were frequently used to turn Arabs and Berbers against each other. His comments do not, however, apply to all Arabs in the cultural sense of the term, but to the Bedouins and nomadic groups with similar negative characteristics.

We can thus explain the apparent contradiction between Ibn Khaldun's high opinion of the bravery, virtue and sobriety of *'umran badawi* groups and his condemnation of Bedouins and similar groups who also live outside the towns. The former possess *'asabiya* and are potential empire-builders; the latter do not and are incapable of laying the foundations of state structures that will last. Unlike the semi-nomadic farmers, these camel nomads had no fixed base and were highly mobile. They were therefore often used as soldiers by the dynasties. Having become tools (and often docile tools) of the rulers' policies, the Bedouin and related tribes were in a position to play a destructive role. They would have behaved in the same way and would have acquired the same bad reputation if they had not served the rulers. Rulers presumably preferred to rely upon these turbulent and anarchic mercenaries rather than upon the *'asabiya* of a tribe from which a rival or an embryonic state might emerge.

The dividing line drawn by Ibn Khaldun between *'umran badawi* and *'umran hadari* does not correspond to a distinction between different ways of life. It corresponds to the presence or absence of *'asabiya*. He anathemizes groups which have no *'asabiya* or which have lost it because they can only play a negative role. He unstintingly praises the virtues of groups which can found empires because they have *'asabiya*.

We can now see the importance of the concept of *'asabiya*, around which the whole of Ibn Khaldun's thought revolves. And we can begin to see the meaning of his political preoccupations.

Medieval North Africa was dominated by the structures of military democracy, and *'asabiya* was undoubtedly an important force. But, as E. Rosenthal judiciously remarks, it was merely the motor of the development of the state. Once an empire had been established by a conquering tribe, its *'asabiya* inevitably begins to decline and disappear. As a result, the state which once drew its strength from *'asabiya* begins to decline. According to Ibn Khaldun, it is basically the emergence of *'umran badawi*, luxury and comfort, which leads to the disappearance of *'asabiya* within the ruling tribe. The tribe becomes much wealthier because it is able to levy taxes on agriculture and trade. This new wealth destroys tribal solidarity. As more and more of the profits are appropriated and as inequality between members of the tribe increases, they become increasingly aware of what is happening. It becomes obvious that the ruler and his entourage are the main beneficiaries of the tribe's victories. Increasingly, ties of kinship begin to look like a pretence. Profits are distributed amongst relatively few people and this allows the privileged few to surround themselves with more and more clients. The importance of blood ties declines accordingly.

As the major figures in the tribe become governors and settle in towns away from the capital, they lose their day to day contact with the tribe. They are given charters of *iqta'*. They are well paid and surrounded by clients and kinsmen. Their interests are no longer those of the tribes. They become more like 'feudal lords', and then claimants to the throne.

One of the main reasons for the decline of *'asabiya* is the behaviour of the ruler himself. He is the *de facto* leader of the tribe, but has no legal claims to that position. Once he accedes to the throne, he in theory enjoys absolute power. He wants to unify and centralize a state which is in fact no more than a collection of dominant and dominated tribes. He is a tribal chieftain who wants to found a dynasty. Whereas he once developed *'asabiya* within his tribe and used blood ties to his own advantage, he now needs to destroy a political structure which has become a major obstacle to the establishment of a true absolute monarchy. Important figures in the tribe still regard him as no more than *primus inter pares* and invoke tribal solidarity. Once they realize that it was they who gave him his kingdom, they refuse to obey his orders and attempt to exploit the situation as best they can. A conflict therefore arises between the ruler, jealous of his position, and his former allies, who become more and more greedy for profits and power. Within the ruler's family the conflict is even more serious. His kinsmen refuse to obey him, constantly demand bigger stipends and become claimants to the throne itself.

The ruler thus comes into conflict with his kinsmen and his dependents. He tries to find new supporters amongst clients, mercenaries and slaves who cannot challenge his power by appealing to tribal solidarity. Freedmen and foreigners begin to play an increasingly important role in the government.

'People find it difficult to submit to a large dynastic power at the beginning, unless they are forced into submission by strong superiority. People are not familiar with, or used to, its rule. But once leadership is firmly vested in members of the family qualified to exercise royal authority in the dynasty ... it becomes a firmly established article of faith that one must be subservient and submissive to them. ... The rulers maintain their hold over the government and their own dynasty with the help, then, either of clients and followers who grew up in the shadow and power of group feeling, or with that of tribal groups of a different descent that have become their clients.'[85] 'The ruler shows himself independent from his people, claims all the glory for himself and pushes his people away from it with the palms of his hands. As a result, his own people become in fact his enemies. In order to prevent them from seizing power, and in order to keep them away from participation in power, the ruler needs other friends, not of his own kin, whom he can use against his own people. These new friends become closer to him than anyone else... they are willing to give their lives for him, preventing his own people from regaining the power that had been theirs. ... This, then, announces the destruction of the dynasty and indicates that chronic disease has befallen it, the result of the loss of the group feeling on which the dynasty's superiority had been based.'[86]

All these factors contribute to the destruction of *'asabiya*. Ibn Khaldun's penetrating analysis goes into every aspect of its destruction. Recruiting mercenaries, buying slaves and paying new clients absorbs a major share of the state's revenue, which has already been reduced by the concessions granted to tributaries. The granting of charters of *iqta'* to chieftains of mercenary tribes and to new clients has the effect of creating a new category of 'feudal lords' who, in their turn, begin to challenge the ruler. In order to cover his increased expenditure, the ruler illegally increases taxes on land and commercial transactions. This has the effect of slowing down economic activity, making taxes heavier and reducing tax revenue even further. The subsequent poverty and discontent lead to disturbances which pretenders and discontented 'feudal lords' exploit to their own ends. Antagonisms within the ruling tribe produce major disturbances amongst the various peoples ruled by the state. New mercenaries are needed to suppress sedition, and have to be paid. Tribes in the service of the ruler are granted new charters of *iqta'*. The ruler resorts to illegal methods of taxation in order to compensate for his loss of revenue and to cover his increasing expenditure. Increased taxation, both legal and illegal, of stagnating resources provokes new rebellions. The strongest tribes try to avoid paying taxes. The dissident *Bled essiba* grows at the expense of the *Bled el-Maghzan*, the area controlled and taxed by the ruler's agents. Decimated in the struggle against absolutism, the ruling tribe is scattered to the four corners of the kingdom. It provides the most dangerous pretenders and enemies—the ruler's own kinsmen. Ultimately, the state is supported only by mercenaries and falls into decline.

The dynasty collapses and is defeated by a tribe with a high level of *'asabiya*. In its turn, that tribe will suffer the same fate.

Ibn Khaldun's analysis of the rise and fall of the state is, then, of considerable importance. It concentrates upon the play of *internal* factors. In the context of North African structures, the rise of an empire is intimately connected with the causes of its decline. Once he has reached the throne, the ruler has to destroy the forces that forged his empire in order to transform his authority as a tribal chieftain into absolute power. But the ruling tribe, which is struggling against the ruler, is also his sole power base. Even if he does not rely upon mercenaries, the antagonism between his authority and that of the tribal chieftains will appear sooner or later. In his attempt to weaken tribal power he undermines the basis of the empire.

The conquests of the victorious tribe allow the state to develop, but the very existence of the state implies the break up of tribal structures. The congenital weakness of the North African states is a result of this internal contradiction. The concept of *'asabiya* is, then, eminently dialectical. *'Asabiya* is the motor of the development of the state, *and* it is destroyed by the emergence of the state.

'Asabiya is a socio-political structure which marks the transition from a classless to a class society. The tribal aristocracy holds power only in so far as it is still integrated into egalitarian structures. As the power of the aristocracy grows, it becomes a class whose interests are in contradiction with those of other members of the tribe, and tribal structures begin to break up. To a certain extent, their break-up strengthens the privileged class: it begins to extend its authority over its clients, who become vassals, and to appropriate some of the means of production (land, cattle). The break-up of tribal structures is in a sense progressive, in that it marks the beginning of a transition towards a more progressive and more highly developed mode of production.

But that development is checked because it affects only the ruling tribe and not the population of the state as a whole. Most of the population still live within tribal structures. Although unequally distributed, the political power and wealth enjoyed by the ruling tribe means that they are in a better position to resist the authority of the privileged class. Its ability to extend its power remains limited and it can appropriate only a small proportion of the means of production. It is thus impossible for any new form of economic, social and political organization (one similar to the feudalism of Western Europe) to emerge. The dislocation of tribal structures weakens the ruling tribe. This is serious even when there are no other armed groups in the area and when the ruling tribe is confronted only by groups who cannot fight. Thus, the Mongol and Turkish dynasties were able to retain their power over the 'hydraulic societies' for a relatively long period. But in North Africa, where the vast majority of the population was inserted into the structures of military democracy and where virtually every tribe was armed, the break-up of the ruling tribe soon led to the collapse of empire and tribe alike. The ruling tribe soon falls from power and is overthrown by a tribe which is still strong and whose *'asabiya* has not yet been destroyed by the development of internal contradictions. But once a new state is established, those contradictions will be exacerbated.

Here, then, we have an explanation for the relative instability of medieval North Africa, for the repeated failure of attempts to create a centralized monarchy and for the survival of the structures of military democracy.

7
The Case Against the Townspeople

The above factors provide a perfectly adequate explanation for the break-up of 'asabiya and for the collapse of dynasties based upon it. Ibn Khaldun states the reasons for its collapse quite clearly, but thinks them insufficient. Having made a fully objective analysis, which accounts perfectly well for the facts, he then goes into apparently subjective considerations. He argues that the decline of 'asabiya, and thus of the dynasty, also results from the depravity of the townspeople, who become accustomed to the luxuries of 'umran hadari.

Once they have taken power and are in a position to enjoy the advantages it gives them, the warriors of the ruling tribe begin to live a life of luxury. Their heirs, brought up in the comfort of the cities, no longer have the military skills born of the harsh life of the bled and of battle. Ibn Khaldun eloquently describes the evolution which, in the course of three or four generations, transforms the warrior into an official or a wealthy notable.

Ibn Khaldun displays a deep-rooted prejudice, a profound antipathy, towards the urban population, accusing them of every possible fault and vice.[1] 'Immorality, wrongdoing, insincerity ... trickery ... devoted to lying, gambling, cheating, fraud, theft, perjury and usury ... adultery and homosexuality. ... Indeed, we may say that the qualities of character resulting from sedentary culture and luxury are identical with corruption.'[2]

In contrast, he sees the people of the bled, the herdsmen and mountain-dwellers who retain the customs of 'umran badawi, as having all the virtues: sobriety, energy, courage, stamina, honesty, modesty, probity, etc. There is no real basis for this manichaean opposition between the vices of one group and the virtues of the other. It reveals the intervention into Ibn Khaldun's scientific thought of subjective and partisan prejudices that are in sharp contrast with the concern for rationality he displays in most of his writings.

Ibn Khaldun moves quite illogically from a rigorous analysis of the realities of North Africa and an objective study of its social and political evolution to a vision of conflict between Good and Evil. If reduced to his objective arguments, his explanation of the successive crises that punctuate the history of the Maghreb is in itself clear and satisfactory. Why, then, does he bring in moral arguments which shed no light on the problem? It is not as though there would be no conflict between the ruler and the townspeople if the latter were virtuous. This use of value judgements is in complete contradiction with the conception of history and the analytic method elaborated by Ibn Khaldun.

How are we to explain Ibn Khaldun's excessively harsh view of *'umran hadari* and of the urban population? This damning condemnation is all the more curious in that it comes from a man who not only belonged to a great urban family but was also familiar with and appreciated the values of urban life. He had enjoyed all the refinements of Andalusian culture. He may well have tired of life at court, and he was certainly attracted towards the harsh purity of life amongst the tribes. Having been driven out of Tlemcen, Fez and Granada, he took refuge in the citadel of Qalat Ibn Salamah, where he lived in peace under the protection of a great Arab tribe. Ibn Khaldun was also in close contact with certain mystical movements. Perhaps his antipathy towards the comforts of urban life expresses a certain puritanical moralism and a taste for asceticism? Yet, for most of his life, Ibn Khaldun does not seem to have scorned the advantages of *'umran hadari* or the pleasures of life at court.

Such arguments are not to be dismissed, but they do not solve the problem. Why should Ibn Khaldun resort to ethical arguments to explain things for which he had already provided a scientific explanation? After all, in other areas his concern for objective analysis and his rejection of value judgements led him to reject the normative arguments of religion.

Ibn Khaldun makes a methodical analysis of the process which leads the state to its inevitable downfall. He understands the process, but deplores it. He does of course refer to the biological cycle of all living things—'Dynasties have a natural life span like individuals'—but he cannot stop himself from railing against the townspeople and making them responsible for the collapse of the empire created by *'asabiya*.

It is not that he is nostalgic for *'asabiya* as such. *'Asabiya* has to disappear if royal power is to be established and consolidated. Ibn Khaldun unemotionally explains how the ruler destroys *'asabiya*, whose tribal structures have become an obstacle to the organization of the state. The dynasty is destroyed because it cannot find anything to replace *'asabiya*. As soon as a state has been established, the factors that led to its growth become the seeds of its destruction. The vicious circle which prevents the dynasty from being consolidated on any lasting basis could be slowed down or even broken if only the ruler could rely upon some new political force in his struggle against the tribal aristocracy. A state whose structures are the negation of tribal structures must be based upon non-tribal forces. In North Africa at this time, the only groups to be organized on a non-tribal basis were those found in the towns and surrounding areas. In the towns, where a very mixed population mingled with elements from the tribe that founded the empire, social structures were no longer tribal. Blood ties gave way to other social relations. The great merchants, who often acquired 'a great number of estates or farms',[3] gave the royal family financial support because 'the owner of property and conspicuous wealth ... needs a protective force to defend him.'[4]

The vicious circle that leads to the decline of the empire might be broken if only the ruler could count upon the support of the urban population in his struggle against the tribal aristocracy. As Ibn Khaldun points out, this population has considerable economic influence: 'Desert tribes and groups are dominated by the urban population. ... As long as they live in the desert ... they need the inhabitants of the cities. ... They must be active on behalf of their interests.'[5] The urban population of North Africa did not, however, constitute a stable political force that could give the king victory over the 'feudal' lords. It is in fact because of their weakness that Ibn Khaldun attacks the townspeople. He criticises their taste for luxury on the grounds that it destroys their military prowess: 'Sedentary people have become used to laziness and ease. They are sunk in well-being and luxury. They have entrusted defence of their property and their lives to the governor and the ruler who rules them and to the militia which has the task of guarding them.'[6] 'Man is a man only in as much as he is able to procure for himself useful things and to repel harmful things. ... The sedentary person cannot take care of his needs personally ... he has no courage as a result of his life in luxury ... and becomes dependent upon a protective force to defend him.'[7]

Ibn Khaldun lists what he sees as the negative features of urban life and comes to the conclusion that the townspeople are militarily and therefore politically impotent. The ruler cannot rely upon them. On the contrary, they often create additional problems for him. The contradiction between state and tribe and between monarch and tribal aristocracy thus leads to the rapid collapse of both parties and the fall of the empire.

Most modern historians lay the blame for the Maghreb's difficulties at the feet of the nomads. Their destructive role was, however, an effect rather than a cause. The underlying causes of the region's instability related to its overall political and social structures. If we have to find a 'guilty party' it would in fact be more reasonable to invoke the part played by the townspeople in the successive crises that affected North Africa.

According to Ibn Khaldun, there is no doubt as to the guilt of the townspeople: they are indirectly responsible for the failure of the various attempts to create a centralized monarchy. The obviously exaggerated and emotional nature of his condemnation of urban life is an expression of his political pessimism rather than of an aversion towards the progress of civilization as such, or the refinements of *'umran hadari* which he personally appreciated. Ibn Khaldun reached the conclusion that the fall of empires is inevitable and not accidental. The factors that led to the collapse of the empires of the past have not disappeared. They are still present and will lead to similar disasters in the future.

There are a number of reasons for thinking that Ibn Khaldun came to this pessimistic conclusion late in life. For a long time he appears to have held very different views. The violence of his denunciations of those who are responsible for so many past, present and future disasters is a reflection of his lost hopes and his personal feeling of helplessness. His personal ambitions had been ruined. More importantly, there was no longer any hope that North Africa as a whole might at last enjoy a long period of peace and prosperity. Political stability alone could have produced peace and prosperity and for a long time Ibn Khaldun had obviously hoped that a powerful monarchy would make it possible.

Ibn Khaldun often appears to be a convinced supporter of royal power and argues that it should be strengthened. 'Royal authority is something natural to human beings, because of its social implications.'[8] 'People . . . cannot persist in a state of anarchy . . . they need a person to restrain them. He is their ruler. As is required by human nature, he must be a forceful ruler . . . royal authority of this kind is a noble institution.'[9] Ibn Khaldun's apologia for royal power is all the more remarkable in that Islamic religious ideology recognizes only the authority of the Caliphate (God's representative on earth), whose temporal authority derives from its spiritual role. This is why Ibn Khaldun takes such pains to demonstrate that the religious law does not censure royal authority and *asabiya*.[10] Although he never wrote a treatise on the art of government (others had done so long before him), Ibn Khaldun devotes several long passages to a description of the ideal monarch, and he does not place any great emphasis on spiritual qualities. The ideal ruler is simply an enlightened monarch who is strong and benevolent and who does not resort to the illegal practices of 'injustice'. According to Ibn Khaldun, sovereignty means caring for the well-being of the people.

Ibn Khaldun is, then, very different from the picture painted by certain modern authors (such as Gautier) of a cynic who recognizes only the role of might and intrigue and who is incapable of understanding anything but tyranny.

Ibn Khaldun did have a real ideal: the founding of stable, well organized states in which the sovereign could keep a tight rein on disruptive elements. Similar ideas can of course also be found in the work of many other Arab writers. But it should be remembered that Ibn Khaldun belonged to a family of officials who had long been attached to the Hafsid dynasty and who owed both their fortune and their rank to the dynasty. Politically, such officials were bitter enemies of the great tribal chieftains who tried to limit their power and undermine the authority of the sovereign. The Khalduns remained loyal to the dynasty regardless of anger and defeat: the historian's great-grandfather paid with his life for his loyalty to the legitimate rulers of Tunis. His grandfather, along with two servants who had remained loyal to the Hafsid family, saved the Sultan's life by carrying him in their arms to a relatively safe refuge after he had been defeated and left for dead on the battlefield. The family traditions that bound Ibn Khaldun to the dynasty are, then, quite understandable. It should also be remembered that the future historian grew up during the reign of a powerful sovereign and that his personal misfortunes had begun when usurpers challenged the rights of the legitimate heir to the throne. Ibn Khaldun saw many states collapse, and, like everyone else in the Maghreb, suffered as a result of the anarchy that raged in the area and which he describes in such poignant terms. As a historian, he was fully aware of the decline that was gradually overtaking the Maghreb.

The influence of such factors was all the greater in that he had a genuine love for his country. He remained a Maghrebian to the last, even though he spent the last twenty years of his life in Egypt. He kept to his Maghrebian customs, and continued to wear Maghrebian dress.

Significantly, it was his black burnous (a very different garment to those worn by the Orientals around him) which first drew Tamerlane's attention to him in 1401.

It might even be said that Ibn Khaldun felt something like patriotism. In Cairo, for instance, he added a chapter to the *Histoire des Berbères* in which he praises 'the talents that the Berber race has shown both in ancient times and in our own day—the noble qualities that brought them to power and to nationhood.' He never praises any other race in such terms. He lists and praises the glories of the Maghreb, regardless of whether they were created by Berber-speakers or by groups which had adopted Arabic: 'I believe I have cited a series of facts proving that the Berbers have always been a powerful, formidable, brave and populous race, a true race like so many others in this world: the Arabs, the Persians, the Greeks and the Romans.' This is high praise indeed. Ibn Khaldun ends by enumerating the qualities of the Berbers 'who could serve as an example to future races.'

Having such a high opinion of the glories of Maghrebian civilization, Ibn Khaldun was all the more conscious of the difficulties facing his country. What is more, he was descended from a great family who had been driven out of Andalusia when the Christians took advantage of the weakness of the Muslim west. When he returned to Seville, the cradle of his family had fallen to the Infidel and he must have felt great bitterness at seeing the Alcazar and the Giralda, monuments to a glorious but vanished past. Like many of his contemporaries, Ibn Khaldun still dreamed of the golden age of the Maghreb when the Almohads ruled the whole area from Seville to Gabès and when the Christians fled at the sound of the trumpets proclaiming the victory of Alarcos in Spain.

Inevitably, Ibn Khaldun saw the decline of the Muslim west as resulting from the anarchy and political fragmentation that was undermining the Maghreb. In his description of the conquest of Ifriqiyah by Abd el Moumen, Sultan of Morocco and founder of the Almohad Empire, in 1159, he writes that 'Abd el-Moumen listened to the complaints of the people of Ifriqiyah, who were being constantly harassed by the nomads. He sent an Almohad army led by his own son to their aid.'[11] 'Abd el Moumen came to Ifriqiyah and put an end to the troubles there'.[12]

His nostalgia for the Almohads is all the greater in that they were destroyed from within by the opportunism of Ibn Ghanya. Uninterested in founding a state himself, Ibn Ghanya rallied all those who chaffed at the peace imposed by the Almohads and all those who could hope to gain

wealth and power from chaos. His forces caused terrible destruction in Ifriqiyah and the central Maghreb. 'His bandits ravaged the countryside and
terrorized the towns. Ibn Ghanya indulged in all kinds of violence,
oppressed the people and behaved as an insolent tyrant.'[13] Despite the
efforts of the Almohads, Ibn Ghanya enjoyed a long 'career of plunder and
devastation.'[14] 'The Arabs supported him with a truly infernal zeal.'[15]

For many years, the author of *The Muqaddimah* cherished the hope
that North Africa would eventually be unified under the rule of a powerful dynasty. He lived in Tunis, the town where Almohad influences
survived longest. His family served a dynasty which was regarded as the
heir to the Almohad Caliphs. Ibn Khaldun describes the ruler who founded the Hafsid dynasty in 1236 thus: 'All the people of Africa and Spain
looked to him, hoping that he would be able to recreate the power of the
Almohads.' According to Ibn Khaldun, the fact that its founder drove
out Ibn Ghanya is one of the dynasty's greatest claims to fame: 'Abu
Zakarya ... the ancestor of the Hafsid Caliphs and the founder of their
power ... successfully defended the country against Ibn Ghanya, pursuing him whenever he showed himself and gradually freeing the people
and the farmers from the oppression they suffered.'[16]

With the entry of the Marinids into Tunis in 1347, it seemed that the
unity and prosperity of the Maghreb were assured. We have only to read
Ibn Khaldun's description of the conquest to realize the importance he
gave it and the hopes that it raised. He does not display such enthusiasm
in any other passage in his writings. Referring to Sultan Abul Hasan's
entry into Tunis, he writes: 'And so it was that he effected this great conquest and, receiving divine favour, subjugated the kingdoms and extended his rule to all the African states from Mesrata to Sous el-Acsa and
from Sous el-Acsa to Ronda in Spain.'[17]

The Khaldun family's reaction to these events is highly significant.
There is no doubt about their fidelity to the Hafsid dynasty. How could
they fail to welcome a conqueror who was reviving the unity of the
Maghreb? Whereas many of the leading citizens of Tunis were unhappy,
the Khalduns welcomed some of the Marinid Sultan's followers into
their home. We have already seen the important influence these intellectuals from Fez had on the future historian's intellectual development.
Despite the reversals of fortune which led to the conqueror's defeat, the
Khalduns remained loyal to his cause. Despite the dangers, they shel-
tered the secretary of the Marinid Sultan when the Moroccans were
driven out of the city.

The hope that a great and stable state would reunify the Maghreb and restore its former glory often finds expression in Ibn Khaldun's writings. Being a native of a country and a city which had been very badly affected by the prevailing anarchy, he unstintingly praises rulers who succeeded in re-establishing the rule of law and order. Writing of events that occurred shortly before he was born, he comments that 'Now that the disturbances caused by the insurgents had died down and that the country no longer rang with the cries of sedition, the Sultan could look to the frontiers of his kingdom and take steps to wipe out the last traces of insubordination. His main ambition was to subdue the Jarid and to deliver the people of that remote area from the claws of those ravening wolves and snarling dogs—the rulers of the towns and the Arabs of the deserts.'[18]

The period of calm during which Ibn Khaldun grew up was followed by a long period of turmoil in Ifriqiyah. This is Ibn Khaldun's description of the actions of the Sultan who put an end to it: 'This state of affairs lasted until God chose to dispel the darkness of oppression with the light of justice and to deliver the people from tyranny, famine and terror. He inspired Sultan Abul Abbas, Emir of the Faithful, to capture the capital and seize the Caliphate to which he was the legitimate heir.'[19] 'Having forced the tribal chieftains to obey him, he drove out the adventurers and freed the countryside and the towns from oppression. His victory gave the empire great superiority over the Arabs and allowed it to extend its authority over all its subjects. The people could cultivate their land in peace. The roads which had for so long been infested with bandits no longer represented a threat to travellers. The gates of divine mercy opened at last and poured forth happiness on to the people.'[20]

There is of course an element of flattery in all this. Ibn Khaldun did dedicate his *Histoire des Berbères* to the sovereign in question. But the description also reflects the author's innermost feelings. He is always ready to praise the actions of powerful rulers who restore order to their kingdoms. He has in a sense left us a list of the monarchs he admired most: Bolguin Ibn Ziri, the founder of the power of the Zirids, Yousof Ibn Tachf, creator of the Almohad Empire, Abd el-Moumen, Yarmoracen, founder of the kingdom of Tlemcen, Yacoub Ibn Abd el-Hack, the architect of the Marinid kingdom, in short all those whose 'fine qualities carried them to the heights of glory, those who ruled the whole of their kingdoms and whose orders were promptly obeyed.'[21] History has confirmed Ibn Khaldun's judgements. On the other hand, he does not conceal his scorn for inadequate kings, even if he served them as a minister.

Speaking of a sultan he had seen rebuked by an all-powerful Grand Vizier, he states that 'I witnessed the scene, and I was convinced that Mansur's character was weak and that he was fated to experience the most humiliating disgrace.'[22]

Such texts prove that Ibn Khaldun wanted to see the establishment of a powerful and lasting monarchy which could put an end to the instability and disorder and extend its authority throughout most if not all of the Maghreb. Such a monarchy would free North Africa from the vicious circle of the rise and fall of increasingly short-lived tribal states. Its emergence would imply the successful resolution of the contradiction between a unified monarchic state and tribal structures. That in turn would imply the emergence of a state based upon non-tribal forces.

In Western Europe, and in France in particular, the only reason that the king could overcome feudal particularism was that he could rely upon the new political force represented by the bourgeoisie, the negation of feudal structures. Royal authority was originally restricted to the top of the pyramid of relations of vassalage: the king's authority over his most powerful vassals was purely theoretical and his authority over the population as a whole was mediated by a host of seigneurial concessions. Without the support of the bourgeoisie, which wanted to destroy a feudal order in which there was inadequate room for it, the king would have been unable to short circuit this hierarchy of authorities, each of which was subordinate to the next, and gradually establish his direct authority over society as a whole.

In North Africa, the cohesion of tribal structures meant that it was impossible to exercise royal authority over everyone; royal authority thus remained superstructural and was poorly integrated into the tribal mosaic. On the other hand, the king had no non-tribal power base in his struggle against his own kinsmen.

Ibn Khaldun's hostility towards the townspeople in fact represents a political attitude. His prejudices would not have been so great had not their importance doomed to failure his wish for a lasting monarchy.

The subjectivism of Ibn Khaldun's criticisms of the urban population derives from his inability to find a rational explanation for their weakness. Unable to grasp the objective causes, he falls back upon dubious psychological explanations which contradict the rest of his analysis: given that the townspeople cannot constitute a political force, they must be depraved cowards.

Ibn Khaldun half realized that this impotence lay at the heart of the basic historical problem of North Africa: the violence of his sweeping criticisms of the townspeople proves that the extent of the problem did not escape him. He clearly understood that if the rulers were to be successful in their struggle against the tribal structures, they would have to gain the support of the townspeople. He realized that tribal organization in the towns was very weak and he is not criticising the townspeople for their lack of *'asabiya*. On the contrary: he justifies the king's moves to destroy *'asabiya*.

Most of the faults Ibn Khaldun attributes to the urban population are ethical and a matter of subjective judgement. When he attacks the townspeople for their 'cowardice', he pinpoints a historical reality: their inability to resist the tribal aristocracy. This is a political judgement rather than a technical comment on their lack of military prowess. When, on the other hand, he makes the essential point that the *'umran hadari* towards which the townspeople are evolving is simply a search for luxury and well-being, he is in fact criticising them for being non-productive and for not creating new economic forces.

Basically, Ibn Khaldun criticises the urban population of medieval North Africa for not constituting a bourgeoisie. Obviously he could not formulate the concept of the bourgeoisie with any clarity. Only the existence of a basic antagonism or class difference between the tribal aristocracy and the great merchants would have allowed him to see that they were fundamentally different.

There was, however, no basis for any such antagonism, as neither group was trying to gain control of the means of production, which were still owned by the tribal communities. Antagonism between the tribal aristocracy and the merchants could develop only if 1) the tribes broke up, 2) the chieftains gained authority over both the tribesmen and their property and 3) the merchants ceased being intermediaries with distant countries and tried to control the domestic means of production.

These essential preconditions did not exist in North Africa: there was no basic antagonism between the tribal and merchant aristocracies. Indeed, they often co-operated with one another. Ibn Khaldun could not formulate any conception of a bourgeoisie because no such class existed in the various societies with which he was familiar. Even in Europe, it existed then only in embryonic form. Nor did he have the historical hindsight with which we can appreciate the decisive role of the bourgeoisie in economic and social evolution. Ibn Khaldun was a fourteenth-century Maghrebian, not a nineteenth or twentieth-century European.

What is extraordinary is that Ibn Khaldun intuitively realized that the main reason for the failure of every attempt to centralize and consolidate the monarchy was to be found in an urban population whose structures were very different to those of the population of the *bled*. In grasping the historically negative nature of the townspeople, he was describing the absence of a bourgeoisie. The amazing thing is that he pointed to an absence even though he had no way of knowing what would have filled the gap, had the basic structures of society been different.

Ibn Khaldun's rigour and logic led him to realize that something was missing but, in the circumstances, it was impossible for him to go any further than that. In an attempt to explain the inexplicable, he therefore falls back upon metaphysical arguments and ethical criteria. Attempting to find an explanation for the historical failings of the townspeople, he falls back upon arguments about the essential nature of the urban population and sees it as the root of all evil.

Such value judgements, which now look like a major breach of scientific objectivity and a major distortion of historical method, have to be seen in context. Seen in that light, they indicate an extraordinary clarity of historical vision.

In the context of medieval North African society, the non-existence of a bourgeoisie is not, strictly speaking, a 'gap'. North Africa's social structures were in fact quite coherent: the vast majority of the population lived in their tribes, and the towns represented only an unstable, weak and de-tribalized faction. The fact that tribal structures were still preponderant and that the means of production could not be appropriated by a privileged minority meant that no bourgeoisie could possibly exist. In terms of this economic and social structure, its non-existence was quite logical.

Nonetheless, Ibn Khaldun realized that something was 'missing' because, like any society, Maghrebian society was characterized by internal contradictions. They were not, admittedly, as serious or as clearly defined as those which characterized Western Europe and which led to its outstanding social and economic development.

It was only in Western Europe that two clearly defined and mutually antagonistic classes developed. In the Maghreb (and in many other areas) no such classes emerged and the principal contradiction was the periodic one between tribal structures and a state which was trying in vain to improve its own structures (the negation of those of the tribe). Such attempts were, as we have seen, short-lived and the contradiction therefore could not develop far. It aborted whenever the establishment of a state began to give birth to a privileged minority definitely distinct from the tribal group. For centuries North Africa was characterized by the structures of military democracy and never made the transition from a classless society to a class society. This was not due to any refusal to change, but to the repeated failure of all attempts to establish a centralized monarchy and constitute a stable privileged minority. Despite the impetus given it by the international gold trade, the historical development of North Africa stalled because of the survival of tribal structures.

Ibn Khaldun contrasts the short-lived Maghrebian kingdoms with the longevity and apparent stability of the great empires of Antiquity and of the medieval Orient. He had only a limited knowledge of their history, and the relative inaccuracy of his information led him to overestimate their strength. The political implications of Islam and of the Caliphate also led him to stress the need for a stable state. The example of the eastern empires and of these principles of stability allowed Ibn Khaldun to see that there was something anomalous about the relative instability of the kingdoms of North Africa. His methodical search for an explanation of the anomaly may not have revealed the reasons for the longevity of other states; but it did explain why the Maghrebian rulers could not establish their power on any stable basis. According to Ibn Khaldun, the heart of the problem lay with the impotence of an urban population incapable of providing a counterweight to the role of the tribal aristocracy.

The violence with which Ibn Khaldun denounces the urban population expresses more than disappointment at seeing his hopes for a stable and lasting state destroyed. According to Ibn Khaldun, the townspeople are 'responsible' for much more than that: their lack of creativity in the field of economics blocks the development of civilization. The *'umran hadari* to which their taste for luxury and comfort leads is characterized only by the growth of consumption. The rise in consumption is both artificial and fragile. It is artificial in that it does not result from increased production and represents only the squandering of wealth extorted from the population as a whole. It is fragile in that it depends upon the vicissitudes of the political and economic powers which extort that wealth. Ibn Khaldun therefore blames the townspeople for the absence of social and economic development. We can see nowadays that the underlying reasons for the stagnation of North Africa and for its political crises are indissociably linked with the system as a whole, and with the survival of tribal structures in particular. If, however, we accept a more limited vision and a more immediate causality, it is true that, in so far as it did not form a bourgeoisie, the urban population was 'responsible' for the stagnation of Muslim civilization in the Middle Ages. But Ibn Khaldun obviously could not use the concept of the bourgeoisie to elucidate the anti-economic role played by the townspeople.

He realized that the palingenetic cycle of the rise and fall of *'umran hadari* was as abnormal as the short, cyclical existence of the empires, and that the two were closely linked. On several occasions he compared the life of the state to that of a man: birth, maturity, death. But he also realized that in other countries the cycles were not so short and that civilization there could develop over a longer period. His reference to biological fatality obviously does not satisfy him. If he saw the destiny of North Africa as something natural, why should he attack those he held responsible for it so savagely? It seems possible that he half realized that civilization is not necessarily doomed to repeat the same cycles and that its development can be interrupted and then reach higher levels. The violence of his subjective reactions expresses a rejection of fatalism and an intuitive belief that progress is not inconceivable, even though that belief is never clearly formulated. It could not be formulated in a society which looked turbulent but which was in fact stagnating. At a time when religious ideology was becoming a reactionary force, Ibn Khaldun tried to understand the society in which he lived and instinctively rebelled against the notion that progress would always be blocked by unavoidable failures. That rebellion gives us the true measure of the man.

Perhaps without even being really aware of it, Ibn Khaldun had the extraordinary prescience to raise what now seems a fundamental problem. For centuries it was almost impossible to even conceive of this problem, and historians only began to raise it once a vital stage in the history of mankind had been reached, namely the industrial revolution. The problem of the stagnation and cultural decline of a brilliant civilization is not specific to North Africa alone. In different ways, it dominates the precolonial history of every country in Africa, Asia and America. In that sense, the work of Ibn Khaldun takes on an international relevance.

Ibn Khaldun was not a prophet and he could not see into the future. His insights did not derive from his philosophical or religious views (as we shall see, the two contradicted one another). They are the product of a rigorously objective approach to the problems of North Africa and of an undeniably scientific investigation into them. It is in this sense that the work of Ibn Khaldun marks the appearance of the science of history.

Part Two

The Birth of History

1

Thucydides and Ibn Khaldun

Given the modernism and vigour of the thought of Ibn Khaldun it is all too easy to forget that we are dealing with a fourteenth-century historian.

The rediscovery and translation of *The Muqaddimah* in the nineteenth century coincided with the rise of historical science and sociology in Western Europe. Many authors were struck by the similarity between Ibn Khaldun's work and their own preoccupations. Accordingly, they drew comparisons between the work of the Maghrebian historian and that of modern historians and sociologists. Although Ibn Khaldun emerges well from such comparisons, they still stressed his shortcomings.

Given that the work of late nineteenth-century historians was often solely concerned with factual history, *The Muqaddimah*, which is more concerned with the underlying causes of historical evolution, looked like a philosophy of history or a sociology. Historians were more interested in discussing Ibn Khaldun's philosophy or speculating as to its possible universal significance than in looking at his work historically. Because of their philosophical preoccupations, they failed to examine *The Muqaddimah*'s methodology and the conception of history that informs it. More importantly, they failed to explain why this extraordinary historical work should have appeared in the fourteenth century.

The only way to bring out the originality of Ibn Khaldun's method and conception of history is to situate them in relation to the work of classical and medieval historians. The development and spread of history in Western Europe, together with the modernism of *The Muqaddimah*, tends to make us forget that historical thought is not a stable or natural category of human intelligence.

Manifestations of an embryonic concern for history do of course appear very early on. Long before the second millennium, the Babylonians were drawing up lists of the major achievements of their kings and dynasties for administrative purposes. Somewhat later, the Hittites began to write annals recording the great events in their political and military life. In a rather different way, sacred literature also displayed a certain interest in the history of human groups: the Bible, for instance, records the tribulations of the Hebrews and the development of their institutions.

Although relatively widespread, such annals and religious writings are only very rudimentary manifestations of what might be termed historical thought. The latter implies knowledge of events as they really happened and an explanation of the links between them. Most annals, however, consist solely of lists of events, and even if it is dated, an isolated event which is not related to anything else remains unintelligible.

In other countries, the conception of a past created by and for God precluded any possibility of explaining events. Theological preoccupations prevented historical thought from developing. This is why the most brilliant civilizations of the past were almost totally devoid of historical thought. India, for instance, never gave any importance to human historicity on the grounds that it was unworthy of attention compared with the progress of the transcendental spirit. Cosmic thought, the notion of One Being and of the circularity of time and events, and the concept of knowledge by and for God led to the repression of historical thought.

China also exemplifies the failure to develop historical knowledge. As well as having relatively accurate traditions which provide information about the distant past, China produced the oldest known collection of historical writings: the Chou King (tenth century BC). From the seventh century BC onwards an uninterrupted sequence of dated annals was kept, and commissions of official historians drew up dynastic histories that go even further back. Under the Han dynasty, a general history of China was written by Sseu Ma Tsien (b. 145BC). His work was carried on by Pan Kou. Under the Sung dynasty, the work of synthesis was continued by Sseu Ma Joung Kouang and the philosopher, Tchou Hi. The existence of a prolific and long-standing tradition of historical work relates to the existence of a centralized government and a powerful bureaucracy. The art of writing had been known for a long time and Chinese culture was very advanced.

Chinese historical thought does not, however, appear to have developed beyond the stage of annals, narratives of past events and encyclopaedic lists. Its stagnation appears to result from a number of causes. On the one hand, history was regarded as being conducive to moral edification and to education, which was of course of vital importance to Chinese culture. On the other hand, the enormous bureaucracy of the mandarins accumulated their carefully compiled archives purely for administrative purposes. The dominance of ethics and administrative practice was further reinforced by a philosophical ideology: the notion that there was a harmony between the human and the cosmic orders. The movement of the cosmos was held to result from the eternal interaction of two antithetical principles. The notion of universal reversibility and the idea of a mechanical evolutionism, a closed circuit which ended with the eternal return, blocked the development of historical thought in China. Equally, the conception of an Emperor who regulated the natural order and acted as an intermediary between Heaven and men helped to prevent historians from looking into the real causes of events.

India and China, the two most brilliant civilizations of the past, thus exemplify the total or partial suffocation of historical thought beneath the weight of ideology and social organization. These are not exceptional cases, but manifestations of a tendency which was to remain quite generalized until the nineteenth century. Until relatively recent times, historical thought—an attempt to rationalize man's past—was a somewhat exceptional phenomenon. Unlike other intellectual disciplines such as philosophy, it developed late and in discontinuous fashion. Most great civilizations have given rise to philosophers, artists and scientists. Such thinkers are far from rare. The number of great historians who wrote prior to the eighteenth century can, in contrast, be counted on the fingers of one hand. Their claim to fame is not based upon the volume or documentary interest of their work but upon their methodology and their conception of history. The advances they made were not, moreover, permanent gains. Those who came after such great historians and imitated them often proved unable to build upon the foundations they had provided. This is particularly true of the heirs of Thucydides and Ibn Khaldun.

If historical thought is to develop and flourish, it requires a complex set of favourable circumstances and social, political and intellectual preconditions which rarely existed before the nineteenth century. The mental functions required for the development of historical thought are themselves no more complex than those which produce artistic work or philosophical thought.

How else are we to explain the fact that so few major historical works were produced in the past and that they were produced in so few countries? As the examples of India and China show, historical thought is easily stifled by ideology. Even though rationalist and materialist conceptions were for a long time hampered by ideology, scientific activity did benefit from the impetus given it by technical progress and by the need to solve technical problems. History, in contrast, has almost no immediate utility. For a long time philosophy was a somewhat docile servant of theology and art a client of religion, which provided the basis for the ideology of all civilizations.

Philosophy can to a certain extent escape the social and political conditions of the day, but it is impossible for a historian to think on the basis of concepts alone. The philosopher can always state that it is not possible to understand reality. But such an attitude is the negation of history itself.

The object of history—knowledge of past events as they really happened—implies a form of rationalist or even materialist thought which breaks completely with religious ideology. The development of historical thought presupposes that man takes responsibility for his own past and implies that he makes an effort to understand the drama of his historical existence. Prior to the nineteenth century, these preconditions were met only in Ancient Greece (thus influencing the Greek and Roman world) and in medieval Muslim civilizations. In both cases, a great number of historical works were produced, and history played an important role in the development of culture.

History really appeared with Thucydides (460-395 BC). Historical thought had of course made great progress by the time of Herodotus (480-425 BC) and was gradually disentangling itself from legends and mythology. But being still concerned with preserving 'the wonderful stories of the past', it had only a vague notion of temporality and causality.

The work of Thucydides, in contrast, marks a decisive stage in the development of human thought. For the first time, a conscious attempt was being made to understand human actions. After a description of the immediate and underlying causes of the Peloponnesian War, Thucydides gives a very sober account of its course. A sober and passionate quest for truth replaces the supernatural elements and the curious or charming digressions of earlier writers. Man becomes conscious of his role in the City and of his role in history. There is no longer any room for the supernatural or for the intervention of the gods. All things are governed by laws. Once events are no longer merely chance happenings or the result of divine intervention, they have to be understood. And if facts are to be connected with one another, the historian must first be certain of their veracity. Truth becomes the main criterion of the value of the historian. But whilst this concern for truth is a necessary precondition for the emergence of historical thought, it is not in itself a sufficient precondition.

Although it continued to play an important role in Greek and Roman thought, history did not remain at the level it had reached with Thucydides. Historians became more and more concerned with literary style. Their ideal was no longer understanding. They wanted to write true-seeming accounts of the past that were skilfully written and honestly interpreted, for the edification of the reader.

The search for truth remained of course the historian's prime duty but, quite aside from the fact that it was often embroidered to please patrons, the truth they sought was only partial. Deliberately so. All ancient historians were of the opinion that some facts were worthy of being recorded while others were of no interest, that it would be in bad taste to include certain facts in a work of history. The sign of a good historian was his ability to give everything the importance it deserved. According to Lucian, the facts have to be carefully chosen; bad taste and childish exuberance are to be avoided.

What are the criteria governing this choice? They vary, depending upon which literary genres constitute history at any given moment. Each genre—ethical, hagiographic, political, romantic, picturesque, theological ... —has its own well-defined traditions. A style suitable for a romantic history is not suitable for a more serious genre. The choice of events that merit attention is equally variable. An examination of social and economic conditions does not belong within the category of facts worthy of attention, except perhaps from the point of view of exoticism. Social and economic facts belong to the domain of the philosopher, the moralist and the theologian, and they see them from a purely normative point of view.

The selection of facts in accordance with genre criteria and the reduction of historical reality to the narrow dimension of political and military events means that history becomes a literary narrative which has little room for explanations. At best, the authors look for immediate or apparent causes, and 'happy' or 'unhappy' outcomes, but they do so within the confines of a genre which precludes any mention of causes or explanations that are incompatible with its nature. Thus, the theological historian sees divine intervention as the basic explanation of the events he is recounting. A more romantic writer will stress the role played by women. Such authors are historians only in so far as they look for themes or inspiration in the past. According to Cicero, for instance, history is a means of adding interest to a speech.

A stylish exposition is considered an essential way of ensuring that the lessons to be learned from history will bear fruit. Authors are often advised to follow the accepted custom of introducing digressions so as to make their books more entertaining. Thus, modern critics find the following virtues in Livy, who was one of the greatest of Roman historians: 'A concern for aesthetics . . . form, composition and style in accordance with the Ciceronian canon . . . extreme sensitivity . . . a vivid imagination . . . knowledge of the human soul . . . narrative and pictorial gifts . . . the threefold ability to instruct, please and move the reader . . . general culture . . .'.[1] Such talents are more typical of the orator or of a writer of fiction than of the historian in any modern sense.

There are of course exceptions. Polybius (210-125), for instance, traces the development of the Roman Empire, analyses the reasons for its power and tries to go beyond literary concerns, using geographical observations to illustrate his comments. But he cannot resist the temptation to make rhetorical and moralistic digressions. Although he does stress the need to explain the facts, he never goes beyond immediate causes, intentions and comments about the outcome of events. He is more interested in saying how things happened than in explaining them. When it comes back to underlying causes, Polybius falls back upon Fortune. In his description of the object of his work, the development of the Roman Empire, he writes: 'It is my task as an historian to put before my readers a compendious view of the part played by Fortune in bringing about the general result.'[2] Anything out of the ordinary and anything that represents a real change is explained in terms of chance, Fortune or the intervention of a god.

St Augustine (354-430) is another major exception. His *City of God* is the source of historical thought in the Christian west. The Bishop of Hippo introduced a new and very important element into historical thought: he broke with the concept of circular time and the eternal return which characterized the work of the historians of the Ancient world. According to St Augustine, time is continuous and irreversible, a continuum stretching from original sin to the last judgement. History thus acquires a general meaning. Along with the notion of the irreversibility of the past, he brings out the decisive historical role of human actions. Man will be saved or damned by his own actions. *The City of God* also marks an extension of the dimensions of history: St Augustine in fact provides an overall picture of Roman history and a general sketch of Ancient civilization.

In some senses, *The City of God* marks an advance in historiography but in others it marks a regression. The parallel examination of historical evolution and of social and cultural conditions does not lead to an explanation of the former in terms of the latter. For St Augustine, divine intervention is the motor of history. *The City of God* is, then, a theological and apologetic work which uses historical arguments rather than a work of history. St Augustine never tries to explain the fall of the Roman Empire. He tries to justify it and to situate it within what he sees as history: the process which takes man from Adam's sin, through the ordeal of evil and finally to redemption. In this symbolic tale, the efficacy of divine action replaces human actions. St Augustine studies the earthly city, not in order to understand it as such, but in order to find portents of the future triumphs of the City of God. Despite its considerable positive contributions (of which so much will be made thirteen hundred years later), St Augustine's work is inferior to that of Thucydides, who refused to look at anything other than human actions and refused to look for explanations outside human nature itself.

In Byzantium, Greek and Roman historical thought survived mainly in moralizing form in a profusion of chronicles, annals, panegyrics and tracts.

There were few qualitative differences between historical thought in the Greek and Roman world and in Muslim civilization. Religious preoccupations had a major influence on it in Islam: history was reckoned one of the 'Arab sciences'—those founded upon Revelation and tradition —along with religious jurisprudence, rhetoric, grammar and poetry. The main task of the Muslim historian was to recount the life of the prophet, the various stages of Islamic conquests and the development of the Caliphate. Muslim history was also a literary genre, and Ibn Khaldun's criticisms of the work of his predecessors could equally well be applied to the work of both classical and medieval historians in Europe: inadequate explanations, a taste for fanciful or improbable stories, superficial judgements, overindulgence in apologia, lack of interest in social and economic life, an over-exclusive concern with style and rhetoric, a tendency simply to enumerate unrelated facts and dates. The similarity in general characteristics of historiography in Greece and Rome and in Muslim civilization may reflect some indirect connections between the two cultures (perhaps via the intermediary of Syrian authors?); but it has far more to do with comparable intellectual conditions. The basic conception of history is very similar in both cases: a skillful narrative account of the past written for the benefit of posterity.

The primary aim of the best historians is still truth, but only a partial truth. The historian chooses which facts to report. The modern approach to history is of course still selective, but it covers all forms of human activity and selects only *significant* facts and events. For centuries, however, historians examined only very restricted and obviously 'noble' areas (military, political and artistic life, the deeds of kings and nobles). As a result, causality could be established only in a very partial sense.

This brings us back to Thucydides, the first true historian. His superiority over those who came after him is obvious. Until the nineteenth century, only Ibn Khaldun had improved upon Thucydides. Thucydides invented history but Ibn Khaldun turned it into a science.

According to Thucydides, the search for truth is an artistic rather than a scientific matter. His history is basically a work of art. He seeks for truth in the same way that Greek sculptors sought it in marble. *The Peloponnesian Wars* displays two characteristics that are essential to any work of art: the greatest possible truth (which according to Thucydides is not the same thing as accuracy), and the greatest possible generality. Thucydides is looking for that higher truth which Aristotle attributes to poetry. The war between Athens and Sparta was of particular interest to the historian in that its violence revealed the workings of the human soul and the eternal forces that rule mankind. That, according to Thucydides, is how the past sheds light upon the future and how the present sheds light upon the past.

The drama of war gives rise to those conflicts within the human soul which the Athenian historian sees as the true cause of conflict. Like a tragedy or a Socratic dialogue, Thucydides's writing has the extraordinary power to abstract ideas and make them live by putting them into the mouths of men. 'We are not free to moderate our desire to command': when put into the mouth of Alcibiades, this expression sums up the essential theme of *The Peloponnesian Wars*. Like all others, that conflict was caused by the boundless will to power which Thucydides sees as the essence of man. In Thucydides's account, the Peloponnesian War becomes 'the most intelligible war in history. It becomes an archetype which sheds light on all subsequent wars by suggesting either a parallel or a contrast.'[3]

Like Praxiteles's sculptures, this quest for the eternal truth is not without a certain artifice based upon generalisations and insights: 'I have ... put into the mouth of each speaker the views that, in my opinion, they would have been most likely to express, as the particular occasion demanded.' The speeches he puts into the mouths of his actors and which reflect their truth are designed to draw out from each particular event the substance which makes it an eternal lesson. The speeches show the role of human will power or, rather, the will which imposes itself upon men and changes the course of the world at decisive moments.

Thus, Thucydides's world is one which has been entirely re-thought; his history is a reconstructed history, eternally true and always with us. 'His arguments are so closely connected with truth that it is impossible to say whether they uncover the truth or produce it.'[4] It need scarcely be pointed out that this rational reconstruction of history, which has the 'directness of a theorem',[5] is a long way from historical science. 'Thucydides develops the eternal themes of life and death as experienced by the men who build, defend and destroy the City. He brings them to life and makes them as vivid as the Parthenon friezes.'[6]

'I followed an unusual method of arrangement and division into chapters ... I chose a remarkable and original method'.[7]

These lines from the foreword to *The Muqaddimah* may look like an expression of authorial vanity or an attempt to appeal to the generosity of a patron. In fact they simply reflect the author's legitimate pride and his striking awareness of the originality and importance of his own work. Again, we have here a sign of his lucidity. Some sections of Ibn Khaldun's work do of course have features in common with other Muslim historians. In his *Histoire des Berbères*, for instance, the facts are grouped into chapters, each dealing with a different dynasty, and great importance is given to military matters. But it should not be forgotten that, unlike *The Muqaddimah*, which was written in very special circumstances, the *Histoire* and other sections of the 'Universal History' were written at the request of rulers. They therefore had to use the classical forms of contemporary historiography. Ibn Khaldun's original ideas and conceptions are to be found in *The Muqaddimah*. It is *The Muqaddimah* that gives the various chapters of *Histoire des Berbères* their meaning. We will therefore concentrate mainly upon *The Muqaddimah*.

The structure, form and conception of *The Muqaddimah* are very different from those of the writings of other Muslim historians and of classical Greek and Roman writers. For the latter, history is primarily a literary exercise: an entertaining narrative account, often mannered in style, and interrupted by picturesque or evocative digressions. The style of *The Muqaddimah*, in contrast, is very direct: there are no attempts to entertain and no flights of fancy. Ibn Khaldun avoids allegories and uses a technical vocabulary in preference to noble or poetic language. *The Muqaddimah* is not designed to amuse or entertain the reader. It is a meditative work, an attempt to understand. The failure to conform to the stylistic canons of traditional eloquence does not, however, reflect any clumsiness on the part of the author: Ibn Khaldun was also the author of highly sophisticated poems written in an irreproachably elegant style.

Ibn Khaldun pays little attention to the requirements of literary convention in *The Muqaddimah* because, unlike Thucydides, he is simply not concerned with artistic matters. He is not interested in uncovering the eternal workings of the human soul or in using the 'speeches' of tragic actors to reveal some profound truth. He is less concerned with major events or with the psychological reactions of prestigious figures than with social evolution and its general mechanisms, even though the latter are often obscure and have none of the prestige of tragedy. Ibn Khaldun deals with the structure of groups rather than with the personality of great champions. Without underestimating the importance of spiritual forces, he reveals the material factors which turn them into active political forces. He rejects the tragic and grandiose history of princes and battles in favour of a singularly prosaic history in which great events are the product of matters relating to economic life and social organization.

In the opening lines of *The Muqaddimah* Ibn Khaldun stresses the differences between his work and that of his predecessors: he is not interested in moving or charming his reader, in moralizing or convincing, or in serving any administration or government. 'The science of history does not belong to rhetoric, one of the logical disciplines ... the subject of which is convincing words by means of which the mass is inclined to accept a particular opinion or not to accept it. It is also not politics, because politics is concerned with the administration of home or city in accordance with ethical and philosophical requirements.'[8] 'As far as the subject under discussion is concerned, the result ... is just historical information ... it leads to one result only: the mere verification of historical information.'[9]

Ibn Khaldun rejects the notion that history has any immediate utility for either ethics or politics, a notion which dominated historiography from its beginnings until the eighteenth century. He is one of the few historians to have studied history as an end in itself and to have arrived at a clear conception of the originality of the discipline both in terms of its ends and its basic methodology.

Ibn Khaldun's new conception of history is initially revealed by his attempt to make a critique of historical methodology. He was the first to make a critique of this importance. Using specific examples from the work of his most important predecessors, Ibn Khaldun lists the reasons for their errors. The usual reason is 'partisanship for opinions and schools.'[10] The implications of Ibn Khaldun's criticisms of 'reliance upon transmitters'[11] are extremely far-reaching if we recall that at the time all the 'hadiths' (stories about how the Prophet reacted in various circumstances) which formed the basis of religious tradition were based upon chains of authority: A relies upon the authority of B, who has it from C, who has it from D and so on . . . the morality of each transmitter being such that there is no reason to doubt his sincerity or the accuracy of the facts he reports. Other reasons which make untruth unavoidable in historical accounts include 'unfounded assumptions as to the truth of a thing'. 'People as a rule approach great and high-ranking persons with praise and encomiums. They embellish conditions and spread the fame of great men.'[12]

There is no shortage of extraordinary and fanciful events in the writings of historians who want to produce literary effects. Ibn Khaldun violently attacks their taste for the miraculous. Speaking of the dragons and genies whose doings punctuate many historical accounts, he comments that 'The genies are not known to have specific forms and effigies. They are able to take on various forms. The story of the many heads they have is intended to indicate ugliness and frightfulness. It is not meant to be taken literally.'[13]

There is nothing particularly original about his denunciation of the white lies put about by historians who are trying to entertain their readers with fascinating stories. The best historians of the classical world had already denounced such lies: both Lucian and Polybius state that the historian's only duty is to devote himself to the truth. But that is their only criticism of existing historiography. Ibn Khaldun does much more than simply denounce falsehood—a necessary step but one which is in itself inadequate. When he examines historical accounts, he uses not only a logical approach but also what might now be termed history's auxiliary sciences: economics, geography, demography, military strategy and tactics, etc. Criticising reports that Moses counted six hundred thousand soldiers in the ranks of the Israelite army, Ibn Khaldun points out that such a small country could not possibly have maintained an army of that size. Moreover, such an army could not be drawn up in battle formation. If the Israelites really did have such a great army, they would have conquered vast areas of territory. Finally, it was demographically impossible for such an army to have been raised in the first place. A census had shown that Israel's population was numerically small and there were limits to its possible growth rate. Ibn Khaldun's use of auxiliary sciences is of course fairly rudimentary, but it does reveal an interesting intellectual frame of mind and a certain broadmindedness. His criticisms of his predecessors' conceptions of history are much more significant. 'They forget to pay attention to historiography's purpose.'[14] Speaking of the dynastic histories so common in Arabic literature, Ibn Khaldun comments that 'it is pointless for an author of the present time to mention the sons and wives, the engraving on the seal ring, the surname, judge, vizier, and doorkeeper of an ancient dynasty, when he does not know the origin, descent or circumstances of its members.'[15]

Speaking of the work of Ibn el-Muqaffa, an eighth-century historian, he writes: 'The statements of Ibn el-Muqaffa, and the excursions on political subjects in his treatises ... touch upon many of the problems of our work. However, he did not substantiate his statements with arguments as we have done. He merely mentioned them in passing in the flowing prose style and eloquent verbiage of the rhetorician.'[16] According to Ibn Khaldun, the historian's basic standpoint vitiates his best efforts: he had all the basic information at his disposal but, although he wanted to get at the truth, he could not get anywhere because he did not even realize how to pose the problems. He did not really understand the meaning of History. Abu Bakr al-Turtushi also dealt with areas very similar to those touched upon in *The Muqaddimah*, but 'His work is merely a compilation of transmitted material similar to sermons in its inspirational purpose ... He sets aside a special chapter for a particular problem, but then tells a great number of stories and traditions and he reports scattered remarks by Persian sages and by Indian sages. ... In a way al-Turtushi aimed at the right idea, but did not hit it. He did not realize his intention or exhaust his problems.'[17]

He also attacks historians who have a purely narrative conception of history, which he regards as 'superficial': 'Their information . . . concerns species the genera of which are not taken into consideration, and whose specific differences are not verified. With the information they set down they merely repeated historical material which is, in any case, widely known, and followed earlier historians who worked on it. . . . When they then turn to the description of a particular dynasty, they report the historical information about it mechanically and take care to preserve it as it had been passed down to them, be it imaginary or true. They do not turn to the beginning of the dynasty. Nor do they tell why it unfurled its banner and was able to give prominence to its emblem, or what caused it to come to a stop when it had reached its term. The student, thus, has still to search for the beginnings . . . '.[18] Ibn Khaldun then uses a striking metaphor to sum up the poverty of a narrative history whose only ideal is the accuracy of the facts it selects and recounts: 'They presented historical information about dynasties and stories of events from the early period as mere forms without substance, blades without scabbards.'[19]

What is Ibn Khaldun's conception of history? It goes far beyond narrative history, a literary genre which provides only an account of the facts. According to Ibn Khaldun, 'It takes critical insight to sort out the hidden truth; it takes knowledge to lay bare truth and polish it so that critical insight may be applied.'[20] The historian must not restrict himself to the eternal forms of history and must concentrate upon its 'inner meaning'. This implies 'speculation and an attempt to get at the truth, subtle explanations of the causes and origins of existing things, and deep knowledge of the how and why of events.'[21]

This concern for explaining and understanding and this dismissal of utilitarian or artistic concerns are basic characteristics of Ibn Khaldun's work. No historian before him had ever argued in such specific terms or so convincingly that the true nature of history is the *understanding* of man's past. Providing a narrative account of the past is merely a preliminary to that essential function. Gathering information is an essential stage, obviously, but not an end in itself. The historian has to be able to explain the facts and arrive at a rational understanding of the past.

But the need to arrive at 'deep knowledge of the how and why of events' means that the historian has to break out of the confines of the various literary genres which make up the heterogeneous body known as narrative history. It is this extraordinary concern for understanding that leads Ibn Khaldun to take such a total or overall view of history.

Earlier historians had restricted themselves to the 'great events' of political and military life and looked for the causes that determined them in palaces and armies. The facts of economic and social life were left to the philosophers and theologians, who examined them in purely normative terms, and to the jurists and administrators, who dealt with them in utilitarian terms. Ibn Khaldun's work marks a major change in historical thought in that it brings together areas of knowledge that had previously been almost totally separated: 'It should be known that these are related matters: the strength and weakness of a dynasty, the numerical strength of a nation or race; the size of a town or city, and the amount of prosperity and wealth. This is because dynasty and royal authority constitute the *form* of the world and civilization which, in turn, together with the subjects, cities and all other things, constitute the *matter* of dynasty and royal authority.'[22]

Ibn Khaldun's main criticism of earlier historians, a criticism which could be applied to all historians from Herodotus to the eighteenth century, is that they failed to recognize the links between political and military history and social and economic evolution. In his account of the errors that introduce untruth into historical accounts, he remarks that 'another reason making untruth unavoidable...is ignorance of the nature of the various conditions arising in civilization.'[23] Rosenthal translates *'umran* as 'civilization', although it is much wider than that and covers economics, culture and politics.

'History refers to events that are peculiar to a particular age or race. Discussion of the general conditions of regions, races and periods constitutes the historian's foundations. Most of his problems rest upon that foundation, and his historical information derives clarity from it.'...[24] 'The scholar in this field needs to know the principles of politics, the true nature of existent things, and the differences among nations, places and periods with regard to ways of life, character, qualities, customs, sects, schools and everything else.'[25] This is not merely a matter of avoiding anachronisms or of adding local colour to the narrative. Ibn Khaldun sees the study of social and economic conditions as the basis of historical criticism, and this implies a new conception of history.

'The normative method for distinguishing right from wrong in historical information on the grounds of inherent possibility or absurdity is to investigate human social organization, which is identical with civilization. ... If we do that, we shall have a normative method for distinguishing right from wrong and truth from falsehood by means of a logical demonstration that admits of no doubts. . . . We shall have a sound yard-stick with the help of which historians may find the path of truth and correctness where their reports are concerned.'[26]

The link between understanding the past and studying social and economic conditions, which Ibn Khaldun rightly sees as basic to his work, comes out very clearly in this passage: 'I chose a remarkable and original method. In the work, I commented on civilization (*'umran*), on urbanization and on the essential characteristics of human social organization in a way that explains to the reader how and why things are as they are, and shows him how the men who founded empires managed to do so.'[27]

We can now see the difference between the ideal of an account of events that are thought worthy of interest—a somewhat passive ideal—and the definition of history given by Ibn Khaldun: 'History, in matter of fact, is information about human social organization.'[28] This, the first sentence of the first volume of *The Muqaddimah*, marks a qualitative transformation in historical thought: it ceases being literature and becomes a science. Ibn Khaldun, who can legitimately be considered the first theoretician, makes a clear distinction between the two conceptions. 'On the surface, history is no more than information about political events, dynasties and occurrences of the remote past, clearly presented and spiced with proverbs. It serves to entertain large, crowded gatherings. . . . The inner meaning of history, on the other hand, involves speculation and an attempt to get at the truth, subtle explanations of the causes and origins of existing things, and deep knowledge of the how and why of events. History, therefore, is firmly rooted in philosophy. It deserves to be accounted a branch of philosophy.'[29] 'Information about human social organization' . . . this definition governs the whole of Ibn Khaldun's work.

The title of the work itself reflects his prime concerns. It should be noted that Ibn Khaldun does not use either of the Arabic terms (*akhbar* or *tarikh*) which are normally used to describe history in the traditional sense. Etymologically, *akhbar* means information about remarkable events, and thus comes to mean the events themselves. *tarikh* appears to derive from a word meaning lunar month, measurement of time and, by extension, dating, annals, historical work.

Ibn Khaldun seems to have wanted to distance himself from the traditional concept of history in the very title of his work: 'Book of Lessons and Archive of Early and Subsequent History, Dealing with the Political Events Concerning the Arabs, Non-Arabs and Berbers, and the Supreme Rulers Who Were Contemporary With Them.'[30] This translation is on the whole acceptable, but unfortunately it does not capture the very specific meaning of *Ibar*. The word is obviously difficult to translate, but it is also very important. Some authors have even suggested that Ibn Khaldun's book should be referred to as the book (*Kitab*) of *Ibar*. *Ibar* is the plural form of *Ibra*, which derives from a root meaning to go from one point to another, to overcome an obstacle.[31] This somewhat ambivalent term is often used by philosophers and mystics to mean grasping the inner reality of something. *Ibra* can sometimes mean disregarding the material appearance of an individual or a system of thought in order to grasp its spiritual essence.

Ibn Khaldun was trained as a philosopher and he seems to have chosen this term to describe the attempt to understand and explain that typifies his work. In a sense, *Kitab al-Ibar* means the book which allows us to move from the external form of history to its true reality, to its inner characteristics. Ibn Khaldun makes *Ibar* almost synonymous with understanding and logically explaining historical events.[32] *Ibar* can be translated as an attempt to understand; it can also be translated as a search for the deeper meaning of things.

2
Historical Materialism and Dialectical Conceptions

'I proceeded from general causes to detailed historical information. Thus, this work contains an exhaustive history of the world.'[1]

As we have seen, Ibn Khaldun tries to differentiate between the necessary and the contingent, the general and the particular. His approach thus corresponds to one of the prime functions of History: were it not for the imbrication of general and necessary developments and apparently accidental events, there would be no need for history.

In his attempt to differentiate between these two elements of historical reality, Ibn Khaldun deals with general causes in *The Muqaddimah* and studies the destiny of each Maghreb dynasty in his *Histoire des Berbères*. The study of North African history thus becomes something very different from a list of accidents and isolated, unrelated events. These events become meaningful when seen in the context of the evolution of the states.

Ibn Khaldun does not however superimpose preconceived ideas or a metaphysical schema upon the historical evolution of the Maghrebian states. The content of the first volume of *The Muqaddimah* is itself the result of a close study of the various states which developed in the medieval Maghreb. It is a synthesis produced by a judicious combination of specific facts and generalizations. The use of objective generalization allows Ibn Khaldun to break with a purely factual conception of History. In the case of the Maghreb, a purely factual approach would have been especially sterile: the political confusion and the repeated failure of attempts to centralize and consolidate the monarchy mean that a study of each dynasty would only produce a list of unrelated facts.

As we have seen, Ibn Khaldun explains specific events in political and military life and in the evolution of the states in terms of general causes. Those general causes are to be found in *'umran*, the totality of economic, social and cultural activities.

It will be recalled that St Augustine also related a sequence of political events, namely the fall of the Roman Empire, to Ancient civilization as a whole and attempted to explain the whole in terms of underlying causes. But for him, those underlying causes were governed by the will of God.

Ibn Khaldun lived in a society in which the influence of religious ideology was no less powerful than in Christian countries. But when it comes to divine intervention (and this is a basic problem for any Muslim thinker—the great Arab conquests of the seventh and eighth centuries are as much religious events as military events), he takes a very different view from St Augustine.

True, each chapter of *The Muqaddimah* ends with a formula expressing veneration of God and acceptance of his will. But whilst there is no reason to doubt the sincerity of these expressions of piety, they are simply the ritual formulae found at the end of all literary or historical chapters in Arabic books.

Whilst Ibn Khaldun's piety is not in doubt, it has to be stressed that his historical arguments leave very little room for divine intervention. Thus, he explains the extent and rapidity of the Muslim conquests not only in terms of belief in the true faith, but also in terms of *'asabiya*, a considerable material force still found amongst the Arab tribes.

In one important passage, Ibn Khaldun refutes the theory that the basic explanation for social organization is to be found in a divinely ordained plan: 'People who have a divinely revealed book and who follow the prophets are few in number in comparison with all the heathen who have no divinely revealed book. The latter constitute the majority of the world's inhabitants. Still, they too have possessed dynasties and monuments, not to mention life itself. They still possess these things at this time in the intemperate zones to the north and the south. This is in contrast with human life in the state of anarchy, with no one to exercise a restraining influence. That would be impossible.'[2] He argues that the philosophers are wrong to say that 'Human beings absolutely require some authority to exercise a restraining influence . . . and that such restraining influence exists through the religious law that has been ordained by God and revealed to mankind by a human being. . . . Existence and human life can materialize without the existence of prophecy through injunctions a person in authority may devise on his own or with the help of a group feeling (*'asabiya*) that enables him to force the others to follow him wherever he wants to go.'[3] 'Human social organization is something necessary. The philosophers expressed this fact by saying

"Man is political by nature". That is, he cannot do without the social organization for which the philosophers use the technical term "polis", town.'[4]

Ibn Khaldun does not hold that the organization of society is basically determined by divine prescription: 'Both Bedouins and sedentary people are natural groups.'[5] He is not using 'natural' simply in the sense of 'physical environment', but in the sense of 'secular, normal and material phenomena', as opposed to divine or supernatural phenomena. Although he often stresses the influence of natural and particularly climatic conditions on human behaviour—and to that extent he is a precursor of Montesquieu—he does not regard physical factors as having a determinant effect on social life. Nor does he attribute a preponderant influence to racial factors. Neither race nor climate can explain the major differences to be found amongst different peoples. 'Differences between races or nations ... are caused by custom and distinguishing characteristics, as well as by descent.'[6] Similar opinions can of course be found in the writings of a number of Muslim thinkers. But Ibn Khaldun makes a distinction between determining factors and effects; 'It should be known that differences of condition among people are the result of the different ways in which they make their living.'[7] Such opinions make Ibn Khaldun a precursor of historical materialism.

The importance Ibn Khaldun gives to this passage has to be underlined, as it is not merely a passing comment. I stress it, not because of any modern philosophical prejudice, but because Ibn Khaldun himself gives it such importance. It is the first sentence of the second chapter of Volume II, the section in which Ibn Khaldun lays the basis for his fundamental distinction between *'umran badawi* and *'umran hadari*. The principle behind that distinction, which anticipates historical materialism, provides the basis for the comparative method, a tool which Ibn Khaldun often uses in his attempt to generalize and synthesize.

By using the criterion of the organization of productive life, Ibn Khaldun is able to compare very different societies: in terms of race, religion, geography and epoch, these societies are not the same, although their mode of production is similar. In each of them the mode of production determines broadly similar structures and developments. It is to a large extent Ibn Khaldun's use of the comparative method that allows him to generalize on the basis of a large number of facts and to arrive at his schema for the evolution of states.

Moreover, there are no static or final differences between these various ways of making a living. Ibn Khaldun sees men as evolving from a very rudimentary state to a more developed organization with more sophisticated production techniques and a more extensive division of labour. The effect of the development of production on social and economic organization is one of the basic tenets of historical materialism. As we have seen, the development from *'umran badawi* to *'umran hadari* within the state is an essential feature of Ibn Khaldun's theories.

Ibn Khaldun believes that there is a close connection between the organization of production, social structures, forms of political life, juridical systems, social psychology and ideologies. Again, he anticipates important features of historical materialism. There is a complex interaction among all these elements, but it is the development of the economy that determines the development of civilization as a whole. Ibn Khaldun emphasizes the changes in political organization, the appearance of new forms of intellectual life and the psychological changes brought about by the transition from *'umran badawi* to *'umran hadari*.

Ultimately, Ibn Khaldun examines every aspect of political and intellectual life in the light of social and economic developments. In his description of the Caliphate, the Sultanate and other bodies whose authority extended to both the spiritual and the temporal, and which were in theory governed by religious law, he writes that 'When we discuss royal and governmental positions, it will be as something required by the nature of civilization and human existence. It will not be under the aspect of particular religious laws. This ... is not our intention in this book. There is no need to go into details with regard to the religious laws governing these positions. ... Thus, we shall discuss those matters only as the necessary result of the nature of civilization in human existence.'[8] He even begins to map out the complex relationship between religious organization and social and economic structures: 'Religion and religious organizations constitute the *form* for existence and royal authority.'[9] But he immediately tones down this comment, which might have been open to criticism from the doctors of the law on the grounds that it was not orthodox, by adding that 'Form is prior to matter',[10] thus confirming the primacy of the spiritual. Despite this hesitation, Ibn Khaldun does seem to have grasped the multiple connections that bind together the different sectors of the life of a society: 'Dynasty and royal authority have the same relationship to civilization as form has to matter.'[11]

We have here an explanation of the encyclopaedic nature of *The Muqaddimah*. Ibn Khaldun does not see the world as a random accumulation of isolated objects, but as a coherent whole in which phenomena mutually determine one another. Encyclopaedias were of course common in Arabic literature; writers wanted to display their erudition, and officials made extensive use of such books. But Ibn Khaldun produced something very different. *The Muqaddimah* is not an encyclopaedia in the sense that it is not a compilation of arbitrarily classified isolated elements. It is an encyclopaedia in the sense that it relies upon an overall conception of history and is based upon the principle that the parts are determined by the whole.

If we wanted to analyse the contents of *The Muqaddimah* and arbitrarily separate out its constituent elements, we would find a cosmology, a geographical description of the world with numerous comments on human geography, a theory of politics, a treatise on economics, a rational classification of the sciences, a theory of education and a rhetoric. We would also find studies on prophecy, the mystics, magic and alchemy, long passages on jurisprudence, linguistics and literature, and a discussion of a variety of arts and technologies. Even so, the list is still incomplete: Ibn Khaldun's work also deals with chemistry, algebra, and geometry and discusses agriculture, medicine, architecture and urbanism, military science, aesthetics and theology. Some of the topics discussed are not especially original, but others are of considerable interest. Ibn Khaldun is, for instance, one of the few Arab authors to deal with artistic problems at any length. His views on education are particularly pertinent and innovatory for his time. His studies of mysticism and of the various branches of magic provide a relatively accurate picture of such practices in the medieval Maghreb. The encyclopaedic nature of Ibn Khaldun's work is noteworthy in that it is probably the most complete synthesis of the human sciences to have been written by any Arab author.

Most of the topics covered by this encyclopaedia are studied both analytically and synthetically: each phenomenon is studied in isolation so as to bring out its basic and permanent features, but the facts are also examined in relation to one another so as to explain their interaction from an evolutionary point of view. Their interaction is not examined statically, but in the context of their overall evolution. Each stage in their evolution corresponds to a stage in agricultural activity, that stage itself being determined by factors external to agriculture. Similar studies are made of every important sector of economic, social, political and cultural life.

What we are dealing with, then, is an analytic, synthetic and evolutionary encyclopaedia, a gigantic undertaking for one man. Not every element in this encyclopaedia is equally important or original. Ibn Khaldun concentrates mainly upon political developments and social factors. He does, however, also make a study of economic phenomena. Unlike his contemporaries, the European schoolmen, he does not look at economic activity in normative terms. Having studied its positive aspects, Ibn Khaldun looks at the transition from a closed economy to more highly developed forms of social organization.

His notion of property, to which he devotes a whole chapter, relies upon concrete notions and upon a certain distinction between use-value and exchange-value. The importance of those notions in modern political economy is well known. Ibn Khaldun devotes lengthy passages to the question of supply and demand and their effects on prices. He also sketches a theory of value based upon the quantity of labour required for the production of an object. He stresses that precious metals do not in themselves constitute wealth. They are merely symbols, means of exchange which in themselves have no value: 'It should be known that treasures of gold and silver ... are no different from other minerals. ... It is civilization that produces them in abundance or causes them to be in short supply.'[12]

Ibn Khaldun's conception of the world is not only synthetic, but eminently evolutionary: 'The conditions of the world and of nations, their customs and sects, does not persist in the same form or in a constant manner. There are differences between them according to days and periods, and changes from one condition to another.'[13] The world is not immutable. On the contrary, it is constantly being transformed, the principle of change being inscribed in the very nature of things. The theme of life and death appears frequently in Ibn Khaldun's work. He often draws a comparison between the evolution of empires and the life of a man: 'The life span of a dynasty corresponds to the life span of an individual; it grows up, passes into an age of stagnation and thence into retrogression.'[14] This is no mere allegory, but a profoundly meaningful comparison. Life is in fact one of the most striking demonstrations of the fact that the whole of reality is in flux. Life cannot but be evolution. The negation of evolution is the negation of life itself. A living organism always contains within it the seeds of its destruction. The inevitable development of life leads to the inevitable development of death. The same applies to dynasties: 'It is natural for the causes of senility to affect the dynasty. ... If, then, senility is something natural in the life of a dynasty, it must come about in the same way natural things come about, exactly as senility affects the temper of living beings. Senility is a chronic disease that cannot be cured or made to disappear, because it is something natural, and natural things do not change.'[15]

The dialectical theme of life and death and of their simultaneous unity and opposition is central to Ibn Khaldun's conceptions. Indeed, it is impossible not to be struck by the profoundly dialectical nature of Ibn Khaldun's thought. As we have seen, he does not regard reality as a random accumulation of isolated or independent objects, but as a coherent totality of phenomena which are organically connected and which necessarily and reciprocally determine one another. He also stresses that this complex combination is subject to an equally complex process of evolution.

We recognize here the two primary characteristics of the Hegelian dialectic: the principle of reciprocal action and interconnection, and the principle of universal change and continuous development.

The concept of *'asabiya*, which lies at the heart of Ibn Khaldun's thought, is a force whose nature and evolution are basically dialectical. It is the product of two antagonistic elements: tribal egalitarianism and the power of the chieftain. The development of *'asabiya* is a dialectical process: in an attempt to increase his power the chieftain undermines the communal structures on which it is based. The development of the contradiction between the old tribal structure and the power of the aristocracy leads to the emergence of something new: the development of the state, a form of organization which is superior to the tribe. To take another example: *'asabiya* is the motor of the development of the state, yet in creating the state it destroys itself. The creation and the power of state structures are indissociably connected with the factors that will destroy them. The emergence of a highly developed social and economic organization results in the destruction of *'umran badawi*, which was one of the preconditions for the development of *'asabiya*. As soon as the ruler achieves power, he becomes involved in a struggle against the very forces on which his power is based.

To take one final example of Ibn Khaldun's dialectical logic: in his attempt to extend his power over his tributaries, the ruler has to recruit mercenaries, and in order to pay them he has to increase taxation. The subsequent downturn in economic activity leads to a fall in tax revenue and he tries to compensate for this by increasing taxes once more. Poverty and discontent lead to rebellions. But in order to suppress them, he needs still more mercenaries, more taxes to pay for these, thereby provoking new revolts—and so on. For Ibn Khaldun, the study of the destiny of political entities is the study of the many intertwined and dialectical contradictions which cause them to develop, change and decay.

The frequency with which Ibn Khaldun uses dialectical arguments, especially in the most original passages in his work, proves that they are closely related to his basic intellectual method. It is not anachronistic to describe his thought as dialectical. Once we realize that his conceptions are in fact dialectical, we begin to see their true importance and significance. Once we realize that a concept like *'asabiya* is characterized by an internal contradiction, we begin to understand its origins and its role as the motor of the development and break-up of the state.

It would, however, be pointless to look for a coherent exposition of the philosophical theory of the dialectic in Ibn Khaldun's work. The interaction between the various elements of social, and economic life is clearly described. But Ibn Khaldun never develops philosophical arguments as to the unity of opposites and the struggle between them, even though the concept itself is essential to his thought. The comparison between the evolution of the state and that of human life is of considerable significance, but it remains largely implicit.

Ibn Khaldun's dialectic appears rather in the context of empirical observations and specific historical comments. Similar remarks could be applied to the passages which seem to anticipate historical materialism. Here again, we find empirical conceptions which are not based upon philosophical arguments. They relate only to historical considerations. In contrast, the long passages Ibn Khaldun devotes to philosophy and religion are inspired by traditional forms of philosophical argument and by the religious orthodoxy of the day.

The Emergence of the Science of History

We now have to look at the origin of these dialectical and materialist themes in Ibn Khaldun's work. It might be possible to trace them back to the work of certain Greek and Arab thinkers. Thus, the theory that movement is an essential characteristic of all things can be found in Aristotle's *Physics* and in Avicenna's *Tabi'yatt* and *Hudud*. It is quite possible to break down Ibn Khaldun's thought into its component elements, to reveal its metaphysical basis and trace it back to the theories put forward by various Arab philosophers and their Greek predecessors.

Mushin Mahdi, for instance, sees Ibn Khaldun as a *faylasuf*, a follower of the Islamic-Platonist tradition who developed a theory of history within the framework of the philosophical system developed by the Arab followers of Plato and Aristotle. We will have to come back to this point in some detail.

But it has to be pointed out from the start that Ibn Khaldun's materialist and dialectical arguments do not derive directly from that tradition. If he had really wanted to write a philosophical study, Ibn Khaldun would have tried to base his historical arguments upon the philosophical theories of his so-called predecessors. He was familiar with their work; after all, he did write a treatise on logic and a commentary on the work of Razes and Averroes before writing *The Muqaddimah*. But when he states or demonstrates the principles of his historical method, he practically never appeals to the authority of these great thinkers. As he himself puts it, his arguments are drawn from the nature of things themselves. According to Mushin Mahdi, the explanation for this discretion is that Ibn Khaldun thought that the philosophical basis of his work was obvious, that it was pointless to specify it and hence any statement of principles was superfluous. There is nothing in Ibn Khaldun's writings to support this dubious hypothesis. There is no obvious link between his

theses and those of philosophers who were solely concerned with normative arguments and who never tried to apply their theories to history.
Besides, how are we to explain the fact that, once he has finished dealing
with historical realities, Ibn Khaldun throws himself into lengthy and
explicit philosophical arguments in volume three of *The Muqaddimah*?
Reading these passages, one gets the impression that Ibn Khaldun is less
a supporter of the Islamic Platonist tradition than a strict supporter of
orthodoxy. Again, we will have to return to this problem.

Ibn Khaldun's historical method is basically empirical. It relies upon
observation of the nature of things, and does not derive directly from any
philosophical theory. This is why his work seems so extraordinarily
modern. Breaking with the methods of the schoolmen, he bases his arguments upon his own observations and upon carefully verified information. Ibn Khaldun is not trying to write a Philosophy of History. He is
an extraordinarily acute observer of reality and his conceptions derive
from objective generalizations based upon his own observations and erudition.

He is able to make objective generalizations because he has no interest
in normative judgements, and no ideological prejudices. He resolutely
privileges rational observation over abstract reasoning. The origin of
these dialectical conceptions and arguments, which foreshadow historical materialism, is not to be found in any philosophical theory, but in
observation and in a truly scientific study of history. As Ibn Khaldun
intuitively realized, the reality of history is a dialectical process of
evolution.

In comparison with the historical thought of Antiquity and of the Arab
and Christian Middle Ages, Ibn Khaldun's work marks a decisive change
—no less than the emergence of the science of history.

Many authors, however, see *The Muqaddimah* as having a very different significance and argue that it is a work of philosophy. According to
Mushin Mahdi, for instance, Ibn Khaldun remained faithful to the principles of the traditional political philosophy which governed the Muslim
City, and basically wanted to advance knowledge of a real society that
was sick and imperfect. He sees Ibn Khaldun as a physician who studies
a sick body in order to cure it by treating it and by introducing reforms
that would bring it closer to the ideal society of political philosophy.
According to Mushin Mahdi, *The Muqaddimah* is intended to explain
those factors which prevent existing communities from evolving towards
the perfect regime.[1]

This appraisal of Ibn Khaldun's intentions is both debatable and unjustified. Ibn Khaldun never in fact suggests any remedies. He proposes neither reforms nor solutions. If the basic ambition of his work is, as Mushin Mahdi suggests, to reform society, why does he mention no reforms? And were there in fact any remedies for the sickness undermining the Maghreb?

Ibn Khaldun did, as we have seen, have a political ideal, but as his research progresses he gradually abandoned his illusions. Having studied its social and political organization in depth, he obviously realized that the causes of the unrest in North Africa were inseparable from its fundamental structures. Whilst there is no reason to doubt that Ibn Khaldun believed in the traditional ideal of the Muslim City, there are no grounds for arguing that *The Muqaddimah* is merely the product of normative intentions or reformist ambitions. Indeed, it is probably wrong to do so.

According to other authors, Ibn Khaldun's work is a cyclical philosophy of history valid for all periods and all countries, and which in a sense prefigured Paul Valéry's celebrated text on the mortal nature of civilizations. If they are to be believed, Ibn Khaldun's world view can be reduced to the following general propositions: history is simply a repeated cycle of the evolution of civilization and state, with each cycle ending in decline and catastrophe. The development of each civilization leads to its collapse as the social solidarity on which the state is based is destroyed by the luxury that corrupts its citizens. Historical evolution is thus basically determined by psychological factors. Ibn Khaldun's philosophy is, then, extremely fatalistic and pessimistic. His cyclical concept of the eternal return prevents him from developing any truly historical thought.

Our examination of Ibn Khaldun's work means that we can invalidate this schema on a number of counts.

On the one hand, we have seen that the notion that psychological factors have a determinant role in history does not really correspond to anything in Ibn Khaldun's theories. On the other hand, we have demonstrated that his theories are not universally applicable and have no 'eternal value'. He stresses the differences between the Maghreb and the countries of the Middle East, pointing out that the crucial concept of *'asabiya* is specific to North Africa alone. But he also shows that *'asabiya* itself is not an eternal phenomenon: he argues that the same socio-political structure did once exist in the Middle East but had disappeared by the fourteenth century.

When Ibn Khaldun speaks in universal terms, he is simply making very general comments which are far removed from the theories he advances with regard to the Maghreb or certain periods in the Middle Ages. Such universalism is, of course, in accordance with the precepts of his religion. Thus, he argues that states have collapsed in the past and will continue to collapse in the future, but he does not argue that the causes and modalities of their decline are the same as those which brought down the kingdoms of the Maghreb: 'The authority of the dynasty at each stage becomes successively narrower than it had been at the beginning. This process continues, stage by stage, until the dynasty is destroyed. The fact can be exemplified by examination of any dynasty, large or small. This is how God proceeds with kingdoms until the pre-destined dissolution comes upon them as upon all his creatures. "Everything perishes except his face".' (Koran 28.88).[2]

Whilst it might be possible to argue that Ibn Khaldun's work contains a philosophy of history, that philosophy does not necessarily have any universal significance.

Ibn Khaldun's theories do not, then, represent an *a priori* metaphysic that is simply applied to world history. They derive from a rational study of conditions in the Maghreb between the ninth and fourteenth centuries. They are a historical synthesis of events that occurred in a specific place and at a specific time, rather than a philosophy of history.

Ibn Khaldun describes and explains the birth, maturity and death of the successive states that existed in the Maghreb throughout most of the Middle Ages. However, does not the fact that these successive phases are studied at such length in *The Muqaddimah* itself suggest that Ibn Khaldun did have a cyclical conception of history?

If that were the case, there would be nothing original about his work: the cyclical conception of temporality dominated historiography for a long time, the work of St Augustine being a notable exception. In philosophy, for instance, Aristotle, Plato and a number of Muslim thinkers all developed the thesis that historical phases were repeated in cycles. The belief that history was simply a process of eternal renewal and the myth of the eternal return stifled historical thought for centuries. If the essence of history is repetition, there can in fact be no point in looking for underlying causes. The notion of circular time blurs the distinction between past, present and future and considerably restricts man's historical role. He becomes merely an actor reciting a pre-written role. Men's view of their own evolution, of time and of history is always related to their conception of human action. The notion of linear and irreversible time was very slow to emerge. The idea that temporality defines the singularity of every event is essential to the development of modern historical thought. Once history is no longer seen as repetition, the notion of long-term historical evolution emerges and it becomes necessary to look for the immediate and underlying reasons for every event.

Ibn Khaldun's theories do emphasize cyclical phenomena and the close similarity between the destiny of the various Maghrebian states of the Middle Ages. Does this invalidate the claim that he is one of the greatest historians to have written prior to the nineteenth century? Is not his conception of history considerably less advanced and less modern than that of St Augustine?

The author of *The City of God* certainly considered time to be irreversible. For St Augustine, human history has a general meaning: although its different phases are not simply repeated one after the other, they remain so many stages in a general process of evolution, with each stage providing the starting point for the next. But this notion of evolution derives from religious conceptions rather than from any objective and rational generalizations on the basis of historical events. St Augustine is less concerned with discovering the meaning of secular history than with using selected facts from the real past to support the belief that man's history is a gradual evolution from Adam's sin to the Last Judgement. With St Augustine, historical thought actually regresses, in that divine intervention becomes the essential factor in history and the evolution of mankind becomes dependent upon a divinely ordained predestination.

Nowadays we consider cyclical conceptions as the complete antithesis of scientific historical thought because we have a broader perspective on the past, and because the major and absolutely unprecedented events of the nineteenth and twentieth centuries have given a new meaning to what once looked like slow and confused developments. At a time when historical evolution is speeding up and constantly changing, the subjective belief in history as a process of eternal renewal cannot help looking like the antithesis of history.

The fact that a historian writes of cyclical phenomena proves that his work is pre-scientific and pre-modern only in so far as the cycles he detects do not correspond to any real historical evolution and in so far as his cyclical conceptions prevent him from looking into the real causes of past events.

But Ibn Khaldun's analysis of the cyclical evolution of the Maghrebian states does not rely upon a metaphysics which is elaborated *a priori* and then applied to certain selected events that confirm it. He describes and studies a historical period which is *objectively* characterized by repeated attempts to establish a centralized monarchy and by the repeated decline of states after a brief period of stability. The repetition did take place: a series of states were established by a number of tribes which, despite their diversity, represented the same socio-political forces, and then they were undermined by the same internal contradictions.

For several centuries, this palingenesis was an objective reality; there were no long-term developments. The development of the internal contradictions was blocked and they could not develop into a higher stage.

Ibn Khaldun does not try to use historical arguments to justify a cyclical philosophy elaborated in abstract and absolute terms. He tries to explain a series of confused events, looks for causes, and arrives at a schema of cyclical phenomena. He makes objective and rational generalizations on the basis of events which really did occur over and over again. The cycle he describes does not, as we have seen, apply to North African civilization as a whole, but only to those tribal groups which established dynasties.

The medieval Maghreb is a mosaic of interacting tribes, all of which are evolving. Their evolution is sometimes simultaneous, but usually the tribes evolve at different rates. Its history is the product of their mutual interaction. As Ibn Khaldun shows, new tribal states develop in opposition to older states, but also in opposition to other tribes which are trying to extend their influence over conquered peoples. The victory of one tribe puts a more or less permanent end to the activities of its competitors. The establishment of a dynasty and the extension of its authority over a group of tribes prevents some of them from evolving and reduces others to servitude, but it also strengthens the dynasty's tribal allies. When the dynasty falls into decline, they are thus able to make a bid for power.

Ibn Khaldun does of course concentrate upon the model evolution of tribes which exemplify the complete cycle. But he also stresses that the vast majority of tribes still have very rudimentary forms of organization. Their development is therefore blocked by the influence of more powerful tribes. Ibn Khaldun shows that the chieftain's dominance over a group of tribes often blocks the development of forces which might otherwise have led them to a greater historical destiny: 'Meekness and willingness to pay imposts and taxes are obstacles to achieving royal authority.'[3] 'A tribe which, because it is closely allied to a dynasty, becomes submerged in luxury will never achieve royal authority.'[4]

He stresses that although the development of a tribe finds expression in a variety of phenomena, there is nothing inevitable about it. It can be blocked at any stage by an encounter with a more powerful tribe.

Ibn Khaldun does not, then, reduce the history of cyclical phenomena to the repeated evolution of a model-state moving automatically through the stages of youth, maturity and decline. He presents the history of the Maghreb, dominated as it is by tribal structures, as a struggle among interacting political organizations which are all trying to establish their supremacy but have all reached different stages of development. To put it metaphorically, Ibn Khaldun sees the history of the Maghreb not as the repetition of the life cycle of a single human being moving from youth to maturity and then to decline and death, but as a struggle between a group of men of different ages. The young try to shake off the authority of their elders and to overthrow the adults. Not all the young men will win and only a small number of them will be victorious, but all the old men are sure to be defeated sooner or later. Those who are in the prime of life are in the best position to force the young to obey them and so to take power from their elders.

There is nothing mechanical about Ibn Khaldun's view of North African history. It is the product of mutual interaction between tribal groups whose internal evolution is to a large extent determined by that interaction. Ibn Khaldun's conception of history combines a series of relatively independent causes and factors which evolve at different rates. It centres upon the interaction between the internal and external factors affecting each tribe in the complex mosaic of North Africa.

Despite the importance of the cyclical phenomena which did objectively characterise the Maghreb in the Middle Ages, Ibn Khaldun's conceptions do not derive from a circular notion of time. Writing as he was during a period of stagnation, he could not of course develop any clear notion of a long-term historical development consisting of qualitatively different stages. He does not, however, subscribe to the myth of eternal return. He stresses that history does not result from a play between eternally similar elements and is not a process of eternal renewal. Indeed, on several occasions he stresses the major changes that can occur: 'Often, someone who has learned a great deal of past history remains unaware of the changes that conditions have undergone. Without a moment's hesitation, he applies his knowledge of the present to historical information and measures the historical information by the things he has observed with his own eyes, although the difference between the two is great. Consequently, he falls into an abyss of error.'[5]

It will be recalled that Ibn Khaldun justifies his desire to look into the underlying causes of the history of his country and his times in terms of the importance of such major changes in historical conditions: 'When there is a general change in conditions, it is as if the entire creation had changed and the whole world had been altered, as if it were a new and repeated creation, a world brought into existence again. Therefore, there is need at this time that someone should systematically set down the situation of the world among all regions and races, as well as the customs and sectarian beliefs that have changed for their adherents.'[6]

It should also be recalled that a number of widespread ideologies in medieval Islam were based upon the theory that historical events were repeated in cycles. The Shi'ites and many Sufis (ascetic mystics) developed prophetic views because of their belief in history as a process of eternal renewal. If, as has sometimes been claimed, Ibn Khaldun's analysis derived from a cyclical conception of time, and if he thought that history consisted simply of a repetition of eternal cycles, he would surely have supported it by appealing to the authority of Sufi doctrine.

Not only does he make no allusion to cyclical beliefs in his study of the evolution of the Maghrebian state: on several occasions he criticises them harshly from a historical point of view. 'They mostly speak in riddles and parables. Occasionally, they make a minimum of explicit statements, or their commentators make explicit statements. ... They say that in pre-Islamic times there had been error and blindness. Truth and right made their appearance through prophecy. Prophecy was followed by the Caliphate, and the Caliphate, in turn, was followed by royal authority. Royal authority, then, reverted to tyranny, presumptuousness, and worthlessness. They said: And since it has been observed to be God's procedure to have things return to their original state, prophecy and truth will by necessity be revived through sainthood. Sainthood will be followed by the stage that properly comes after it (the Caliphate). This in turn will be followed by the time of the Antichrist, which will take the place of royal authority and the rule of power. Then, unbelief will return to the old position it occupied before the coming of the prophecy of Muhammad.'[7] Having discussed the obscurantism and contradictions of one 'prediction work' based upon such beliefs, Ibn Khaldun concludes that 'The most likely assumption is that the whole work is incorrect, because it has no scientific basis, astrological or otherwise.'[8]

Ibn Khaldun, then, condemns belief in prophecies based upon the theory of eternal return. He also restricts the field of application of his theories to determinate countries and periods. Finally, he demonstrates that North African history cannot be reduced to a simple or mechanical process and that it results from the interaction between a large number of tribes, each of which is subject to change. It would therefore be not only difficult but incorrect to reduce his thought to a cyclical philosophy of history. The schema for the evolution of a model state which develops, declines and dies does not derive from the projection of a philosophical theory on to historical reality, but from a rational observation of the facts and from rational and objective generalizations made on the basis of those facts.

As we shall see, Ibn Khaldun does put forward a number of philosophical arguments, notably in the third volume of *The Muqaddimah*. For the most part, they derive from doctrines which were quite widespread in the Muslim world of the fourteenth century and cannot be regarded as specific to Ibn Khaldun. Ibn Khaldun's historical thought is much richer than his philosophical conceptions. Looking at all the most original and important elements of his work, we have to conclude that he is a great historian and no philosopher.

According to some modern commentators *The Muqaddimah* is not a historical but a sociological work. This might be a minor observation, were it not that the notion of Ibn Khaldun as a mere *Kulturhistoriker*[9] is based upon a narrow and distorted view of his work.

Ibn Khaldun does of course place considerable emphasis on social and economic conditions and he is one of the first—if not the first—of thinkers to examine society in terms not purely practical or normative. But we have only to glance at the way certain sociologists classify his work to see that they have broken this down and reassembled it in terms of their own preoccupations.

Issaway,[10] for instance, has edited a selection of extracts from *The Muqaddimah* and arranged them as follows: 1) methodology, 2) geography, 3) economics, 4) public finance, 5) population, 6) state and society, 7) religion and politics, 8) knowledge and society, 9) theory of being and knowledge.

Ibn Khaldun never made any such methodical study of philosophical, social and economic questions. He wrote no such treatise. On the one hand, this classification derives from a very recent concept of sociology and political economy and, on the other hand, Ibn Khaldun's main ambition was to explain historical events and not to produce a methodical study of society as a whole. His approach is logical and methodical, provided that it is seen in terms of his true concerns. Thus, Ibn Khaldun never studies public finance as such. Having briefly demonstrated its importance in the life of the state, he discusses the financial problems that the government has to resolve as the state develops and relates them to other evolutionary factors which determine the strength or weakness of a dynasty at different stages in its development.

Ibn Khaldun concentrates upon political factors and their underlying causes. He is trying to understand the destiny of states and not to produce a description of all the different elements of social life. This explains the gaps in his sociological analysis: for example, he makes only a very brief study of the egalitarian tribe in which there is no *'asabiya* because, although widespread, such tribes cannot found states. He makes practically no mention of the tribal council (*jam'*), which was both a symbol and an expression of tribal egalitarianism, simply because it is not a major political force. On the other hand, he does make a detailed study of *'asabiya* which, as we have seen, is of considerable importance in the development of the state.

If we argue that the originality and importance of Ibn Khaldun's work are restricted to the overtly sociological passages found in it, we miss a vital feature of his thought: the attempt to locate the underlying causes of the historical events that occur as social structures evolve. The view that his writings can be divided into a philosophy and a history is a distortion of his thought and deprives it of most of its value. Ibn Khaldun does not paint a picture of social and economic conditions as a sort of backdrop against which events unfold. The important point is that he tries to explain events in terms of the evolution of their social and economic base. But, consciously or unconsciously, certain supporters of colonial ideology are reluctant to see a North African thinker as the creator of the fundamental and 'dangerous' science of history.

It is true that Ibn Khaldun seems somewhat uncertain as to the relationship between the study of civilization and the study of historical events, and that in some passages he seems to regard the former as an autonomous science auxiliary to historical research. But in other passages and in practice he stresses the unity of these two projects. He objected to the traditional conception of narrative history because it concentrated exclusively on important political events, and realized that the originality of his 'method' derived from the link that he established between the study of events and the study of social structures. 'I chose a remarkable and original method. In the work, I commented on civilization, on urbanization, and on the essential characteristics of human social organization, in a way that explains to the reader how and why things are as they are, and shows him how the men who constituted a dynasty came upon the historical scene.'[11] There can be no doubt but that Ibn Khaldun was fully aware that the originality of his conception of history lay in the combination of a study of *'umran* and of political and military events. It is his 'original method' that he regards as a science, not traditional narrative history.

In medieval Muslim civilization, the so-called 'Arab science' of history was no more scientific than rhetoric, poetry or religious jurisprudence. Narrative history was not classified as one of the intellectual sciences inherited from the Greeks, partly because it had considerable religious importance (history is the science of Islamic tradition) and partly because it did not conform to the Greek philosophers' definition of science. Being an enumeration of specific contingent facts chosen on the basis of subjective criteria, narrative history could not be considered a manifestation of scientific thought. On the contrary, it was one of the most typical forms of 'spontaneous thought'. In the chapter he devotes to the 'intellectual sciences',[12] Ibn Khaldun simply adopts this traditional classification, which excludes history on the grounds that it was unanimously regarded as a literary and narrative genre.

He does, on the other hand, regard his own conception of history as one of the intellectual or true sciences: 'The subject is in a way an independent science. This science has its own peculiar object—that is, human civilization and social organization. It also has its own peculiar problems—that is, explaining the conditions that attach themselves to the essence of civilization, one after the other. Thus, the situation is the same with this science as it is with any other science, whether it be a conventional (traditional) one or an intellectual one.'[13]

The modesty Ibn Khaldun shows here is noteworthy. Muslim thinkers held that there were three preconditions for the emergence of a new science: it had to have its own peculiar object (*mawdu'*), its own peculiar problems (*masa'il*) and its own goal (*ghaya*). Ibn Khaldun mentions these three requirements very briefly: his new science has an object—*'umran* or human society—and it has its own problems—the facts relevant to the essence of civilization (ie. historical events). But as for its goal, 'It leads to one result only: the simple verification of historical information.'[14]

It seems, although this is only a hypothesis, that Ibn Khaldun more or less consciously avoids raising the question of the status of his science at the philosophical level. In the passage we have cited he does no more than allude to the problem and looks at his science from an extremely narrow point of view, seeing it merely as a means to verify historical information. Traditionally, history was regarded as one of the 'Arab' or revealed sciences and it had considerable religious importance. Any attempt to prove that it was one of the intellectual sciences would have been regarded with suspicion by the Doctors of the Faith. To do so would have been a delicate and dangerous undertaking. It may be for this reason that Ibn Khaldun demoted the new science he had created to the status of an auxiliary discipline.

Whatever the explanation, this limited definition does not fit in with the great emphasis he places on the unity between the external form of history ('information about political events'[15]), its narrative and literary form, and its inner meaning, namely 'speculation and an attempt to get at the truth, subtle explanation of the causes and origins of existing things, and deep knowledge of the how and why of events.'[16] This notion of the inner or essential meaning of history is inseparable from the study of society. Here Ibn Khaldun is not simply outlining an auxiliary discipline. The new science he is talking about and which he invented is simply the science of history. History ceases to be a branch of literature and becomes a science. 'History, therefore, is firmly rooted in science. It deserves to be accounted a branch of science.'[17]

Taha Hussein has criticized De Slane for translating *'ilm* as 'science' and argues that it really means knowledge in a very general sense. He argues that the sentence should read: 'History, therefore, is firmly rooted in wisdom. It deserves to be accounted a branch of wisdom.' Strictly speaking, Taha Hussein is quite right, but his claim that Ibn Khaldun never intended to make history a science in any real sense rests upon an anachronism. In the fourteenth century, the concept of 'science' was very ill-defined, and the sciences were almost indistinguishable from philosophy.

It is not surprising that Ibn Khaldun could not formulate the concept of science with any clarity. Even today, history is not always regarded as a science. But what Ibn Khaldun sees as the essential or inner meaning of history does correspond closely to what has since the nineteenth century been known as historical science.

It certainly cannot be denied that Ibn Khaldun realized that his conception of history constituted a new branch of knowledge. His attitude is highly significant. In both the Muslim world and in the medieval Christian world, science was seen as a static whole which could neither be extended nor developed. It was thought impossible to use new discoveries to extend scientific knowledge. All that could be done was to learn, refine and adapt what was already known. The dogmatic belief that science was a finite body of knowledge was based upon an unbounded admiration for the Ancients, and reinforced by extremely powerful religious ideologies. In the Muslim world, for instance, innovation and research were considered synonymous with rashness and heterodoxy. The Koran was the perfect, intangible expression of knowledge. Ibn Khaldun's criticisms of his predecessors, his awareness of having created a new science or a new branch of knowledge show exceptional intellectual courage, as they were formulated at a time when paralysis was beginning to affect every area of life.

To sum up: history, in the sense that Ibn Khaldun uses the word, is indeed a science: it has all the characteristics that distinguish a science from an art or from any other intellectual discipline. The emergence of the science of history in the mid-fourteenth century, a period of intellectual stagnation and even decline, is a truly extraordinary event. We have to look, next, at what made it possible.

3
Historiography and the Rationalist Heritage

The emergence of the science of history in the work of a thinker who had no real followers and who wrote five hundred years before the emergence of history in Europe is a truly remarkable event. Ibn Khaldun's work is so obviously superior to that of any other historian writing before the nineteenth century that it is tempting to see him as a 'lone star' and his work as 'an astonishing book which is not related to anything else.'[1]

Ibn Khaldun was not a prophet, however, and there is nothing miraculous about *The Muqaddimah*.

Historical thought was much more important in the Arab world than in any other pre-industrial society. It was stifled in India and it atrophied in China. It certainly played an important part in the culture of the Christian world; but in the Arab countries of the Middle Ages it was absolutely essential to the intellectual formation of any 'gentleman'. It was important in fashionable and literary life, in political-administrative activities as well as in religious life. L.E. Gardet has pointed out that 'One of Islam's characteristic features is that it was for centuries steeped in history'.[2]

In most cases there is of course little qualitative difference between historical thought in the Greek and Roman world and in Muslim countries: in both cases, it took a literary or anecdotal form. But there are, so to speak, considerable quantitative differences. The importance of history in Muslim culture can be gauged from the fact that more than thirteen hundred books by Arab historians are recorded as having been produced between the ninth and the thirteenth centuries (this figure does not include summaries). History never penetrated cultural life in Greece, Rome, Byzantium or, *a fortiori*, medieval Western Europe to anything like the same extent. In the medieval Arab world, historiography was much more developed. This quantitative development is not unrelated to the qualitative mutation in historiography represented by Ibn Khaldun's work.

We have first to explain the great importance of history in Muslim culture.

Even before the appearance of Islam, the Arabs had shown a certain interest in historicity. Their oral literature shows the care with which they studied their genealogies and the importance they gave to epic accounts of tribal battles.

Like Christianity, and perhaps even more so, Muhammad's doctrine led to the emergence of a historical conception of man's life and destiny. The notion that time had a definite beginning and an end destroyed the cyclical conception of temporality and established an idea of time which encouraged the development of historical thought. Human history was no longer a process of repetition but one of evolution. Muhammad believed that his coming marked the end of a process punctuated by the appearance of other prophets. In a sense, that in itself allowed the historian Ibn Qutaybah to evaluate the importance of religion from the standpoint of universal evolution. Muhammad also asserted that his prophetic function depended upon his knowledge both of past history and of the future.

Despite its complexity, the Koran (which was originally written to be read by only a small group of men) could not provide any explicit answer to the many problems raised within a community that had grown to the size of a vast empire. The study of how the Prophet had behaved in different circumstances thus became a particularly important means of elucidating the judgements of the doctors of the law. Historians made considerable efforts to collect, discuss, verify and interpret the *hadiths* which, together with the Koran, formed the basis of the orthodox tradition. Obviously, the requirements of religion often blunted their critical abilities, but constant reference to spiritual and political history did forge thinkers for whom a basic historical approach was a constant necessity. In order to decide which *hadiths* were genuine, they had to use historical methods and textual criticism, and look critically at eye-witness accounts. In the ninth century, Bokhari collected almost three hundred thousand *hadiths*, but rejected all but a dozen of them after establishing that the others were false. So the historian's role was very important. He had to establish the details of every incident in the life of the Prophet and the circumstances surrounding it, gauge the relative accuracy of various accounts, and the authenticity of the texts. History thus became the science of Tradition. Its importance in Arab culture can be measured by the fact that the earliest surviving prose work in Arabic is a life of the Prophet written by Ibn Ishac in 763.

History was not, however, restricted to a purely religious function. The expansion of Islam was very different to that of Christianity, which was usually the work of poor people who made individual and often clandestine conversions. The expansion of Islam was spectacular, both in political and material terms. Right from the beginning, there was an organized state whose ruler, the Caliph, held religious, political and military powers. Especially in early times, the history of the Islamic religion is indistinguishable from political and military history, and the Muslim historian therefore had the task of writing accounts of the astonishing conquests which carried the Prophet's Word from Aquitaine to Turkestan. These historical accounts were also designed to fuel the enthusiasm of the defenders of the Faith. Books which used the political success of the faithful to prove the value of religion were responsible for many conversions.

The rulers and their court officials also required the historian to trace the history of the different races who made up the empire and to record the circumstances in which they had been converted: their legal and fiscal status differed greatly, depending upon whether they had been converted voluntarily or by force.

The historical events which followed the death of the Prophet, the wars of succession and the murder of the prophet's son-in-law Ali all had serious consequences and were studied in great detail.

With the general spread of culture and above all with the development of a civilization based upon the written word, history became even more important. Chinese papermaking and bookbinding techniques were brought to Baghdad at the end of the eighth century. Every ruler, every town and every mosque wanted a library. Rich private citizens took great pride in their collections of rare books. History held pride of place in these collections and it is said that the library of the Fatimids in Cairo contained almost two million books of all kinds, including no less than twelve hundred copies of Tabari's *History*. This passion for books did much to encourage the writing of history. Muslim historians had a wide readership and huge amounts of often accurate documentary material, even if they did sometimes misuse it. Historiography was without doubt one of the most distinguished and brilliant branches of Muslim intellectual life.

A vital part of Muslim culture, history was studied at elementary school and in institutes of higher education. History books were extremely popular with young people, and during the Middle Ages it was impossible to imagine a 'gentleman' who did not have a broad knowledge of history, if only because it allowed him to make sparkling conversation. Every speech was spiced with allusions to historical events and historical anecdotes and no one could afford not to know them. According to Ibn Khaldun, 'History serves to entertain large crowded gatherings.' A knowledge of history was a passport to social success, but it also brought down the blessing of Heaven on its possessor. Being an essential part of the 'Arab sciences', history was thought to lead to wisdom and to an understanding of matters of tradition and religious life. It also provided a training for political, administrative and military life. The famous Caliph Mohawiha inaugurated a tradition which was to be carried on by other Muslim rulers: during the first part of the night he was said to receive 'story-tellers' who recounted the great deeds of the Arabs and of other races, and explained to him the policies adopted by the rulers of the Ancient world. Having rested for the second third of the night, he would then have books dealing with war, tactics, strategy and the principles of government read to him until dawn. 'History is a discipline widely culti-vated among nations and races. It is eagerly sought after. The men in the street, the ordinary people aspire to know it. Kings and leaders vie for it.'[3]

History took many very different forms: biographies, especially of the Prophet, biographical dictionaries, town annals (the annals of Damascus, written in 1175, ran to eighty volumes), dynastic histories, chronicles, great universal histories—only the most famous of the many Muslim his-torians can be mentioned here. In the second half of the eighth century, Ibn Ishac and el-Ouaquidi produced works dealing primarily with the life of the Prophet. Ibn Qutaybah, Dinawara and Yaqoubi inaugurated the genre of universal history, whilst Baladhori devoted himself to writ-ing the history of Islam and its conquests. But the true founder of Mus-lim historiography, to whom all later historians refer, was Tabari (839-923) who wrote an immense history of the world, beginning with Adam and ending with the tenth century. His work is an immense source of documentation and displays a real feel for accuracy and truth. Although he usually restricts himself to relating events and traditions, he was also capable of writing colourful and fluent narratives. Mention should also be made of Couli's memoirs of the Abassid dynasty and of

Thabit Ben Sinan's detailed history of the tenth century. The widely-travelled and open-minded Masiudi produced one of the most interesting histories of the period. The historians of the thirteenth century included Ibn Kallikan, Prince Ibn el-Athir and Abul Fida, who were all primarily biographers.

Historiography was thus highly developed in the medieval Muslim world. Ibn Khaldun's work is not, then, an aberration, but the culmination of a long-standing historical-literary tradition. His thought took shape against this background, and the abundant documentation upon which *The Muqaddimah*'s comparative method is based derives largely from the considerable historical output that was so typical of the Muslim world.

Ibn Khaldun's work is not, however, simply a continuation of this fertile tradition. *The Muqaddimah* represents a real mutation in historical thought. Its author was the first historian to look for the underlying causes of events in economic conditions and in the evolution of social structures.

The conception of history evolved by Ibn Khaldun is so novel and revolutionary that its importance was not really appreciated. His contemporaries and later Arab historians revered Ibn Khaldun, but the aspects of his work they most admired were those closest to traditional conceptions of history. The only other author to have studied historical developments in terms of social and economic factors was Qudamah b. Jafar, who lived in the tenth century. But Franz Rosenthal, who mentions him as the only example of an Arab historian who reminds one of Ibn Khaldun, comes to the conclusion that there is no connection between their work. Ibn Khaldun is not known to have had any predecessors, and there can be no real doubt as to his originality.

The material he used derived partly from his own erudition, but mainly from his own observations and from his concrete experience as a politician. What distinguishes him from other historians is his interest in causality. Not content with immediate causes, he looked for underlying causes in areas ignored by traditional historical thought. If, on the surface, history is no more than information about historical events, its inner meaning involves speculation and an attempt to get at the truth, subtle explanations of the causes and origins of existing things, and deep knowledge of the how and why of events. 'Showing how' is the basic ambition of Ibn Khaldun, and that ambition determined his method. 'I commented on civilization ... in a way that explains to the reader how and why things are as they are.'[4] 'The normative method for distinguishing right from wrong in historical information on the grounds of inherent possibility or absurdity, is to investigate human social organization, which is identical with civilization. ... If we do that, we shall have a normative method for distinguishing right from wrong and truth from falsehood in historical information by means of a logical demonstration that admits of no doubts.'[5]

In his account of military operations and of the causes of victory, Ibn Khaldun seems to anticipate Spinoza by three hundred years: 'Superiority in war is, as a rule, the result of hidden causes. The occurrence of opportunities as the result of hidden causes is what is meant by the word "luck".'[6] Elsewhere he writes that 'No one can stand up against the authority of the truth, and the evil of falsehood is to be fought with enlightening speculation.'[7]

Although Ibn Khaldun is one of the few historians writing before the nineteenth century to have taken rationalism as far as this, other thinkers associated with the great rationalist movement which forms the most brilliant branch of medieval Muslim philosophy made similar, if not greater, efforts in domains such as the natural sciences, medicine, chemistry and mathematics.

From the seventh century onwards, the great economic expansion, the intense commercial activity and the great social transformations that resulted from the establishment of the Arab empire went hand in hand with major intellectual developments. The active and well-travelled merchant aristocracy of the great cities saw religion as a dynamic and stimulating ideology rather than as a form of renunciation. Some famous theologians such as Muhammad Shaibani, one of the founders of the Hanafite rite, developed theories similar to those that the Calvinists were to elaborate three hundred years later in Europe: it is the duty of the religious to succeed in business, profits are a gift from Heaven; becoming wealthy is a means of praising and serving God.[8]

In the intellectual field, practical research and scientific investigation were encouraged and the rationalist movement therefore spread. It was stimulated by the scientific and philosophical heritage of Greek thought: the Arabs rescued it from oblivion and preserved it from what would otherwise have been almost certain destruction. A number of classical Greek works were translated and edited with commentaries. But far from simply translating and imitating Greek thought, the Arabs enriched it by adapting it to new circumstances. By breathing life into the classics,

Arab authors in fact created something new. The combination of elements of Greek philosophy and Islamic religion gave birth to a new current of ideas.

Several great Arab philosophers were also scientists in the true sense of the word. Following the path of rationalism, they rejected mythical or religious explanations in at least some areas and consciously began to explore reality. Although there were a few exceptions (like Razi, the great doctor and philosopher, who appears to have come very close to atheism), true disciples of the Greek materialists were very rare. Few thinkers were truly anti-religious, but many others rejected obscurantism and went ahead with their research, convinced that a rational quest for truth would confirm the revelations of religion. Al-Kindi, al-Farabi, Ibn Sina (Avicenna), and, in the West, Ibn Bajja (Avenpace) all worked along these lines, as did Ibn Rochd (Averroes), the last of the great rationalist philosophers. Inspired by a boundless faith in the strength of reason and the rationality of the world, he argued brilliantly that there was no real contradiction between religion and reason. He shed great light upon the symbols, mysteries and miracles he rejected, at least for those capable of grasping the subtleties of his thought.

Ibn Khaldun was greatly influenced by these thinkers. In his youth, he was influenced by the teaching of Abelli, the great logician. Later, when he was living in Granada, he wrote commentaries on the work of Ibn Rochd and Razi. It is certain that the concern for understanding and for investigating underlying causes that characterises his historical method derives largely from the work of the great rationalist thinkers. Most of *The Muqaddimah* bears the mark of rationalism and its influence is particularly clear in those passages devoted to criticisms of historiography.

The link between Ibn Khaldun's historical work and the thought of the great rationalists is not straightforward, however. They wrote long before Ibn Khaldun and are typical of the period between the ninth and eleventh centuries. The great rationalist current gradually dried up, despite a final flowering in the work of Ibn Rochd (1126-1198). For more than a century, a reactionary movement had been developing in religion, and various mystical tendencies overcame rationalism.

Some authors, such as Mushin Mahdi, argue that Ibn Khaldun is a direct heir to the rationalist philosophers, or even that he is the last of them. But although it has the advantage of simplicity, it is difficult to support this thesis. In the long passages he devoted to philosophical problems, Ibn Khaldun looks much more like a supporter of orthodoxy, or even of the theories put about by religious reactionaries, than an heir of the rationalists or Ibn Rochd, even though he had studied the latter's work. As a historian, the author of *The Muqaddimah* was clearly influenced by rationalist works written several centuries before his time; but he was also influenced by the reactionary religious movement that was at its height in the fourteenth century and which was perhaps stronger in North Africa than anywhere else.

The reasons for this obscurantist reaction are complex. It was to a large extent a result of the downturn in economic and social development in the Muslim world as a whole. Islam had once been a dynamic religion, but it was now becoming an oppressive ideology. Religious thought stagnated as the society around it became paralyzed. It was also influenced by the ruling classes' fears of progressive interpretations of religion.

Until roughly the beginning of the eleventh century, the doctors of the law (*ulama*) had to show a certain tolerance towards free thinkers, who were sometimes supported by certain rulers. But that tolerance came to an end when political, social and economic difficulties in the Maghreb introduced movements which found their ideological expression in major heresies. Despite the subtlety of their heterodoxy, their dissident nature was enough to attract discontented elements. The cause of orthodoxy thus gradually came to be identified with that of the ruling classes who, in order to ensure that they had reliable officials and sympathetic judges, encouraged the religious leaders to use their influence in the schools. The *madaris*, which had originally been liberal private colleges, became tools for the surveillance of intellectuals and bases for a generalized reaction against the scientific and rationalist movement. Gradually, theological preoccupations came to dominate the whole of intellectual life. Any research which offended against religion was banished.

This religious reaction was not directed against the mystical movements which called upon men to renounce the world and escape from reality: these represented no great threat from a social point of view. Sufism, a mystical doctrine influenced by Christian monasticism, Persian illuminism, and the cult of local saints spread rapidly amongst both the rural and the urban masses. This mysticism was always fairly favourably regarded and was finally integrated into orthodoxy by the works of Ghazzali, the arch-enemy of the rationalist movement in philosophy. Sufism then took on a major role in intellectual life as a whole. Under its influence, teaching in the *madaris*, which had already become purely scholastic, declined into illuminism and anti-Arab speculation.

From this point onwards, the intellectual life of the Muslim world was increasingly characterized by a decline in scientific research and by a return to traditional literary formulae. The numbing effect of the spread of mysticism combined with traditional piety to produce increasing intolerance: the social prescriptions of religious law were interpreted in the strictest sense possible.

The eleventh-century Maghreb was a particularly devout country in that it followed the austere Malikite rite. Conditions were not favourable to the survival of the rationalist tradition. The enlightened education Ibn Khaldun received in his youth was very much the exception. He had the good fortune to enjoy the broad education he recommends for others because of his family background. Its Andalusian origins may also have helped. The social position of his family meant that he himself could have access to the thought of the great rationalists even though it had long been banned from public schools. In the pious and narrow-minded atmosphere of Tunis, the arrival of Andalusian thinkers and intellectuals at the Marinid court must have seemed like an extraordinary breath of fresh air. We can therefore well understand the joy the young Ibn Khaldun found in knowledge when Abelli, a family guest, introduced him to logic and rationalism. Ibn Khaldun's rationalism is very exceptional for his time. It is a reflection of his family background, a social rank which made him relatively independent and, of course, of his own efforts and intellectual gifts.

The Effect of Religious Reaction

Ibn Khaldun should not be seen, however, as a rationalist philosopher who had somehow strayed into the fourteenth century. Although greatly influenced by Abelli and others in his youth, he was also influenced by the religious reaction. His membership of the ruling class, his status as a great landowner and his political role all made him lean towards orthodoxy. Moreover, as a judge and preacher, he belonged to the social group most strongly behind the movement towards reaction and mysticism. The ground for his retreats in the sanctuary of the mystic Abu Madyan and for his conversion to Sufism had presumably been long prepared by the example of a father who devoted much of his life to research into mysticism.

Ibn Khaldun's involvement with the mystical movement explains the presence of strikingly anti-rationalist arguments in *The Muqaddimah*. There is a striking contrast between the passages marked by classic rationalism and those marked by mystical obscurantism.

Ibn Khaldun never hesitates to condemn the 'errors' and 'dangerous writings' of Averroes and Avicenna in the most violent terms, even though he had once admired them. He even goes so far as to question the value of logic and philosophy as such: 'What use do these sciences and the pursuit of them have?'[1]

Turning away from the enthusiasms of his youth, he condemns logic itself, not for its formalism, but because it is a vehicle for rationalism and threatens tradition and the dogma that 'The intellect has nothing to do with the religious laws and its views.'[2] Although he asserts the primacy of the principle of causality at the beginning of *The Muqaddimah*, he finally rejects on religious grounds the principle of the intelligibility of reality. He seems to argue that the ways of God are unfathomable and to want to defend the omnipotence of God against the claims of militant rationalism. He condemns those who try to go beyond sensual perception and visible phenomena in an attempt to reach the true essence of things, that being the realm of the divine: 'Existence is too wide to be explained by such a view. "And He creates what you do not know".'[3] When he is dealing with actual historical problems on the other hand, he has no hesitation in stating that 'The accidents involved in every manifestation of nature and intellect deserve study. Any topic that is understandable and real requires its own special science.'[4]

Conversely, he attempts to prove that man cannot form concepts in any adequate manner and that he cannot distinguish between good and evil or true and false without the help of revealed laws: 'The essence of the *spiritualia* are completely unknown. One cannot get at them, nor can they be proven by logical arguments.'[5] Logic cannot grasp metaphysical realities and merely describes man's ability to think. It is therefore 'a technical procedure and can be dispensed with in most cases.'[6]

Such explicit condemnations of philosophy invalidate Mushin Mahdi's hypothesis that Ibn Khaldun was basically a philosopher working in the Islamic Platonist tradition.

Ibn Khaldun even goes so far as to recommend that his readers refrain from the study of the sciences: 'We must refrain from studying these things, since such restraint falls under the duty of the Muslim not to do what does not concern him. The problems of physics are of no importance for us in our religious affairs or our livelihoods. Therefore, we must leave them alone.'[7] He then recommends that the reader should take refuge in religion and trust to divine inspiration: 'If you are . . . hampered in your understanding of problems . . . entrust yourself to God's mercy. . . . If you do that, God's helpful light will shine upon you and show you your objective.'[8] When it comes to history, however, he argues that man must rely upon his own judgement and that all truths can be perceived by the intellect.

Ibn Khaldun devotes long passages to upholding mystical theories and to championing religious reaction. Other passages which, although shorter, are not without their importance bear witness to his open-mindedness and to the faith in rationalism which inspires most of his work.

These contradictions raise a major problem which most commentators have failed to detect, or have simply avoided. Being primarily concerned with bringing out the modernism of Ibn Khaldun's work—and they are of course right to do so—most of them see him as a rationalist philosopher and ignore the many passages which contradict that view. But Ibn Khaldun is no Descartes or Montesquieu.

In view of their length and their importance, it is remarkable how little effect the passages inspired by religious reaction have on Ibn Khaldun's historical method as such. On the other hand, Volume Three of *The Muqaddimah*, which deals mainly with philosophical problems, jurisprudence, theology and literature is completely dominated by religious and mystical theories. Although the mystical influence appears to be restricted to these areas, it cannot be ignored.

Ibn Khaldun does not apply his scientific method in the systematic account of the various domains of spiritual and intellectual life given in Volume Three of *The Muqaddimah*. Religion becomes the touchstone for all his judgements, and they are all value judgements. As a historian, Ibn Khaldun subscribes implicitly and at times explicitly to a rationalist philosophy, but as a philosopher he is a convinced follower of Ghazzali. In his hostility towards philosophy he goes even further than Ghazzali, arguing that it cannot even be a servant of theology.

It is, however, obvious that Ibn Khaldun's main contribution to science—and this is the source of his greatness—does not derive from his religious attitude or from his orthodox theological training. On the contrary, it derives from the work of the rationalists.

How are we to explain the existence of two such different intellectual attitudes in the same book? There is no interaction between the two: these contrasting intellectual attitudes apply to two distinct areas. How are we to explain this clear-cut distinction?

It has sometimes been argued that Ibn Khaldun was a freethinker who allayed the suspicions of powerful and intolerant bigots by masking his true opinions under arguments drawn from mysticism. In his discussion of historical problems that have religious implications, he does more than once give the impression that he is breaking off the argument and refusing to state his opinions clearly. At other times, he takes refuge behind the contradictory opinions of third parties. It has therefore been claimed that he is using Ibn Rochd's method of *taqiya*, which denies access to the author's innermost thoughts to anyone who cannot follow a philosophical argument. But Ibn Khaldun does not seem to disagree with any point of dogma. And although marked by rationalism, his historical comments are both quite comprehensible and to the point.

There is absolutely no basis for the hypothesis that Ibn Khaldun was a free-thinker wearing a mask of orthodoxy. If he were such, how could he have held important religious positions during a period of intolerance? He would surely have refused them if their intellectual implications had been intolerable to him. His contemporaries, meanwhile, stress that he had the reputation of being very devout and of being a convinced believer in Sufi doctrine and in Malikism.

When Ibn Khaldun returned to Tunis in 1378, after having written most of *The Muqaddimah*, he did fall foul of Ibn Arafa, the mufti. Some modern commentators see his departure for Cairo in 1382 as a flight from a cabal organized by Ibn Arafa and his religious supporters.

There is no factual basis for this accusation of free-thinking. The quarrel between the two men seems to have resulted from personal difference, from a rivalry between teacher and courtier. There were also more specifically political reasons for Ibn Khaldun's departure from Tunis: Abul Abbas, the Sultan of Tunis, had just declared war, and his enemies included the Dawawidah, amongst whom Ibn Khaldun had played such an important role. Perhaps he was reluctant to fight against his old friends. Perhaps he had been asked to win them over, had failed to do so and therefore fled in fear of being disgraced. The attractions of a great intellectual centre may also have had a lot to do with his departure for Cairo.

There is no reason to doubt Ibn Khaldun's piety, and he was never a victim of religious intolerance. Indeed, when he settled in Egypt, which was much more tolerant than the austere and pious Maghreb, he was noted and even criticized for the intransigence of his religious zeal.

It is also possible to explain the contradictions in Ibn Khaldun's thought in terms of a change in his opinions. According to this view, Ibn Khaldun studied the rationalist philosophers in his youth but then rejected his earlier interests as being impious and devoted himself to religion. Most of his philosophical and anti-rationalist arguments are to be found in Volume Three of *The Muqaddimah*; and we know that these later sections were written in Cairo, long after the first two volumes.

Ibn Khaldun's intellectual views probably did change considerably as he grew older. In his youth, he was as we saw greatly influenced by the rationalist philosophers of Fez, and particularly by Abelli. It is possible that he later rejected theories to which he had once been attracted because of his lack of experience. Thus, he states that 'The science of logic ... contains things that are contrary to the religious laws. ... This science has only a single fruit, namely, it sharpens the mind in the orderly presentation of proofs and arguments, so that the habit of excellent and correct arguing is obtained. ... Therefore, the student of it should be aware of its pernicious aspects as much as he can. Whoever studies it should do so only after he is saturated with the religious law and has studied the interpretation of the Koran and jurisprudence. No one who has no knowledge of the Muslim religious sciences should apply himself to it. Without that knowledge, he can hardly remain safe from its pernicious aspects.'[9]

Ibn Khaldun's life in Cairo was increasingly dominated by his religious and legal activities. Perhaps his leanings towards mysticism were also strengthened by a great personal loss: his wife and children were drowned when the ship taking them from Tunis to Cairo was wrecked in 1384.

Ibn Khaldun taught the religious sciences in a number of important schools. In 1398, he was even appointed head of the Baybars Institute, a famous Sufi foundation. On several occasions, he was appointed to the Malikite judgeship and was, he says, criticized for the austerity and zeal he showed as a judge. An intransigent puritan, he even had the taverns closed down. Those voluptuous feasts in the Alhambra gardens were a thing of the distant past. His austerity was not always favourably regarded, and he was removed from his position as judge on more than one occasion. He appears to have felt very bitter about the loss of his position.

Apart from the extraordinary episode of his meeting with Tamerlane in 1401, the latter part of Ibn Khaldun's life appears to have been that of a pious and austere old man who was concerned primarily with theology and the religious sciences. It is not, then, surprising that most of the additions and alterations to *The Muqaddimah* relate to the third volume, which deals with intellectual and spiritual matters, or that they seem anti-rationalist and reactionary compared with his work as a whole.

Although only to be expected, the effects of old age do not, however, explain everything. Even before he began to write *The Muqaddimah*, Ibn Khaldun had taught the religious sciences and held posts in the judiciary. He was already greatly influenced by the Sufi mystics: the periods he spent in retreat in Abu Madyan's sanctuary are adequate proof of this. Yet none of that prevented him from writing an admirably rationalist work which is dominated by an attempt to discover the underlying causes of political events. And if Ibn Khaldun was consciously rejecting the philosophical enthusiasms of his youth, surely he would have altered the rationalist passages (those dealing with historical method) in order to bring them into line with the later sections?

It is not in fact possible to make any radical distinction between these two aspects of Ibn Khaldun's thought. Nor is it possible to explain away one or other of his intellectual attitudes. It is inaccurate to suggest that he was a rationalist philosopher; Volume Three of *The Muqaddimah* contradicts any such view. It is equally absurd to see him only as a mystic; that argument flies in the face of the most original aspects of his work. Contradictory as they may be, both elements have to be taken into account.

The only valid approach is to look at Ibn Khaldun's thought dialectically and to see it as a contradictory body of work. Philosophically, Ibn Khaldun was a pious and strict Muslim for whom knowledge of the supra-sensible world would leave no room for the exercise of reason and whose belief in divine revelation was absolute. But when it came to looking at the concrete world, Ibn Khaldun argued as an empiricist, for methodological rather than doctrinal reasons. Though no rationalist in any philosophical sense, his training as a logician allowed him to go beyond mere statements of fact and to arrive at a truly scientific method. It helped him to reach materialist conclusions but did not imply any questioning of his religious convictions.

Taken as a whole, Ibn Khaldun's thought does not, then, form a coherent system. It would in any case be anachronistic to ascribe to a fourteenth-century thinker problems and solutions which were simply not available to him. The 'materialism or idealism' dilemma is a very recent one and it did not arise in Ibn Khaldun's day. We have to assume that what *for us* is a fundamental problem was for a fourteenth-century thinker very ill-differentiated. He would not even be aware of the contradictions in his position. When we read statements such as 'It should be known that differences of condition among people are the result of the different ways in which they make their living',[10] we are now reminded of a whole philosophical system. But for Ibn Khaldun, there were no such philosophical implications: it is simply a rational generalization arrived at on the basis of many observations and much fruitful work.

These contradictions are by no means peculiar to Ibn Khaldun. The thought of many medieval writers, be they Arabs, Jews or Christians, is typified by a similar lack of overall cohesion. They frequently indulged both in philosophical arguments more or less tied to theology, and in sciences that used empirical methods to investigate reality. Although it was not realized at the time, the latter did imply a certain materialism. Any thinker who was both a philosopher and a scientist was therefore torn between two contradictory ideological tendencies.

Despite his devout mysticism, Ibn Khaldun now looks very different from any other thinker of the classical or the medieval period. His writings now look strikingly modern. His main concerns, or at least those which now seem the most original and which he himself considered the most novel and personal, are in fact those of a twentieth-century philosopher. Ibn Khaldun was basically raising the same problems as any modern historian, and was using similar methods to resolve them: he looked for underlying causes in social and economic structures. A modern historian is of course far better equipped to solve such problems. He is working in the twentieth century, a hundred years after the most important event in history—the industrial revolution—and therefore has a much broader and complex perspective than that available to Ibn Khaldun.

Ibn Khaldun did succeed none the less in addressing the problems of what is now regarded as *the* method for historical research. His conception of history as being dominated by economic and above all social problems is almost as broad as our modern conception. Ibn Khaldun did not of course have the conceptual tools of the modern historians, but *The Muqaddimah* still represents a strong reaction against what might be termed anecdotal history. For a twentieth-century historian, this fourteenth-century thinker remains a man with recognizably similar concerns, a fellow worker and, in some ways, a master.

We do not normally find such modernism in the thinkers of the past, except perhaps in the very greatest of them, and they are usually philosophers. Without wishing to underestimate their value, it has to be said that Ibn Khaldun's modernism and his superiority over his contemporaries are much more significant. Philosophy developed long before history: even in Antiquity, thinkers were able to deal with the great problems of metaphysics, and even today their writings have lost none of their value. But unlike philosophy, history could not work at a purely abstract level. There were many obstacles in its path and it developed very slowly. Basically, modern historical thought dates only from the nineteenth century. The unexpected appearance of an authentically modern conception of history in the fourteenth century thus poses a truly exceptional problem.

Ibn Khaldun's concern for understanding is quite different from the usual preoccupations of a professional historian who is writing an account of events to which he himself is indifferent. Ibn Khaldun was a politician, a soldier and a diplomat. He was a minister and a councillor, an eye witness to historical events. He himself had instigated historical events and altered their course. He had been personally affected by the decline of the Maghreb. He realized that his personal setbacks were simply minor aspects of a general phenomenon and he wanted to *understand* that phenomenon. Ibn Khaldun was a diplomat, and his sense of history was sufficiently developed for him to look beyond current events and to go back in time to find precedents, to discover causes and events similar to those he had seen with his own eyes. He became a historian because he was a man of action who sought to understand his destiny. He thus introduced new elements into historical thought.

In order to understand and in order to move from immediate to underlying causes, he had to broaden the perspective usually adopted by historians. As a statesman, he knew that the outcome of history is not really decided in palaces or on battlefields. Having been trained as a philosopher and a logician, he looked for causal factors in various aspects of social and economic life. Philosophers, moralists and theologians had, of course, often commented upon such topics. But their comments were basically normative and abstract; they described society as it should have been and took very little interest in society as it really was. Being a man of action, Ibn Khaldun looked more at concrete realities.

Such arguments provide, however, only a partial explanation of how the science of history could emerge in the work of a fourteenth-century Maghrebian. Ibn Khaldun was not the first man of action to have taken to writing history. Thucydides was elected a General and took part in the Peloponnesian wars. But he did not try to explain historical developments in terms of concrete social and economic developments. He was interested in the rational motives behind men's actions.

Ibn Khaldun wanted to understand, but so, surely, did all those other thinkers who had for centuries been pondering over the destiny of men and society? Why do their writings not have the same interest as Ibn Khaldun's work? Despite their value, they are still marked by outdated intellectual methods: a modern historian's approach to the Peloponnesian war is very different from that of Thucydides, and the questions he asks about that war are very different to those asked by the Athenian historian.

In his approach to history, however, Ibn Khaldun does think and argue like a *modern scientist*. The questions he asks are basically those that we are now asking and the causes he uncovers are very similar to those which interest us. It is this modern scientific attitude that makes Ibn Khaldun so very different from most medieval thinkers. But for all that he was still a man of the fourteenth century, and no less an important part of his intellectual activity was closely connected with his religion. Because of his religion, he raised problems which others before him had already formulated in much more secular and rational terms. Ibn Khaldun's originality lies not only in the modernism of his historical thought, but also in the hiatus between his scientific approach to history and his religious convictions.

Given that for centuries little distinction was made between scientific activity and religious speculation, the same contradiction applies to all the scientists of the past. But in their work the contradiction is much less pronounced than it is in Ibn Khaldun. From a scientific point of view, these philosopher-scientists were far less modern than Ibn Khaldun; but they were also much less influenced by religion.

We can now see the split between the scientist and the mystic in Ibn Khaldun very clearly. In the work of certain other thinkers of the past, there was a close connection between scientific reasoning and philosophical or logical method. That interpenetration is typical of what is known as 'pre-modern scientific thought'. According to the Aristotelian conceptions which indisputably dominated the Middle Ages both in Christendom and the Muslim world, science is, so to speak, the servant of logic. Logic prescribes the rules scientists have to follow in their search for truth, and the rules the logician imposes upon the scientist derive from logic alone. They are less concerned with developing knowledge of real phenomena than with drawing the right deductions from universal principles. Scientific observation is, then, based upon metaphysical presuppositions. Logic generalizes the results of observation in such a way so as not to invalidate the *a priori* metaphysical construct. Pre-modern scientific thought is characterized by a constant contradiction between research which attempts to find a solution to concrete problems and metaphysical speculation, between the discovery of objective truths which should lead to truly scientific generalizations and a desire to integrate the results of scientific investigation into a logical system which has been accepted *a priori* in order to establish a working hypothesis. Its scientific approach relies upon formal logic rather than upon concrete analysis. It starts out with a revered philosophical system and attempts to integrate the results of observation into that system at all costs.

This complete faith in a rationalist metaphysics and a formal general and abstract concept of logic means that phenomena are explained solely in terms of argument based upon abstract premises. Platonic reflection theories which argue that the world of sense perception is merely an unstable and deformed shadow of the Ideal (which alone is real and worthy of serious attention) must lead intellectual activity into a complete impasse. No attempt is made to understand the real world. Thus, in *The Republic*, Plato does not study the real City, but tries to show what the ideal City should be. In the Muslim world, his disciples Avicenna, Averroes and above all al-Farabi also devoted themselves to studying the Ideal City and to adapting it to the context of Islam.

The omnipotence of this rationalist metaphysics, combined with an equally powerful theology, led to the paralysis of history. History could mean only a narrative account of the past. Research into underlying causes was not directed towards analysis of the evolution of concrete facts, but towards abstract and normative arguments about the ideal society. This was a complete negation of any historical approach. Given the dominance of pre-modern scientific thought, it is not surprising that the development of historical method was so restricted.

Ibn Khaldun's intellectual structures were very different: his philosophical preoccupations were largely derived from his scientific observations. His investigations did not start out from a system of logic.

Ibn Khaldun belonged to a 'reactionary' religious movement which was directed against the rationalist philosophers. As we noted, he went even further than Ghazzali and condemned the use of logic. It was his absolute faith in religion and its doctrines that led him to reject all philosophical constructs. He thought it quite pointless and almost blasphemous to speculate as to the nature of the Ideal City. Revelation alone could provide the answer to such questions.

But at the same time Ibn Khaldun was not a pure mystic who submitted fatalistically to the will of God without trying to understand it. He was a man of action living in a very imperfect City which was despicable but real. Although he knew perfectly well what the Ideal City should be, he had to act within the context of earthly society and he therefore tried to understand that. Its anarchy, perversity and disorder were such that it did not bear comparison with the Ideal City. Nor could the causes of events on earth be deduced from the nature of the celestial City. Ibn Khaldun therefore tried to understand the world in which he lived on the basis of the concrete elements provided by his observation of society. In a very important passage, Ibn Khaldun underlines the need to observe concrete facts and to ignore considerations inspired by rationalist metaphysics: 'Scholars are, of all people, the least familiar with the ways of politics. The reason for this is that scholars are used to mental speculation and to a searching study of ideas which they abstract from the *sensibilia* and conceive in their minds as general universals, so that they may be applicable to some matter in general but not to any particular matter, individual, race, nation or group of people. Scholars, then, make such universal ideas conform in their minds to facts of the outside world. All their conclusions and views continue to be something in the mind. They come to conform to the facts of the outside world only after research and speculation has come to an end, or they may never come to conform to them. ... In their case, one expects the facts of the outside world to conform to them, in contrast with the intellectual sciences, where, in order to prove the soundness of views, one expects those views to conform to the facts of the outside world.

'Thus, in all their intellectual activities, scholars are accustomed to dealing with matters of the mind and with thoughts. They do not know anything else. Politicians, on the other hand, must pay attention to the facts of the outside world and the conditions attaching to and depending upon politics. These facts and conditions are obscure. They may contain some element making it impossible to refer them to something exemplary and similar, something contradicting the universal idea to which one would like them to conform. The conditions existing in civilization cannot always be compared with each other. They may be alike in one respect but differ completely in others.

'Now scholars are accustomed to generalizations and analogical conclusions. When they look at politics, they press their observations into the mould of their views and their way of making deductions. Thus, they commit many errors, or at least they cannot be trusted not to commit errors. ... The average person of a healthy disposition and a mediocre intelligence ... restricts himself to considering every matter as it is, and to judging every kind of situation and every type of individual by its particular circumstances. ... Most of this speculation stops at matters perceivable by the senses. ... Such a man can, therefore, be trusted when he reflects upon his political activities. He has the right outlook in dealing with his fellow man ... This situation makes one realize that logic cannot be trusted to prevent the commission of errors, because it is too abstract and remote from the *sensibilia*.'[11]

This text is of considerable importance. It marks the break between Ibn Khaldun's method and pre-modern scientific thought, which he criticizes severely. He stresses the need for direct observation of specific concrete facts and the need to 'consider every matter as it is and stop at matters perceivable by the senses.' His method is not simply empirical. He does not bring together a random collection of unmethodical observations. He is basically trying to explain the facts as a whole. Although Ibn Khaldun is in philosophical terms a supporter of strict religious orthodoxy and although he denies that reason can assure man of salvation or explain the universe, he still wants to understand the society and the time in which he lives. Although he denies that reason has any efficacy in the spiritual domain, he adopts an eminently rationalist method as a means to explore and explain reality. The rationalism of the great Arab philosophers had influenced him so much that it inevitably reappeared in his work as soon as he moved away from the spiritual domain. He therefore falls back upon an implicitly rationalist method to deduce general principles from his observations. And at times he does not shrink from systematizing this method or from establishing 'a normative method for distinguishing right from wrong and truth from falsehood.'

Ibn Khaldun is not concerned with justifying his deductions by appealing to authority or to revered metaphysical principles. He restricts himself to stating the material facts and looking for the laws that govern their evolution. His arguments are essentially based upon 'necessity and the nature of things'. By 'necessity' Ibn Khaldun means basically natural necessity, a factor he states but does not try to explain. 'Necessity' in this sense implies that things bear the seeds of their own transformation within them. It can also mean a necessary precondition in the sense (e.g.) that man has to eat in order to live. These necessities are not in themselves sufficient causes. Their effect can be interrupted by other factors and they apply only to material life. When he enters the domain of the spiritual, however, Ibn Khaldun wholly abandons his rationalist method: 'To establish the truth and soundness of information about factual happenings, one requirement to consider is the conformity of the reported information with general conditions. This is more important than, and has superiority over, personality criticism [appeals to authority]. For the correct notion about something that ought to be [this refers to the injunction of religious law] can be derived from personality criticism, while the correct notion about something that was can be derived from personality criticism and external evidence by checking the conformity of the historical report with general conditions.'[12]

The intellectual structure of Ibn Khaldun's work is, then, singularly complex and original. On the one hand, he is a mystic who is prepared to countenance all kinds of obscurantism in order to defend the cause of his religion. On the other hand, he lays claim to the heritage of the great rationalist philosophers. We are not dealing with an absurd, static or paralyzing opposition between two irreducibly antagonistic attitudes, but with a contradiction that was both dialectical and productive.

Although he in theory renounces his rationalist background in order to defend his religion, Ibn Khaldun does not thereby give up his attempt to understand. He rejected the rationalist metaphysics that paralyzed scientific research because of his mysticism—and it was that which allowed him to make considerable advances. It was precisely his total faith in Muslim dogma as to the ideal and the beyond which ensured the objectivity of his study of a secular society so radically different from the Ideal City.

So, in this very exceptional case, it would seem that the influence of the religious reaction, which had such negative effects elsewhere, was relatively positive. It had a positive effect in that it repressed the rationalist metaphysics which, by asserting that abstract reasoning was the only source of knowledge, had sterilized research into and formulation of the laws governing reality. But—and this is the important point—for Ibn Khaldun, the mystical attitude was restricted to the spiritual domain alone. Ibn Khaldun did not take refuge in fatalism. He struggled to understand the realities of his time. Although he had abandoned it as a dogma or metaphysic, Ibn Khaldun retained his rationalism as a method of investigation and deduction, and oriented it towards the empirical observation of a real society.

Ibn Khaldun thus escaped the ambiguities which characterize premodern scientific thought. Once it had been repressed by the wave of mysticism, philosophy could no longer dominate scientific research. Ibn Khaldun's work is characterized by the almost total disappearance of one major element in pre-modern scientific thought, that which made no distinction between the sciences and philosophy and so made science dependent upon philosophy. *The Muqaddimah*, in which scientific method and philosophical speculation are separated out, marks the appearance of modern thought and the birth of the science of history.

Conclusion

It was taken for granted that the work of this great historian could suddenly appear like a jewel in the midst of medieval Muslim culture, in which history played such an exceptionally important role in social, religious and political life. But we now see that the situation in the Maghreb and the peculiarities of historical development in this part of the Arab world did in a sense provide a favourable background for the emergence of his thought.

Certain historical conjunctures and situations are more favourable than others for the development of historical thought. Unlike the Middle East, where major historical events were, so to speak, the result of 'foreign policy' (the Crusades, the great Turkish and Mongol invasions, the struggle against Byzantium), and unlike Spain, where Christianity and Islam clashed, medieval North Africa was a relatively isolated part of the Muslim world. Its evolution was brought about by mainly internal factors (St Louis's expedition to Tunis in 1270 was merely an isolated episode without any major repercussions). The only conflicts were those between states with almost identical structures. But their rise and their fall were governed by domestic causes.

It was probably this situation that led Ibn Khaldun to take a very different view of history from that of traditional historians. As he could scarcely blame foreign conquerors for the fall of the North African dynasties, he *had* to look for historical factors other than those studied by narrative history. The great political instability of the Maghreb in the Middle Ages led him to look for an overall explanation that could make sense of a jumble of unrelated facts.

In his search for internal general causes he began to analyse certain social structures and to apprehend problems which he might not have noticed at all, had he been dealing with historical events dominated by external causes. The contrast between the sophisticated civilization of the cities and the harsh conditions of tribal life may also have led him to a certain awareness of economic and sociological phenomena.

As we have seen, Ibn Khaldun's clarity of scientific vision also owes something to the contradiction between rationalism and mysticism. Although both tendencies existed throughout the Arab world, with the latter becoming dominant in the eleventh or the twelfth century, in North Africa the two did not come into conflict until much later. Ibn Khaldun is living proof that rationalism was still an active force, that it had not yet been completely stifled.

The forms taken by these antagonistic tendencies were more extreme in the Maghreb than elsewhere. Ibn Rochd (Averroes) lived for many years in Morocco and died there. He was the last of the great Arab rationalists, and took rationalism further than anyone else. His influence on other Moroccan thinkers was to be felt for a long time. Ibn Khaldun's teacher Abelli had been his pupil. But religious reaction was also very strong in the Maghreb, which adopted Malikism, one of the most austere and rigid forms of Islam. These characteristics of the Maghreb and its history all contributed to the development of Ibn Khaldun's thought.

But whilst important, these general characteristics are not enough to explain the appearance of a work as extraordinary as *The Muqaddimah*. We therefore have to evoke more specific factors, many of them relating to the personality of Ibn Khaldun himself.

Other historians had also dealt with the past of North Africa. But none of them seems to have raised the problems studied by Ibn Khaldun, and not one of them arrived at his conception of history. The author of *The Muqaddimah* seems to have had no precursors and, what is more significant, he does not appear to have had any real successors, despite the fame of his work. It took a truly exceptional mind, in terms of both intellect and mental structures, to arrive at this conception of history in the fourteenth century.

Ibn Khaldun was at once an orthodox and mystical believer and a great rationalist thinker. At a time when the religious reaction had been triumphant for more than a century, he was still able to assume the heritage of the rationalist movement. Although that heritage had been repressed at the level of philosophy, it could still be used as a guide for empirical investigations. Ibn Khaldun was, then, an exceptional thinker for his time. And although his conception of history appears very modern, he remains quite exceptional in modern terms. The conceptions adopted by modern historians are an integral part of a powerful scientific movement which has not been dominated by metaphysics for more than two hundred years. In the fourteenth century, however, the only way for Ibn Khaldun to establish the autonomy of his scientific method was for him to break logic's hold over the sciences by appealing to religious orthodoxy. Modern historians do not, of course, have to make any such appeal to mysticism.

But if Ibn Khaldun's scientific thought was to develop, his basic rationalism had to overcome his mystical tendencies, and his desire to understand had to be strong enough for it not to be stifled by fatalistic obscurantism.

The birth of Ibn Khaldun's conception of history thus corresponds both to a certain stage in the development of the contradiction between rationalism and religion and to a specific point in his own intellectual development. In later life, his theological interests do in fact seem to have gained the upper hand over his concerns as a historian.

Although it owed much to a tradition of historiography and was a response to specific features of the medieval Maghreb, *The Muqaddimah* was in many ways the product of this ephemeral conjuncture. It was written by a man of exceptional intelligence at a time when he was prepared to abandon metaphysics, to generalize on the basis of his erudition and his experience as a statesman and a soldier, and thus arrive at a truly scientific understanding of the times in which he lived.

The historical thought of Ibn Khaldun, the last of the truly great thinkers of medieval Muslim civilization, is like the last, exceptionally ripe fruit on a tree most of whose branches are dead and whose growth is about to be stunted for several hundred years to come.

What relevance does Ibn Khaldun have in the second half of the twentieth century?

His work not only throws light on the situation in the medieval Maghreb and bears witness to the birth of scientific historical thought in the Arab world. The research, analysis and synthesis of this brilliant Maghrebian of the fourteenth century also helps us to gain a better understanding of what is probably the greatest and most dramatic problem of our day: underdevelopment.

Underdevelopment is of course a very modern phenomenon. In every Third World country it is characterized by the imbalance between a rapid demographic growth brought about by the 'health revolution' and an economic growth rate held back by a number of economic and social factors. It is basically a twentieth-century phenomenon, but it results from older causes. Some of the causes of underdevelopment relate to the phenomenon of colonialism, but others have to be sought in the distant past of those countries which have become underdeveloped. Although less obvious than recent factors resulting from the action of the colonizers, they should not be forgotten, if only because they paralysed economic and social developments for centuries, and thus facilitated colonial domination. *The Muqaddimah* raises the question of the underlying causes of underdevelopment.

The Muqaddimah describes and explains the situation in the Maghrebian states at a very important moment in their history. The period of their former glory was coming to an end and was giving way to a period of stagnation interrupted only by indecisive crises.

Ibn Khaldun's analysis allows us to understand how the social and economic development of the Maghreb was paralysed, not by external or chance factors, but by internal causes: it deals with a *structural* crisis which relates to the survival of predominantly tribal structures and their corollaries—the impossibility of any private appropriation of the means of production and the privileged minority's inability to constitute itself as a clearly differentiated class capable of dominating the rest of the population in any lasting fashion.

Ibn Khaldun's emphasis on the political impotence of the urban population and the mediocrity of its economic role raises a major problem which is not restricted to the countries of the Maghreb alone. It typifies the historical evolution of much of the world. Western Europe owes its exceptional development to the violence and the clarity of the dialectical social antagonisms which gave birth to a capitalist bourgeoisie in a tightly structured feudal society. Although Africa, Asia and pre-Columbian America all gave rise to brilliant civilizations, they did not produce the conditions required for the formation of a true bourgeoisie.

It should be stressed that Ibn Khaldun's analysis of North Africa does not provide grounds for seeing Islam itself as an obstacle to change. A number of authors, however, make a point of describing Islam as 'the religion of fatalism and resignation'[1] and as a major reason for the stagnation which affected the Muslim world for centuries.

This argument is a survival from the imperialist ideologies of the Crusades and cannot really be taken seriously. If 'Islamic sclerosis' were in fact a major factor, how are we to explain the sudden rise of Muslim civilization, the 'Arab miracle' which lasted for almost five hundred years? Those who, in an attempt to legitimize modern colonialism, try to explain it in terms of the survival of the heritage of Rome and Byzantium greatly exaggerate the positive aspects of Roman and Byzantine colonization, which in fact ended in 'fraudulent bankruptcy.'[2] The extreme rapidity with which Islam spread to countries that were still subject to the oppression of the Christian emperors shows that it held out the possibility of definite progress and relative liberation.

There is every indication that for several centuries varied and undoubtedly creative capacities developed in the Muslim world. These successes cannot, however, be attributed to the influence of Islam alone: Islam was superimposed upon extremely varied economic and social structures. Just as Christianity was the religion of slave, feudal and capitalist societies, Islam left its mark upon a wide variety of tribal, semi-feudal and 'hydraulic' societies. Islam is an important historical factor, but it is not primordial.

Some authors point to the many social and economic implications of Islam and argue that Muslim societies were much more influenced by religion than European society. They forget that in the Middle Ages, the influence of Christianity was at least as great as that of Islam. But whereas in Europe, the industrial revolution and its aftermath led to a weakening of religious factors, those factors remained influential in Muslim countries simply because their rate of economic and social development was slower.

It is only relatively recently that the ideal of renunciation and resignation which is now seen as a permanent feature of Islam became so important. If this tendency did in fact exist in earlier periods, it played only a minor role. On the contrary, commercial success and profit-making were seen as religious obligations. Until the eleventh century, this dynamic tendency was very influential, and it can be argued that Islam was to a certain extent a stimulus to trade and economic activity. Gibb stresses the slow process which gradually transformed the internal structures of Islam.[3] Only when economic development was slowing down and when decline was setting in did *zuhd* or resignation and fatalistic renunciation become the dominant form of religion. The ideology of a stagnating society cannot remain dynamic. In so far as its own development was paralyzed, Islam became a paralyzing force.[4]

The situation studied by Ibn Khaldun lasted for several hundred years. Indeed in some ways it lasted until the nineteenth century and thus divided the period of development from the colonial period.

Morocco turned in upon itself and retained its medieval structures. Thanks to tribal resistance, it succeeded in avoiding domination by the Portuguese and the Spanish. The conquest of America was a further contributory factor in that it diverted the attention of the Iberian powers away from the Maghreb.

The rest of North Africa came under the rule of the Turks, who were less fearsome masters than the Christian feudal lords. The greater part of the structures described by Ibn Khaldun survived none the less. In Morocco, a series of dynasties (Beni Ouatta, Saadeines, Alouites) followed one another, but their authority was in fact restricted to the plains. In the central and eastern Maghreb, the dominance of the Turks put an end to the political cycles of the past. Tribal structures persisted and the tribes went on fighting one another, some trying to avoid paying taxes, others forcing their enemies to pay them tribute. Still others succeeded in asserting their dominance, with or without support from the Turks.[5]

Ibn Khaldun's work helps us to understand why the advances made in the Middle Ages came to an end and gave way to such a long period of stagnation. *The Muqaddimah* reveals the causes which made possible the decisive factor in the underdevelopment of the Maghreb: the colonial conquests of the nineteenth century. Those conquests were not the result of the power of the conquerors alone. Structures which had existed for hundreds of years facilitated the process considerably.

France had great difficulty in conquering Algeria and would probably never have succeeded in doing so if Abd el-Kader, who was the leader of a group of tribes backed by a powerful religious brotherhood, had been able to coordinate the actions of all the country's forces. But like other Maghrebian leaders before him, Abd el-Kader came up against the opposition of some great tribal chieftains. The contradiction between state structures and tribal structures which Ibn Khaldun had analysed was now no longer simply an internal conflict as it had been in the fourteenth century. The French were able to use it to their advantage. They succeeded, though not without great difficulty, in defeating the forces ranged against them by supporting and using the tribal chieftains (particularly in the *Constantinois*) and giving them power. It was these Algerian chieftains rather than the French troops who overthrew Abd el-Kader's fledgling state.

When the European imperialists reached Morocco, the Alouite dynasty had already gone through the stages of development and stability, and was entering a period of decline very similar to that described five hundred years earlier by Ibn Khaldun. The mountain tribes were refusing to pay taxes, and a number of pretenders were fighting for control of the *Bled el-Maghzan*. Although in many ways classic, these insurrections had very novel results, thanks to the role played by the great foreign powers. The colonization of Morocco also was considerably facilitated by the support given to the French troops by the great tribal chieftains. The long-standing antagonisms between royal and tribal or semi-feudal power again worked to the advantage of the imperialists.

Ibn Khaldun's analysis of *'asabiya*, a dialectical structure whose basic and indissociable elements are tribal egalitarianism and the role of the chieftain, allows us to see why so many of the chieftains chose to serve the colonists. Colonialism gave them the means to extend their previously limited authority over the population. They were able to appropriate much of the common land and transform its occupants into sharecroppers or agricultural labourers. The privileged minority became integrated into a new system which allowed them to appropriate a much greater proportion of the surplus produced by the population.

The tribal structures which had characterized North Africa for centuries were in this way broken up and finally destroyed for ever. Although very different from the bourgeoisie which had slowly emerged in Europe, a privileged minority of North Africans and foreigners finally succeeded in appropriating the means of production which had for the most part been owned by village or tribal communities for centuries. In North Africa, as in other parts of what we now call the Third World, the system of military democracy and the 'asiatic mode of production' gave way to a capitalist system very different from that prevailing in the developed countries. At the same time, class struggles, which had for centuries been embryonic and confused, became very clear-cut and began to develop rapidly. Internal contradictions which had previously been aborted took on an unprecedented violence.

Although it had been blocked for a long time, historical evolution now speeded up considerably. The structures described by Ibn Khaldun had made colonization possible, and they were destroyed by it. Their after-effects, however, continued to be felt and became combined with other, newer factors. It is this combination of older internal causes and more recent external factors which determine the appearance of underdevelopment in the twentieth century. *The Muqaddimah* is thus of contemporary and universal significance in that it sheds light on underlying factors whose importance has been underestimated. It helps to clarify the role of colonialism and modern neo-colonialism. The work of Ibn Khaldun, a brilliant Maghrebian of the fourteenth century does not only mark the birth of the science of history. It is also a major contribution to the history of underdevelopment.

Notes

Preface

1. For the benefit of readers who are unfamiliar with the transliteration of Arabic, it should be pointed out that the 'Kh' in Khaldun is pronounced like the German 'ch' or the Spanish 'j'. In linguistic terms, it is a voiceless velar fricative. 'Khaldun' must not be pronounced as 'Caldun'.

2. P.K. Hitti, *Récits de l'histoire des Arabes*.

3. G. Marçais.

4. A. Toynbee, *A Study of History*, Oxford 1934, vol. 3, p. 322.

5. There is no room here to go into the definition of underdevelopment in any detail or to make a detailed analysis of its complex causes. I deal with these questions in my *Géographie du sous-développement*, Paris 1965.

6. See M. Daumas, *Histoire générale des techniques*, 2 vols. Paris 1962, 1965.

7. *Géographie du sous-développement*, pp. 222-228.

8. The over-restrictive spatial nature of the term results from the limitations of nineteenth-century documentation. It now seems necessary to find a new and non-geographical term to describe a mode of production which existed, albeit with major variations, in Africa, Asia and America.

9. Beginning with an article by J.F. Hammer-Purgstall in *Le Journal asiatique*, 1822. De Slane's French translation appeared between 1844 and 1862. Franz Rosenthal's translation of *The Muqaddimah* appeared in 1958.

10. Notably E.F. Gautier in his *Le Passé de l'Afrique du nord*, Paris 1937.

11. See Maurice Godelier, 'La Notion de mode de production asiatique', *Les Temps Modernes*, mai 1965; 'Le Mode de Production asiatique', *La Pensée*, No. 114, avril 1964, No. 122, août 1965; 'La Notion de "mode de production asiatique" et les schémas marxistes d'évolution des sociétés', *Cahier du centre d'études et de recherches marxistes*.

12. Raymond Aron, *Dimensions de la conscience historique*, Paris 1961, p. 384.

Part One: The Past of the Third World

1. General Characteristics and Fundamental Structures

1. Tamerlane (1336-1406) was, it will be noted, almost the exact contemporary of Ibn Khaldun.

2. G. Marçais, *Histoire et historiens de l'Algérie*, Paris 1930, p. 211.

3. D.M. Dunlop, 'Sources of Gold and Silver in Islam According to al-Hamadani', *Studia Islamica*, XCMLVII.

4. F. Braudel, *The Mediterranean and the Mediterranean World in the Age of Philip I* (Tr. Siân T. Reynolds), London 1966, vol. 1, p. 468.

5. M. Lombard, 'L'Or musulman du VIIe au XIe siècle', *Annales Sociétés Civilisations*, 1974.

6. Ibn Hwqal, *Kamal*, p. 649.

7. For more detail see Y. Lacoste, A. Mouschi, A. Prenant, *L'Algérie passé et présent*, Paris 1960, pp. 103-106.

8. *The Muqaddimah* Volume 2, pp. 283-285.

9. C. Cahen, 'Contribution à l'histoire de *l'iqta*'', *Annales Sociétés Civilisations*, janvier-mars 1953; 'Notes pour l'histoire de l'himaya', *Mélanges Louis Massignon*, 1957.

10. *The Muqaddimah* Volume 2, p. 284.

11. Roughly speaking, *maghzan* means 'state power'.

12. North Africa, where the colonizers had been driven out by a series of insurrections, was one of the very few independent and non-colonized areas to have been conquered by the Arab empire. This to a large extent explains why they had such difficulty in conquering it between 647 and c. 710. The Berbers accepted Islam, but refused to surrender.

13. Marc Bloch, *Feudal Society* (tr. L.A. Manyon), London 1961, p. 248.

14. R. Boutruche, *Seigneurie et féodalité*, Paris 1959.

15. K. Wittfogel, *Oriental Despotism*, New Haven 1957.

16. It is not certain that 'functional' hydraulic societies which actually constructed large-scale works still existed in Muslim countries during the Middle Ages. Such works were rarely undertaken, even in Iraq, where Genghis Khan's invasion resulted in the destruction of many irrigation works. It is however possible that the population had fallen to such an extent that it was impossible to assemble the necessary workforce.

2. A Politician from a Great Family

1. Ibn Khaldun wrote a major autobiography.

2. The name derives from that of Abu Hafs, the founder of the dynasty.

3. From the name of the Beni Abd el-Wadid tribe.

4. The name derives from that of the Beni Merin tribes.

5. *Histoire des Berbères*, vol. 3, p. 23.

6. *Histoire* Vol. 3, p. 24.

7. *Histoire* Vol. 3, p. 23.

8. *Histoire* Vol. 4, pp. 251-2.

9. *Muqaddimah* Vol. 1, p. 66.

10. *Muqaddimah* Vol. 1, p. 64.

11. De Slane Vol. 1, p. xxxi.

12. *Histoire* Vol. 4, p. 300.

13. *Histoire* Vol. 4, p. 180.

14 *Histoire* Vol. 4, p. 100.

15. De Slane Vol. 1, p. xxxiv.

16. De Slane Vol. 1, p. xxxvi.

17. De Slane Vol. 1, p. xliii.

18. De Slane Vol. 1, p. xliv.

19. *Histoire* Vol. 4, pp. 378-81.

20. De Slane Vol. 1, p. xlvii.

21. *Histoire* Vol. 3, p. 69.

22. *Histoire* Vol. 3, p. 450.

23. *Histoire* Vol. 3, p. 70.

24. De Slane Vol. 1, p. xlix.

25. De Slane Vol. 1, p. xlviii.

27. *Histoire* Vol. 3, p. 72.
28. *Histoire* Vol. 3, p. 450.
29. De Slane Vol. 1, p. xlix.
30. Mushin Mahdi, *Ibn Khaldun's Philosophy of History*, London 1957

3. From Condottiere to Historian

1. De Slane Vol. 1, p. xlix.
2. *Histoire* Vol. 3, p. 463.
3. The last third of Ibn Khaldun's life (after, that is, he had written the most original sections of *The Muqaddimah*) is of less interest. It does, however, shed some light on the conceptions he held in 1375-78. We will come back to the last twenty-five years of his life when we analyse those conceptions..
4. François Châtelet, *La Naissance de l'histoire*, Paris 1962.
5. Ibid.
6. *Muqaddimah* Vol. 1, p. 57.
7. *Muqaddimah* Vol. 1, p. 63.
8. Of the Hejira (1297-1387 AD).
9. Of the Hejira.
10. Ibn Khaldun here is referring to the Maghrebian dynasties. He adds that the East was similarly visited by plague.
11. *Muqaddimah* Vol. 1, p. 64. Emphasis added.
12. *Muqaddimah* Vol. 1, p. 65. Emphasis added.
13. *Muqaddimah* Vol. 2, pp. 290-91.
14. *Muqaddimah* Vol. 1, p. 249.
15. *Muqaddimah* Vol. 1, p. 12.
16. *Muqaddimah* Vol. 1, p. 11.
17. *Muqaddimah* Vol. 1, p. 83.
18. *Muqaddimah* Vol. 1, pp. 10-11.
19. *Muqaddimah* Vol. 1, p. 83.
20. *Muqaddimah* Vol. 1, p. 71.
21. Cf. Rosenthal, Translator's Introduction, civ-cvii.
22. The third volume deals with jurisprudence, theology, philosophy, pure and applied science, teaching methods, rhetoric and poetry.
23. Ibn Khaldun later wrote a further section dealing with the history of the Eastern dynasties. This section is generally considered to be less original and there is little connection between its content and that of *The Muqaddimah*.
24. The contents of *The Muqaddimah* are as follows:
Introduction: *The excellence of historiography; An appreciation of the various approaches to history; A glimpse at the different kinds of errors to which historians are liable; Something about why these errors occur*;

Volume One: *The nature of civilization; Bedouin and settled life, the achievement of superiority, gainful occupations, ways of making a living, sciences, crafts and all the other things that affect civilization; The causes and reasons thereof.*

Chapter 1. *Human Civilization in general.*
Chapter 2. *Bedouin civilization, savage nations and tribes and their conditions of life, including several basic and explanatory statements.*
Chapter 3. *On dynasties, royal authority, the Caliphate, government ranks, and all that goes with those things.*
Chapter 4. *Countries and cities, and all other forms of sedentary civilization; The conditions occurring there.*

Volume Two
Chapter 5. *On the various aspects of making a living, such as profits and the crafts; The conditions that occur in this connection; A number of problems connected with this subject.*
Chapter 6. *The various kinds of sciences; The methods of instruction.*

Volume Three. *Jurisprudence, the sciences, scholarship and education, linguistics, rhetoric, poetry.*

4. The Myth of the 'Arab Invasion'

1. C.A. Julien (tr. J. Petrie, C. Stewart), *History of North Africa. From the Arab Conquest to 1830*, London 1970, p. 73.
2. Ibid.
3. Of the Hejira.
4. Of the Hejira.
5. *Muqaddimah* Vol. 1, p. 64.
6. *Muqaddimah* Vol. 3, p. 366.
7. *Muqaddimah* Vol. 1, p. 302.
8. *Muqaddimah* Vol. 1, p. 304.
9. 'Cent vingt ans de sociologie maghrébienne', *Annales* 3, 1946.
10. G.F. Marçais, *La Berbérie musulmane et l'Orient au Moyen-Age*, Paris 1946.
11. Julien, *History*, p. 73.
12. E.F. Gautier, *Le Passé de l'Afrique du Nord*, Paris 1937, pp. 72, 374.
13. E.F. Gautier, *Histoire et historiens de l'Algérie*, Paris 1930, p. 31.
14. He makes a distinction between Sanhadja-speaking Berbers and Zanata speakers, and claims that the former are sedentary whereas the latter are nomads allied to the Arabs. This theory is extremely schematic, and there is no relationship between the ethnic and linguistic characteristics of a group and its way of life. Many Berber herdsmen spoke Zanata, but so did sedentary groups like the montagnards of the Aures. But the sedentary Kabyls and the nomadic herdsmen of the Atlas spoke Sanhadja.
15. R. Brunschwig, *La Berbérie occidentale sous les Hafsides*, Paris 1940, Vol. 2, p. 421.
16. R. Brunschwig, *Les Arabes en Berbérie*, p. 169.
17. C.A. Julien, *History*, p. 73.
18. *Histoire* Vol. 1, p. 7. Emphasis added.
19. A tribe belonging to the Beni Hilal confederation.
20. The Zirid ruler of Ifriquiyah, then at war with the Hammadites.
21. Former governor of the eastern part of Ifriqiyah, which was now independent, and founder of the Hammadid dynasty. His capital was initially the Qalat of the Beni Hammad, but was later moved to Bougie.
22. *Histoire* Vol. 1, p. 34.
23. *Histoire* Vol. 1, p. 29. Emphasis added.
24. The ruler of Tlemcen, on whose behalf Ibn Khaldun himself recruited mercenaries.
25. *Histoire* Vol. 3, p. 454.
26. For the application of this policy in Algeria, see C.R. Ageron, 'La France a-t-elle eu une politique kabyle?', *Revue historique*, 1960.
27. *Saint Augustin*, Paris 1913; *Autour de Saint Augustin, Sanguis martyrum*, Paris 1918; *Les Villes d'or*, Paris 1921.
28. E.F. Gautier, *Le Passé de l'Afrique du Nord*, Paris 1937, p. 114.
29. Ibid., p. 92.
30. Ibid., p. 25.
31. Ibid., p. 24.
32. Ibid., pp. 9, 24.

33. Ibid., pp. 95-101.
34. Ibid, p. 102.
35. E.F. Gautier, *Moeurs et Coutumes des Musulmans*, Paris 1931, p. 722.
36. E.F. Gautier, *Le Passé*, p. 96.
37. Ibid., p. 272.
38. G. Bouthoul, *Ibn Khaldun, sa philosophie sociale*, Paris 1930, pp. 50-51.
39. Julien et Courtois, *Histoire de l'Afrique du Nord des origines à la conquête*, Paris 1951, p. 48.
40. Cf. the statement made to the Senate Commission of Enquiry in 1891 by Camille Sabatier, 'administrator' and one of the 'theoreticians' of policy towards the Kabyls: '*Divide et ut imperes?* And why not? Why not prevent the Kabyls and the Arabs from uniting? The only thing they could unite against is France!'

5. The Crisis of the Fourteenth Century

1. This thesis is so absurd that it is self-contradictory. If the role of the nomads was so negative, how is it that the area enjoyed relative prosperity prior to the eleventh century, when the Berber population consisted largely of nomads and semi-nomads?
2. It is possible that the break between the ruler of Tlemcen and his suzerain lord, the Fatimid Caliph of Cairo, was an indirect effect of the disruption of the gold trade. Ifriqiyah was finding it increasingly difficult to pay tributes to Cairo and to finance trade with Egypt. Marçais points out that monetary reform in about 1050 led to a major crisis in Ifriqiyah (*Les Arabes en Berbérie*, p. 56).
3. *Muqaddimah* Vol. 1, p. 64.
4. H. Terasse, *Histoire du Maroc*, Paris 1950, p. 462.
5. *Muqaddimah* Vol. 2, p. 93.
6. *Les Arabes en Berbérie*, p. 727.
7. The 'share' kept by the tax collector.
8. *Muqaddimah* Vol. 2, pp. 103-104.
9. *Muqaddimah* Vol. 2, pp. 106-107.
10. *Muqaddimah* Vol. 2, pp. 108-111.
11. *Muqaddimah* Vol. 2, p. 123.
12. *Muqaddimah* Vol. 2, p. 136.
13. The *Khammesat* system authorized by Islamic tradition, which is now very widespread, gives the sharecropper only one fifth of the harvest.
14. *Muqaddimah* Vol. 2, p. 338.
15. *Muqaddimah* Vol. 2, p. 345.
16. *Muqaddimah* Vol. 2, p. 97.
17. This prosperity may have come about because for a while the gold trade between Ifriqiyah and the Sudan was re-established and because the routes across the central Sahara were again in use.
18. *Muqaddimah* Vol. 1, pp. 64-5.
19. *Muqaddimah* Vol. 1, p. 64.
20. Ibid.
21. *Muqaddimah* Vol. 1, p. 320.
22. *Muqaddimah* Vol. 1, p. 319.

6. The Development of the State

1. *Muqaddimah* Vol. 1, p. 71.
2. *Muqaddimah* Vol. 1, p. 249.
3. Cf. Rosenthal, 'Introduction', p. lxxvii; G. Labica, 'La Religion chez Ibn Khaldun', *La Pensée*, octobre 1965.

4. Mushin Mahdi, *Ibn Khaldun's Philosophy of History*, London 1957, pp. 193-95.
5. *Muqaddimah* Vol. 1, pp. 84-85.
6. *Muqaddimah* Vol. 1, pp. 249-250.
7. *Muqaddimah* Vol. 1, p. 253.
8. *Muqaddimah* Vol. 1, pp. 250-251.
9. *Muqaddimah* Vol. 1, p. 251.
10. *Muqaddimah* Vol. 2, p. 273.
11. *Muqaddimah* Vol. 2, p. 279.
12. *Muqaddimah* Vol. 2, p. 274.
13. *Muqaddimah* Vol. 2, p. 287.
14. *Muqaddimah* Vol. 2, pp. 291-292.
15. *Muqaddimah* Vol. 2, p. 296.
16. *Muqaddimah* Vol. 2, pp. 276-279.
17. *Muqaddimah* Vol. 2, pp. 356-357.
18. *Muqaddimah* Vol. 2, pp. 296-297.
19. *Muqaddimah* Vol. 1, p. 11.
20. *Muqaddimah* Vol. 1, p. 347.
21. *Muqaddimah* Vol. 1, p. 344.
22. *Muqaddimah* Vol. 1, p. 346.
23. *Muqaddimah* Vol. 1, p. 65.
24. *Muqaddimah* Vol. 1, p. 285.
25. *Muqaddimah* Vol. 1, pp. 327-328.
26. *Muqaddimah* Vol. 1, p. 337.
27. *Muqaddimah* Vol. 1, p. 351.
28. *Muqaddimah* Vol. 2, p. 237.
29. *Muqaddimah* Vol. 1, p. 347.
30. Enan Mohamed, *Ibn Khaldun, His Life and Work*, Lahore 1941.
31. Ayad Mohamed Kamil, *Die Geschichts und Gesellschaftslehre Ibn Khaldouns*, Berlin 1930.
32. Erwin Rosenthal, *Ibn Khalduns Gedanken uber den Staat*, Berlin 1932.
33. *Encyclopédie de l'Islam*.
34. Alfred Von Kremer, 'Ibn Chaldun und seine Kulturgeschichte der islamischen Reiche', *Sitzungsberichte der Kaiserlichen Akadamie der Wissenschaften, Phil-hist. Klasse*, XCIII, Vienna 1879. Khemeri Tahir, 'Der 'Asabiya Begriff in der Muggadima des Ibn Khaldun', in *Der Islam*, 1936.
35. Silvestre de Sacy, *Ibn Khaldun*, Paris 1865.
36. Charles Issawy, *An Arab Philosophy of History*, London 1950.
37. Claude Cahen, *Leçons d'histoire musulmane*, Paris 1958.
38. Arnold Toynbee, *A Study of History*, Oxford 1934, Vol. 3, p. 474.
39. Gaston Bouthoul, *Ibn Khaldoun, sa philosophie sociale*, Paris 1930.
40. Gaston Bouthoul.
41. Kamil Ayad.
42. Bercher et Surdon, *Recueil de textes de sociologie contenus dans les Prolégomènes d'Ibn Khaldoun*, Algiers 1951.
43. Hellmutt Ritter, 'Irrational Solidarity Groups: A Socio-Psychological Study in Connection with Ibn Khaldun', *Oriens* (Leiden), I, 1948.
44. Silvestre de Sacy.
45. Louis Gardet, *La Cité musulmane*, Paris 1954.
46. Khameri, 'Der 'Asabiya Begriff ...'.
47. *Muqaddimah* Vol. 1, pp. 332-333.
48. *Muqaddimah* Vol. 1, p. 333.
49. Ibid.

50. *Muqaddimah* Vol. 1, p. 334.
51. Ibid.
52. *Muqaddimah* Vol. 1, p. 261.
53. *Muqaddimah* Vol. 1, p. 283.
54. *Muqaddimah* Vol. 1, p. 264.
55. *Muqaddimah* Vol. 1, pp. 264-265.
56. *Muqaddimah* Vol. 1, pp. 262-263.
57. *Muqaddimah* Vol. 1, p. 289.
58. *Muqaddimah* Vol. 1, p. 287.
59. *Muqaddimah* Vol. 1, pp. 289-290.
60. *Muqaddimah* Vol. 1, p. 284.
61. *Muqaddimah* Vol. 1, p. 269.
62. *Muqaddimah* Vol. 1, p. 284.
63. *Muqaddimah* Vol. 1, p. 284.
64. *Muqaddimah* Vol. 2, pp. 303-305.
65. In the Arab world, the relationship between protector and dependent was known as *himaya*. See C. Cahen, 'Notes pour l'histoire de l'himaya', *Mélanges Louis Massignon*, 1957.
66. *Muqaddimah* Vol. 1, p. 264.
67. Marc Bloch, *Feudal Society* (tr. LA. Manyon), London 1961, p. 142.
68. *Muqaddimah* Vol. 1, pp. 284-286.
69. *Muqaddimah* Vol. 1, p. 282.
70. *Muqaddimah* Vol. 1, p. 252.
71. *Muqaddimah* Vol. 1, pp. 39, 305.
72. *Muqaddimah* Vol. 1, p. 306.
73. *Muqaddimah* Vol. 1, p. 306.
74. *Muqaddimah* Vol. 1, p. 307.
75. *Muqaddimah* Vol. 1, p. 306.
76. *Muqaddimah* Vol. 1, p. 308.
77. *Muqaddimah* Vol. 1, pp. 303-304.
78. *Muqaddimah* Vol. 1, p. 303.
79. *Muqaddimah* Vol. 1, pp. 303-304.
80. *Muqaddimah* Vol. 1, p. 306.
81. *Muqaddimah* Vol. 1, p. 306.
82. R. Montagne, *La Civilisation du désert*, Paris 1947.
83. *Histoire* Vol. 3, p. 139.
84. *Muqaddimah* Vol. 1, p. 252.
85. *Muqaddimah* Vol. 1, p. 314.
86. *Muqaddimah* Vol. 1, pp. 372-373.

7.   The Case Against the Townspeople

1. See *Muqaddimah* Vol. 1, p. 253f., Vol. 2,, pp. 291-297.
2. *Muqaddimah* Vol. 2, p. 296.
3. *Muqaddimah* Vol. 2, p. 285.
4. *Muqaddimah* Vol. 2, p. 286.
5. *Muqaddimah* Vol. 1, pp. 308-309.
6. *Muqaddimah* Vol. 1, p. 257.
7. *Muqaddimah* Vol. 2, pp. 296-297.
8. *Muqaddimah* Vol. 1, p. 291.
9. *Muqaddimah* Vol. 1, p. 381.
10. *Muqaddimah* Vol. 1, p. 391.

11. *Histoire* Vol. 2, p. 32.
12. *Histoire* Vol. 2, p. 43..
13. *Histoire* Vol. 2, p. 99.
14. *Histoire* Vol. 2, p. 212.
15. *Histoire* Vol. 2, p. 90.
16. *Histoire* Vol. 2, p. 102.
17. *Histoire* Vol. 4, p. 253.
18. *Histoire* Vol. 3, p. 2.
19. *Histoire* Vol. 1, p. 150.
20. *Histoire* Vol. 1, p. 152.
21. *Histoire* Vol. 1, p. 220.
22. *Histoire* Vol. 4, p. 324.

Part Two: The Birth of History

1.   Thucydides and Ibn Khaldun

1. A. Taladoire, *Histoire des littératures* in *Encyclopédie de la Pléiade*.
2. *The Histories of Polybius* (tr. E.S. Schuckburgh), Bloomington, Indiana 1962, vol. 1, p. 4.
3. H. Marrou, *De la connaissance historique*.
4. J. de Romilly, *Histoire et raison chez Thucydide*, Paris 1956.
5. Ibid.
6. Thibaudet.
7. *Muqaddimah* Vol. 1, p. 11.
8. *Muqaddimah* Vol. 1, p. 78.
9. *Muqaddimah* Vol. 1, p. 79.
10. *Muqaddimah* Vol. 1, p. 71.
11. *Muqaddimah* Vol. 1, p. 72.
12. Ibid.
13. *Muqaddimah* Vol. 1, p. 73.
14. *Muqaddimah* Vol. 1, p. 63.
15. Ibid.
16. *Muqaddimah* Vol. 1, pp. 82-83.
17. *Muqaddimah* Vol. 1, p. 83.
18. *Muqaddimah* Vol. 1, pp. 9-10.
19. *Muqaddimah* Vol. 1, p. 9.
20. *Muqaddimah* Vol. 1, p. 7.
21. *Muqaddimah* Vol. 1, p. 6.
22. *Muqaddimah* Vol. 2, pp. 290-291.
23. *Muqaddimah* Vol. 1, p. 72.
24. *Muqaddimah* Vol. 1, p. 63.
25. *Muqaddimah* Vol. 1, pp. 55-56.
26. *Muqaddimah* Vol. 1, p. 77.
27. *Muqaddimah* Vol. 1, p. 11.
28. *Muqaddimah* Vol. 1, p. 71.
29. *Muqaddimah* Vol. 1, p. 6.
30. *Muqaddimah* Vol. 1, p. 13.
31. Mushin Mahdi, *Ibn Khaldun's Philosophy of History*, p. 65.
32. Ibid.

210

2. Historical Materialism and Dialectical Conceptions

1. *Muqaddimah* Vol. 1, p. 12.
2. *Muqaddimah* Vol. 1, p. 93.
3. *Muqaddimah* Vol. 1, pp. 92-93.
4. *Muqaddimah* Vol. 1, p. 89.
5. *Muqaddimah* Vol. 1, p. 249.
6. *Muqaddimah* Vol. 1, p. 173.
7. *Muqaddimah* Vol. 1, p. 249.
8. *Muqaddimah* Vol. 2, pp. 5-6.
9. *Muqaddimah* Vol. 2, p. 305.
10. Ibid.
11. *Muqaddimah* Vol. 2, p. 300.
12. *Muqaddimah* Vol. 2, p. 325.
13. *Muqaddimah* Vol. 1, p. 57.
14. *Muqaddimah* Vol. 1, p. 346.
15. *Muqaddimah* Vol. 2, p. 117.

3. The Emergence of the Science of History

1. *Ibn Khaldun's Philosophy*, p. 291.
2. *Muqaddimah* Vol. 2, p. 128.
3. *Muqaddimah* Vol. 1, p. 287.
4. *Muqaddimah* Vol. 1, p. 286.
5. *Muqaddimah* Vol. 1, p. 58.
6. *Muqaddimah* Vol. 1, p. 65.
7. *Muqaddimah* Vol. 2, p. 188.
8. *Muqaddimah* Vol. 2, p. 224.
9. Von Kremer.
10. *An Arab Philosophy of History*.
11. *Muqaddimah* Vol. 1, p. 11.
12. *Muqaddimah* Vol. 3, pp. 111-118.
13. *Muqaddimah* Vol. 1, p. 77.
14. *Muqaddimah* Vol. 1, p. 79.
15. *Muqaddimah* Vol. 1, p. 6.
16. Ibid.
17. Ibid.

4. Historiography and the Rationalist Heritage

1. Astre, *Les Cahiers du sud*, 1947.
2. L. Gardet, *La Cité musulmane*, Paris 1954.
3. *Muqaddimah* Vol. 1, p. 6.
4. *Muqaddimah* Vol. 1, p. 11.
5. *Muqaddimah* Vol. 1, p. 77.
6. *Muqaddimah* Vol. 2, p. 86.
7. *Muqaddimah* Vol. 1, p. 7.
8. S.D. Goitein, 'The Rise of the Near-East Bourgeoisie', *Cahiers d'histoire mondiale*, 1957.

5. The Effect of Religious Reaction

1. *Muqaddimah* Vol. 3, p. 253.

2. *Muqaddimah* Vol. 3, p. 154.
3. *Muqaddimah* Vol. 3, p. 250.
4. *Muqaddimah* Vol. 1, p. 79.
5. *Muqaddimah* Vol. 3, p. 252.
6. *Muqaddimah* Vol. 3, p. 296.
7. *Muqaddimah* Vol. 3, pp. 251-252.
8. *Muqaddimah* Vol. 3, p. 297.
9. *Muqaddimah* Vol. 3, pp. 257-258.
10. *Muqaddimah* Vol. 1, p. 249.
11. *Muqaddimah* Vol. 3, pp. 309-310.
12. *Muqaddimah* Vol. 1, pp. 76-77.

Conclusion

1. J. Célerier, *Islam et géographie*, Paris 1952.
2. C.A. Julien, *Histoire de l'Afrique du Nord*.
3. Gibb, 'Une Interprétation de l'histoire islamique', *Cahiers d'histoire mondiale*, 1953.
4. See Maxime Rodinsion, (tr. B. Pearce) *Islam and Capitalism*, Harmondsworth 1977.
5. M. Emerit, 'Au Début du XVe siècle; les tribus privilégiées en Algérie, *Annales*, janvier-février 1966.

Index

Printed in the United States
by Baker & Taylor Publisher Services